Edinburgh
Education and Society
Series

General Editor:
COLIN BELL

In memory of Jock Johnstone
1912–1990

WORKERS NOT WASTERS

Masculine Respectability, Consumption
and Unemployment in Central Scotland:
A Community Study

DANIEL WIGHT

EDINBURGH UNIVERSITY PRESS

Edinburgh University Press Ltd
22 George Square, Edinburgh

Typeset in Lasercomp Palatino
by DSC Corporation Ltd, Falmouth, and
printed and bound in Great Britain at the
University Press, Cambridge

A CIP record for this book is available
from the British Library

ISBN 0 7486 0444 8

Contents

List of Figures and Tables

Acknowledgements

My greatest debt is clearly to the inhabitants of Cauldmoss who allowed two complete strangers to make use of their lives for their own ends. Although the villagers had no illusion that this research would in any way improve their circumstances, many were extremely generous with their time and hospitality and nearly all of them were co-operative informants.

Numerous people helped me in the first stage of this project, and they were acknowledged in my thesis. In the production of this book three people have played a crucial role. The friendship, intellectual stimulus and critical appraisal that Anne Marie Bostyn provided as a colleague in Cauldmoss have been maintained to this day. Many of the less pedestrian ideas explored here can be traced back to conversations inspired by her far more theoretical insight than mine.

This text has been greatly improved by the critical reading given it by both Anne Marie Bostyn and Rory Williams, who gave this lengthy task priority in spite of daunting commitments. Their enthusiasm for the subject sustained my efforts in the last few weeks, and both were far too supportive and courteous to comment on major flaws that could not be speedily remedied.

Erica Wimbush, my wife, encouraged me to proceed with this book, fully aware of the evenings, weekends and holidays it would consume and the extra work for her of caring for our daughters Ruby and Megan. Her encouragement and tolerance were essential for the book to be finished.

Finally, I am indebted to Gabriele Wight for painstakingly completing the most tedious task of all: proof reading.

1

Introduction

AN ETHNOGRAPHY OF AN INDUSTRIAL LOWLAND VILLAGE
In a sombre history of twentieth-century Scotland, Harvie
describes:

> an unlovely 'third Scotland' sprawled from South
> Ayrshire to Fife . . . old industrial settlements that
> ought to have been evacuated and demolished . . . but
> were preserved by buses, council housing and lack of
> long-term planning. . . . Somewhat isolated, ignored,
> lacking city facilities or country traditions – even lack-
> ing the attentions of sociologists . . .
>
> (Harvie 1981: 66)

'Cauldmoss' is part of this 'third Scotland'. In so far as can be
discerned from the sparse studies of Lowland Scotland, and from
my own observations, it seems typical of ex-coalmining villages
throughout the central belt. This book is intended as a partial
ethnography of Cauldmoss, which has all the characteristics Harvie
outlines – except the need to be evacuated and demolished. It is
partial in that it focuses on particular themes – respectability,
employment, consumption and unemployment – and only addresses these in respect to men.

There have been several reviews of studies relating to Lowland
Scotland (Eldridge 1974; Aitken and Mcarthur 1979; Turner 1980;

Condry 1983), all of which seem to concur with Condry in his
conclusion that:

> Too much attention has been paid to the islands and
> Highlands, and too little to the anthropological study
> of the Lowlands and the urban areas. Despite the
> theoretical rejection of the urban – rural dichotomy
> researchers have remained firmly encamped in rural
> fields in the far north.

(Condry 1983: 133)

In fact, only one anthropological book about Scotland south of
the Highland line has been published, and that was concerned
with a parish in the Cheviot Hills (Littlejohn 1964). As for ethnographic work specifically on the central belt of Scotland, Condry
only discovered two publications: a one-page comment on joking
relationships in Bo'ness (Girling 1957) and an investigation into
social stratification and church affiliation and participation in
Falkirk (Sissons 1973). Apart from several dissertations and theses (listed by Turner 1980: 3) the only other ethnography of
central Scotland has come from Turner's own research in a fishing village on the east coast of Scotland (Turner 1979a, 1979b). It
was this study that led him to initiate research on 'work' as a
moral category which took Anne Marie Bostyn and myself to
Cauldmoss.

Certain quasi-ethnographic works were helpful in this study
of Cauldmoss (e.g. Heughan 1953; Jephcott 1967) and one particular work was invaluable in providing us with a lengthy local
history of the parish. It is unjust that the author cannot be given
due credit for the detailed research involved, but this would
betray the true identity of Cauldmoss.

Though very little has been written about the culture of Lowland Scotland, a tradition of 'community studies' produced
several detailed ethnographies of working-class culture in England in the 1950s and 1960s. Lockwood (1966) used these as a
source for his influential tripartite typology of working-class
images of society, and in many respects Cauldmoss typifies his
ideal type of 'traditional proletarian', particularly in terms of the
community structure.

The striking cultural similarities between the northern English
working class – as described, for instance, by Dennis *et al.* (1956) –

and the inhabitants of Cauldmoss illustrate how much more important their common experience as an industrial proletariat has been in shaping their culture than have national characteristics, while the resonance of Hoggart's descriptions thirty years later demonstrates his point that 'attitudes alter more slowly than we always realise' (Hoggart 1957: 13). Indeed, the recent concern with postmodernism amongst many sociologists illustrates how the theoretical interests that arise from the metropolitan professional subculture in which most social scientists live can prompt debates largely irrelevant to other sections of the population. According to Simmel's analysis of 'modernity' (Frisby 1985), Cauldmoss is, in many respects, pre-modern.

There have been several analyses of the role of community studies in British sociology (e.g. CCCS 1976; Goldthorpe 1979) and Newby (1983) identified four reasons why they went out of fashion. First, several sociologists demonstrated that the admired characteristics of working-class culture are pragmatic and instrumental in character and likely to be abandoned or modified if their context is changed. Second, there was considerable criticism of what some saw as impressionistic methodology which made comparison difficult, and the whole focus on communities seemed less relevant to contemporary society since urbanisation, the growth of bureaucracy and increasingly centralised decision making were seen to mean 'the eclipse of community' (Stein 1964). Finally there was confusion over the term 'community' itself, which had become discredited by its highly normative usage.

Lee and Newby (1983: 57) identified three main ways in which 'community' has been used: a geographical expression for a fixed locality; a set of social relationships (of positive or negative kind) which take place within a locality, and a particular type of relationship, a sense of identity or common interest within a group. Cauldmoss could be described as a 'community' in all these three senses. I will use the term consistently according to the second definition: 'a set of social relationships which take place wholly, or mostly, within a locality' (ibid.: 57). When referring to the geographic settlement of Cauldmoss, I will use a term such as 'village', and when referring to a sense of common identity or interest, I will specify that meaning.

Notwithstanding the criticisms of community studies, at the time when we were starting our fieldwork Newby concluded:

The most frequently cited ethnographies of working-
class life are now seriously out of date. The community
study as a method of investigating changing patterns of working-class culture is long overdue for a
revival.

(Newby 1983: 27)

THE MAIN THEMES

In his study of a fishing village in Lowland Scotland Turner
found that 'work' constituted one of the most important moral
concepts in the local culture (Willis and Turner 1980). If this were
so for the whole of industrial Scotland, Turner wondered, how
was widespread unemployment affecting this? In 1981 he sub-
mitted a proposal to the Social Science Research Council (SSRC)
'to conduct an anthropological enquiry into moral aspects of the
concepts of work, unemployment, leisure and recreation in a
small Scottish town currently experiencing high levels of
unemployment'.

Having won funding from the SSRC, to be administered by the
Social Anthropology Department at Edinburgh University,
Turner appointed Anne Marie Bostyn and myself to conduct the
research under his supervision. We began our study in June 1982
and formally completed this original research project in April
1984 with the submission of our Final Report to the SSRC (Turner,
Bostyn and Wight 1984). In the meantime both Bostyn and I had
identified specific topics on which to base PhD theses, and we
continued our research to these ends (Bostyn 1990; Wight 1987).
We both lived in Cauldmoss from July 1982 until August 1984
when I left, leaving Bostyn to stay for a further two years.

Beyond investigating the ethics around work, I was interested
in the cultural constraints that shaped how people responded to
unemployment. When they lose their jobs the unemployed remain within other social relationships and they generally
struggle to fulfil the obligations entailed by these. 'Family, friendship, community membership, and citizenship all carry sets of
opportunities and duties' (Fryer and Payne 1986: 240). One of the
questions addressed in this study is how flexibly these duties
were defined in Cauldmoss, and in particular, the extent to which
they took a material form. Economic deprivation, rather than
the absence of a structured work role, has sometimes been

suggested as the main cause of the social and psychological consequences of unemployment. The approach adopted here will focus on the social deprivation caused by lack of money, rather than the denial of unintended consequences of unemployment (Jahoda 1982).

When we set out in 1982 we were eager to investigate the extent to which the unemployed substituted bought goods and services with their own work, and the degree to which an 'informal economy' had developed as a result of mass unemployment. Our concepts of the 'underground' and 'domestic' economies stemmed from a speculative article by Gershuny and Pahl (1980), which caught the imagination of many libertarian-inclined social scientists. The authors suggested that the contraction of the 'formal economy' might expand the 'communal/household' and 'underground' economies, and that many people might find this very rewarding. Following empirical research these ideas were revised (Pahl 1984), and it is now widely recognised that the 'informal economy' is part of, and dependent on, the larger economy (Harding and Jenkins 1989), but the cultural, rather than material, restrictions to informal work have been given little recognition to date.

A related issue was the effect of male unemployment on the sexual division of labour. The increase in female employment, the growth of companionate marriages in some sections of society and general assumptions about the increasing flexibility of gender roles led some sociologists to assume that unemployment would lead men to participate more in house work and child care. The validity of these optimistic assumptions was explored in Cauldmoss.

Integral to the issues outlined above was the topic of consumption. The most widely expressed rationale for employment in our society is the 'need' for money, while the notion of separate 'economies' also problematises the norms and practices of consumption. It was hypothesised that, in response to different economic circumstances, domestic produce could substitute for purchased commodities. How was the concept of material 'need' constructed in this culture, and why was it that the social evaluation of surplus time and patterns of consumption did not allow the former to compensate for reduced spending capacity, for instance through the production of home-brewed beer, vegetables and so on. The value accorded to goods clearly incorporated much more than practical utility. What was the social and symbolic value of particular patterns of consumption?

In the past the capitalist economy was dependent on a disciplined labour force, a dependence that was linked (in a still disputed way) to the positive moral evaluation of disciplined work. How, then, does the contemporary economy's need for sustained high levels of material consumption relate to the normative evaluation of spending patterns? Obviously such a question went far beyond the scope of this research, but it was possible to explore the ethos of consumption within a particular locality in modern Britain.

At the heart of these questions about consumption was the problem of explaining the perpetual inflation of material living standards. How is it that the unemployed and low paid still experience poverty as their forebears did fifty years ago, although their real income is far higher? (cf. Seabrook 1982). This study analyses the values learnt and perpetuated within a community which contribute to the dynamic in consumer demand that has meant needs have kept pace with, and ahead of, nearly two centuries of industrial production.

Although there has been growing theoretical interest in consumption these works are usually devoid of any detailed ethnography, and the reader is left wondering how the ideas relate to the common experiences of ordinary people. Apart from Bourdieu's *Distinction* (1984), it appears that Goldthorpe et al.'s call for a 'new empirical sociology of consumption' (1969: 183) went largely unheeded.

Involvement in Cauldmoss life made it immediately clear how practically all aspects of social life were structured according to distinctions between the sexes. The importance of gender was further emphasised for Anne Marie Bostyn and myself by the way it determined our participation in the village: we spent the great majority of our time with our respective sexes. Once alerted to the significance of masculine identity its relevance to the two main themes already outlined became obvious. The meaning of work for men could be understood in terms of their roles in their families, and men's spending patterns appeared to be, in part, a means of asserting or expressing their masculine identity. Consequently, to understand women's experiences and perceptions of employment and consumption would have involved much more than a simple elaboration from, and modification of, men's circumstances. Women rarely considered themselves 'unemployed' when they were seeking work (see Callender 1987), and most of women's spending was for the whole household which put it in a very different context from that of men. Since I needed to restrict the scope of my research, and for obvious reasons of methods, I decided to focus primarily on the male world of Cauldmoss, though, being a community study, women inevitably feature throughout it.

The sexual segregation in Cauldmoss was such that having researchers of different sexes was invaluable if one was not to rely on the accounts of one sex to learn about the beliefs and behaviour of the other. The data I collected on women were amplified or modified by Anne Marie Bostyn's much fuller participation in their world, and she is in broad agreement with the way these data have been interpreted in this book.

Another feature of social life that soon became apparent in Cauldmoss was the concern to maintain distinctions of social status. The widely found boundary between the respectable and rough in working-class culture has long been recognised but has rarely been accorded much importance by sociologists. This is probably due to the frequent treatment of cultural factors as epiphenomena. It seems that only by using the term 'capital' to discuss factors such as honour, reputation and social status (Bourdieu 1984, 1990) are materialist inclined sociologists ready to take culture seriously. Indeed, it is striking that the things which most concerned people in Cauldmoss on a daily basis were, in terms of mainstream sociological theory, generally considered trivia (see Giddens 1979: 71): for instance the cleanliness of children's clothes, the relative expense of wedding presents, or personal reputation in the village. This was the stuff of status distinctions. Factors deemed to be of sociological importance, in particular occupation, class position and voting behaviour, were usually experienced by villagers as the inevitable parameters of their condition, and therefore rather futile to dwell on. Within these bounds they led their lives, exercised by issues that were subject to their influence.

THEORETICAL APPROACH

Our original approach to this research was highly inductive, and for much of our time in Cauldmoss we collected data relating to all areas of village life in a manner that led us to be described, by a fellow anthropologist, as 'ethnographic hoovers'. Like Cohen, who has vigorously argued for 'grounded theory' rather than 'grand theory' (Cohen 1978), I was primarily interested in the meanings of the actors themselves. These were given precedence over any preconceived notion of a 'larger social system which provides [the community's] dynamics and which, therefore, explains its nature and process' (ibid. 8). My latent theoretical orientation, which emerged in the course of analysis, was Durkheimian, particularly as developed by Douglas (1966, 1970) and Martin (1981). Sahlins' *Culture and Practical Reason* (1976) was also an important influence in focusing my attention on the expression of cognitive categories.

I have, however, been somewhat eclectic in my use of theory which, I hope, is excusable in an ethnography that does not assume causal primacy for any structural factors. Thus I have drawn on Weber's concept of status, which seems to provide the best way to interpret social stratification *within* the village. The focus on the given style of life necessary to belong to a status group inevitably leads the analysis of village life to the realm of consumption, since lifestyles are primarily based on what one consumes (Weber 1948). However, I will argue that the esteem of being a disciplined worker was essential to belong to the status group the 'respectable working class', which therefore entwines social status with production.

To treat the village as if it existed in a vacuum, however, rather than as part of a much wider, complex society, would be naive. The history of Cauldmoss for the last 150 years, the means of livelihood which sustained it in the 1980s, and the profound changes in the population's employment roles around this time can only be explained in relation to the economy of Britain as a whole (see Dennis *et al.* 1956: 37, in particular the footnote). This recognition of macro-structural factors which have shaped the culture of the village could fit into broad Marxist or Weberian perspectives.

There are three principal macro-sociological constraints highly relevant to this book. First there is the stratification of British society as a whole, which of course is variously interpreted by differing groups within it. The position of Cauldmoss inhabitants in this stratification led to their dependence on the labour market, their subordination to their employers and their lack of control over the conditions of their work. The second important macro-process is the way different styles of life, and the esteem attached to them, are generated and proselytised on a nationwide basis. Third, there is the government system of state welfare upon which many people in Cauldmoss were dependent. Particular focus will be placed on the ways in which the inhabitants of Cauldmoss interpreted these external factors, whether they recognised them as significant, and how they shaped their own culture in response to these constraints. A central issue which will not, regrettably, be addressed directly is the influence of the media, and particularly television, in the culture of Cauldmoss.

I will adopt Weber's concept of class as a description of one's economic circumstances, defined by common life chances of wealth and income under the conditions of given commodity and labour markets (Weber 1948: 181). Indigenous notions of class in Cauldmoss will be discussed in Chapter Three.

This picture of Cauldmoss culture is painted with a broad brush, concentrating on classificatory schemes, the actors' formulation of the norms governing their behaviour and a general description of practice in key areas of the men's village life. In a sense, then, this ethnography only provides the background for a fine-grained analysis that should follow, of how individuals are influenced by these cultural principles but also actively construct and modify them, and how they improvise their social interactions in relation to them (Bourdieu 1977). Unfortunately there has not been scope for more intricate analysis of this kind.

METHODS

Participation in village life

Anne Marie Bostyn and I moved into a four-in-a-block council flat in Cauldmoss in the summer of 1982 and both lived there for two years. I then moved but Anne Marie stayed for nearly two more years. During this period I visited the village fairly regularly and returned for two months to conduct our second questionnaire survey.

The local council offered us a three-apartment flat at the furthest end of a line of council houses stretching out from the centre of the village. We took it unaware that it was a 'hard to let flat' largely because of the reputation of the neighbour living upstairs and in part because the whole road was known as "the Gorbals of Cauldmoss", on account of the "problem cases" or "wasters" who were housed there. Being located here meant we initially had far more contact with the other "incomers" who lived on the street than with locally born inhabitants of the village. This had both advantages, for instance being accepted as fellow outsiders, and drawbacks, such as becoming associated with these people by the more established and respectable inhabitants. Overall we appreciated being more remote, and therefore rather less constrained to conform to conventional behaviour, than we would have been anywhere else in village council housing.

The vast bulk of the data collected was in the form of notes made immediately after joining in activities in the village. From the start we tried to maximise our participation, which at first was often self-conscious and contrived but after about six months became increasingly spontaneous and developed a momentum of its own. Every opportunity was taken to visit people or share leisure activities with them, we attended church services, helped with community centre clubs and outings (mainly for children and young people), and joined in evening socials. Beyond this my main involvement in village life came through the pubs, and through accompanying men fishing and collecting fuel. I also joined the local Labour Party which coincided with my political persuasions but was of limited research value (see Chapter Three). Anne Marie Bostyn's main involvement beyond that mentioned above was through a group of close female friends, joining the Women's Rural Institute and playing bingo.

An important sphere in which we did not participate was that of employment. The dearth of local vacancies and consequent resentment had we succeeded in getting a local job led us to abandon this original objective. Therefore the analysis of employment (Chapter Four) is based entirely on data collected in Cauldmoss and describes the meaning employment has to people within their residential community. Had I been able to observe workplace culture a different perspective would have emerged.

Another important limit to the compass of this book is that it excludes those residents of Cauldmoss who lived in private houses and had minimal contact with the village. Although a few participated in our surveys, by and large they played very little part in the social world that we were trying to understand.

Our experiences in Cauldmoss confirmed the advantages of long-term participation in a community. In particular it allowed us to understand the contextual specificity of many of the accounts we had previously recorded. Thus we came to realise that talk of muggings and decapitated horses were expressions of fear and a moral order under threat from "incomers", but that rumours of slaughtered sheep and witchcraft had some basis in people's behaviour.

Long-term participation was particularly valuable in investigating illegal activities. By joining in with a wide range of activities in the village we came to be accepted by most of our informants as unthreatening. Thus frustrating diversions from the specific foci of our studies could be rewarded by the extraordinary frankness of those involved. For instance, after spending three weeks helping out with the children's summer playscheme we had a Friday evening's drinking to conclude the project, during which an unemployed man who (very unusually) had also helped mentioned that he had frequently worked on the side. A few weeks later he unhesitatingly gave me a detailed history of his numerous undeclared jobs and the ways in which he had fiddled the Department of Social Security (DHSS). A more important advantage of participant research when studying illegal activities is the opportunity to join in and incriminate oneself. This can obviously involve moral dilemmas (see Wight 1987), but unless solidarity with one's informants is demonstrated and trust established by taking the same risks as them there is little chance of being told much factual information (cf. Evans-Pritchard 1973: 6).

Several anthropologists have found that joining in indigenous economic activities is the best way of developing a sympathetic relationship with their informants (e.g. Evans-Pritchard 1940: 13; Okely 1992: 16–17). For nearly half the period I lived in Cauldmoss I was signing on for Unemployment or Supplementary Benefit. The bureaucratic hassles of claiming were ethnographically instructive, while our worries about a DHSS inspector judging us to be 'living as husband and wife' were a revealing experience (and ironic having been suspected of being DHSS snoopers ourselves). But more important, this position as claimant demonstrated a communality of interests with many of the people we were studying. Several commented that signing on enabled me to really find out "what like it is on the bru": a woman told me I was "in it with us", and a man said, half approvingly, "Ye've joined the family!"

One of the general difficulties I experienced in participating in Cauldmoss life was trying to maintain small talk. In part this was my unfamiliarity with 'phatic communion' (Malinowski 1923: 313–16), to which I will return shortly, but this was compounded in two ways. First, I tried to be mindful not to express personal views that might influence informants' accounts, and second, it was difficult to reciprocate gossip, which made up much of Cauldmoss conversation. One does not usually gossip unless one's audience is socially closer to oneself than to the person under discussion, which meant that initially we were never in a position to gossip, and even when we were, we felt obliged to keep nearly all we had learnt confidential.

Though it is a well-established practice to find a few intimate informants who provide the bulk of one's data (Evans-Pritchard 1973: 6), it is rarely thought necessary to specify them and their background. This is surprising since the social positions of one's main informants are fundamental to the epistemology of the whole study. For instance after three months in Cauldmoss I reflected that the nine people I had come to know best were all in some way peripheral to village life, being either incomers or condemned as deviant. Such an unrepresentative group resulted, in part, from our location on a road full of "wasters", but it was also due to the greater accessibility of those on the fringe of the 'moral community'. This is particularly the case when an illicit drug can be used as an entrée and means of colluding in illegal activity. Since those at the centre of community life are likely to be the most self-contained in their social world, there is initially a risk of bias towards marginal people and their activities.

Those inhabitants who featured in my ethnographic research can be roughly categorised into three groups: friends; acquaintances who shared particular circumstances or activities with me, and superficially known villagers. Others helped by participating in one of the various surveys, to be discussed in the following subsection.

There were four people I came to know very well and whom I considered friends. All of them lived in council housing, three of the four had been born in the village and three of them were connected by family ties. Tam was a widower in his 70s who started his working life as a miner. In this he was typical of men in his age group, but he had far more children than most, he did not drink alcohol and he had several engrossing hobbies (principally bird fancying), all of which were unusual and made him renowned in the village.

One of Tam's many daughters, Janet, stayed nearby with her own daughter, but she spent much of her time in Tam's house doing the domestic work. Her husband had left her several years before and she now had a boyfriend in the village. Until recently she had worked as a cleaner in the local school, but after a temporary ailment she decided to remain on Invalidity Benefit and divided her time between the work of two households and her main interests which were bingo, breeding canaries, reading and television. Her one child, in her early 20s, had had various part-time low-paid jobs but was currently unemployed. For Janet to have been separated from her husband was unremarkable, though not typical, while her small family, her preference for not continuing in low-paid employment and her interests (other than bird fancying) were all common to women of her age.

Alex, in his 30s, was the boyfriend of Tam's youngest daughter and an incomer, though he had lived most of his life within the central belt of Scotland. As an incomer, and having intellectual and artistic interests, he was not typical of Cauldmoss. However, his previous employment in semi-skilled manual work, his long-term unemployment, the failure of his first marriage and his cohabitation with a Cauldmoss woman were all characteristic of village life. The minor ways in which he defrauded the authorities might have been typical of the long term unemployed, though his involvement in theft, or at least his conviction for it, was less usual. I came to know Alex's girlfriend fairly well; she was typical of unmarried women in Cauldmoss. It was with Alex that I spent most time and developed the closest friendship while in Cauldmoss.

The fourth friend, Maggie, had no kin ties with Tam. In her 30s she had two young sons and a husband who had emigrated from Ireland in his teens. He worked as a lorry driver but was to leave her for another woman (in Glasgow) in 1986. In that same year Maggie was to lose her part-time job as a shop assistant in the local town. Maggie's upbringing in the village, her family circumstances and her husband's employment (prior to 1986) were all very characteristic of Cauldmoss women in her age group.

There were about fifty acquaintances whom I came to know well in particular contexts. Some were neighbours while others I joined in various activities, such as helping out at the youth clubs, drinking in the pubs, digging coal from the burn, going fishing or ferreting, or simply visiting them. The third category, in terms of familiarity, were about 300 villagers or more who, in brief encounters, relayed some information that I noted down, or who were the subject of other's conversation.

Beyond the strictly ethnographic research I conducted semi-structured detailed interviews with two dozen people. These respondents either had particular influence in, or special insight on, the village, or were typical of a particular age group and sex. The former group included the minister, priest, community workers, headmistress, a major local employer, the doctor, one of the shopkeepers, plus a senior official at the Department of Employment. Bostyn also interviewed church elders, other employers, two teachers, an official at the local Job Centre and the DHSS Information Officer for Scotland. The local Department of Employment office was unwilling to help us with our research. The interview schedules are described elsewhere (Wight 1987: Ch. 2).

The surveys

Bostyn and I carried out the first questionnaire survey within the first few months of our arrival in Cauldmoss. It was intended to introduce us to a cross-section of the population, and enable us to map people's cognitive categories in relation to 'work' and 'leisure'. Ten per cent of households in Cauldmoss were sampled (using the 1981 Register of Electors) and, where appropriate, the head of the household and spouse were interviewed. Wherever possible two resident adults were recruited. We achieved an 86.5 per cent response rate in an initial round of interviews, and then made up the sample to be representative by sex and housing tenure. The final sample size was 104 (Table 1.1).

The survey provided a very successful introduction: everyone in the village soon got to know of our project, many respondents subsequently greeted us in the street and chatted, several encouraged us to return for further discussion and some came to be important contacts. While administering the questionnaire there

TABLE 1.1 Sample for first survey.

	Total on electoral register (within our population)	Total questioned	Sample size
Households	619	69	11.15%
Adult individuals	1,304	104	7.98%

were usually long digressions about the village, the state of the economy or individuals' employment histories, which we eagerly noted down. A lengthy report of how the first survey was designed and carried out, its results and how they were analysed can be found as an appendix to our first *Final Report* (Turner *et al*. 1984).

The second questionnaire survey was carried out three and a half years later in November and December 1985, when both Bostyn and I had specific topics we wanted to investigate now that we had more closely defined the subjects of our theses. The second survey was also a vehicle for recruiting people to complete time and money budgets (see below), but since we were not optimistic that many would do this the questionnaire included questions on the use of time and money. We returned to the same households sampled in the first survey but, because many of our questions were about the whole household we only interviewed one person in each house. The final sample was sixty-two. A detailed description of how we conducted the second survey and the time and money budgets can be found in our second *Final Report* (Noble *et al*. 1986).

Twenty-four of the sixty-two respondents in the second survey completed a money budget. This involved recording their weekly expenditure, according to categories drawn from the Family Expenditure Survey, and recording their weekly income. Although we were pleasantly surprised at the number prepared to complete these budgets, once the findings were broken down according to household size and age, employment circumstances and housing tenure the figures were not adequate to make meaningful comparisons.

The problems in analysing the money budgets are described elsewhere (Noble *et al*. 1986: 19–20). They related particularly to the figures for clothing and shoes, large household goods and alcohol. Few people could give a weekly average for the first two categories, and it was a matter of chance whether they had bought such items that week. Only those using mail order catalogues were able to state weekly sums with any certainty. Statements about expenditure on alcohol could not be relied on because, first, the topic was heavy with moral evaluation and, second, accuracy depended on entirely frank financial arrangements between husband and wife. Nevertheless, the budgets did provide valuable information about the details of people's lives, best interpreted as a collection of case studies. The data from these budgets and the questionnaire survey results will be presented where pertinent to the ethnography.

Reflexivity

It is now well recognised that the ethnographer's self influences how the ethnography is produced, and the need for reflexivity is widely accepted both in sociology (e.g. Hammersley and Atkinson 1983) and in social anthropology (Okely and Callaway 1992). It is still rare, however, for much space to be devoted to such analysis in ethnographic texts, in part, no doubt, because funding bodies are unlikely to regard more than a superficial period devoted to this activity as a valuable use of their money and because publishers assume readers want the substantive 'facts' unqualified by these epistemological doubts. Over-stretched by the demands of taking comprehensive field-notes I failed to keep a diary while in Cauldmoss, as advocated by Okely (1975). Nevertheless, I will briefly outline the main features of my autobiography most relevant to how I experienced living in Cauldmoss and to the way its inhabitants reacted to me.

I am a white male from a southern English middle-class family; undoubtedly each of these characteristics shaped the interaction between myself and the inhabitants of Cauldmoss. One consequence of my privileged status was my own ethic towards work. I believed that work should be intrinsically interesting and worthwhile (though well aware that for most people it was not), and that meaningful employment was of much greater value than a marginally higher wage. Linked to these beliefs was my esteem for the diligent application of craft skills. These notions had developed from my experience of the labour market, usually doing agricultural or horticultural work that I had enjoyed (though poorly paid) and had had some control over, and they were incompatible with the thorough alienation experienced by most people in Cauldmoss in relation to their jobs.

Both my parents had degrees and my father was an academic; consequently I grew up in an intellectual household. All of us children were invested with 'a high volume of cultural capital' (Bourdieu 1984), an important aspect of which was my parents' decision not to have a television. A direct consequence of this upbringing was a notion that conversation should be intellectually stimulating (and, implicitly, demonstrate one's stimulating intellect). This left me inept at the 'phatic' conversations that made up most talk in Cauldmoss, since I felt unable to communicate properly if the discussion never went beyond what I saw as inane topics like the weather, and uncomfortable if a conversation became intermittent. The lack of a childhood's television viewing left me unfamiliar with many formative influences in popular culture, which was exacerbated by my lack of contemporary knowledge about football, pop music and television programmes. All this compounded the problem of casual, inconsequential conversations.

During my early teens I had few friends and only tenuous connections with male peer groups as is typical of boys of this age. This was probably linked to the relative isolation of our house, a mile from the nearest village and three miles from my school. I assume that this lack of male company, and the fact that I grew up with two older and two younger sisters, were important contributions to my abnormal socialisation as a man in Britain. Two obvious but important elements of this were that I had never enjoyed or been competent at football, probably the most ubiquitous institution for simultaneously expressing male solidarity and competitiveness, and I did not relish drinking large amounts of alcohol. Although I largely overcame the latter aversion, these were serious handicaps to my participation in the male life of Cauldmoss. At a deeper level, being rather insecure in my own masculine identity and finding the norm of predatory male sexuality problematic probably made me more conscious of the importance of masculine identity in the lives of Cauldmoss men. It may have been that my emphasis on gender in interpreting the meaning of employment and spending patterns was a defence against my subconscious sense of inadequacy as a male, in that by stressing the cultural specificity of masculinity in Cauldmoss I belittled the significance of my not meeting local standards.

Another strand of my cultural preconceptions came from my long-term interest in ecological issues and affinity to an anti-consumerist, bohemian/hippy lifestyle. My conscious attempt to appear more conventional when we moved to Cauldmoss (which succeeded to the extent that some young men thought I was a drugs squad officer), made me highly aware of the norms of respectable presentation. Indeed, we felt severely constrained in almost all our public behaviour, from eating to means of transport to the colours of our window frames. This provides one of many contrasts with anthropological fieldwork in the Third World. In one's own society there is far less tolerance for peculiar behaviour: nearly every eccentricity is remarked on, whereas for First World researchers in the Third World it is more likely to be similarities in behaviour that are noted.

The frugal lifestyle I had previously led (second-hand clothes, vegetarian food, hitchhiking) accentuated my perception of villagers' concerns with purchased commodities. Having previously lived in France, where there was no welfare benefit for the young unemployed, and Jamaica, where there were virtually no welfare payments for anyone, my perspective of poverty when I first arrived in Cauldmoss was very different from local people's. This prompted my curiosity about the social construction of material need.

These aspects of my biography meant that I was less at ease in the village and had less empathy with local values than others might have done. Although it made immersion in this culture at times traumatic, it certainly qualified me as an outsider (Turner 1967: 26–7). A fellow anthropologist who had grown up in a mining district in north east England commented that she would not have noticed half the things I recorded in Cauldmoss because they were so commonplace to her.

Working and staying with Anne Marie Bostyn during my two years fieldwork was extremely valuable, not simply because of the obvious benefits of exchanging ideas with a colleague and the greater access it gave me to a sexually segregated society. It also allowed further exploration of my subjectivity since she was clearly of a different sex and from a very different background: skilled working class in Yorkshire.

Reactions to us, the 'students'

Our project in Cauldmoss had previously been heralded by an article in a local newspaper which printed a tongue-in-cheek description of how anthropologists normally move into undeveloped tribal areas to study 'the primitives'. It was widely read in the village several months before our arrival, by which time the indignation and suspicion which it had aroused had largely been forgotten, but it did not improve our reception. Only a few took it as a joke and planned to set us up: "I'll tell them we eat bairns at Christmas".

Conducting our first questionnaire survey introduced us to a cross-section of the population, and others learnt what we were doing through conversations with us in the village shops and pubs or indirectly through gossip. We explained that we were studying the effects of unemployment and how people cope with it, and, more generally, that we wanted to record their way of life and outlook on the world. Many initial perceptions of us, however, were impervious to this explanation: we were variously called crime reporters, drugs squad, social workers or DHSS snoopers, the different descriptions usually reflecting different villagers' potential involvement with the respective authorities. In general Cauldmoss inhabitants found it improbable that their ordinary lives were the subject of an academic study.

After a month or so we came to be known as 'the students', a phrase we had never used (proud to be research workers) but which was the indigenous category people in Cauldmoss found most appropriate. As students we had an ambivalent status. On the one hand we had obviously been privileged with an education which extended far beyond that of most villagers, and would presumably enter a highly paid professional career on completing our research. Some, mainly older, inhabitants were deferential towards us, which could be extremely annoying when it inhibited them from refusing an interview and instead led to successive excuses that brought us back repeatedly to pester them again. On the other hand we were apparently unemployed (cf. Condry 1983: 110), impoverished much of the time, and not yet 'proper' adults despite being four or five years older than others with steady jobs and young families. One woman asked my age and was astonished to learn I was 25: "Don't you think that's awfi old to be a student?". The advantages of low social status for an anthropological researcher are well known: as students I think we had this standing, although our informants knew that our life chances in the wider society were very different from those of most villagers.

Although many inhabitants regarded us as unemployed, for others our research was self-legitimating simply because it was 'work'. Conducting the first survey was definitely seen as work, and several respondents who did not fully understand what we were trying to do resolved the issue with comments such as "Well, it's a job anyway". During the second survey an old man explicitly stated what others had probably thought: that if he had been *sent* the questionnaire he would have put it straight in the fire, but he was prepared to answer it in my presence because it

gave me a job, even if it was not a proper one. "Bloody world's
rotten with bloody temporary jobs an' this sort o' thing." He was
not prepared to fill in the time or money budgets since the only
value he saw in any of this activity was that it gave me employment:
if he were to complete them himself what would I have to do?

Anne Marie Bostyn's and my residence in the same house
immediately aroused considerable interest, and amongst older
people condemnation. We learnt later: 'most older folk looked at
it as terrible . . . they said, "they should ha' put them in digs – and
they're goin' to talk about *us!*" '. Younger people were shocked
not by our living together unmarried, but by our doing so without having a sexual relationship.

Some people in Cauldmoss remained perplexed throughout
our fieldwork as to what we were really interested in. Our
neighbour told us that if we were to walk about in patched jeans:

> People in Cauldmoss would think that you're tryin' to
> experiment wi' them, to see their reaction . . . They'd
> say, "What's he playin' at now? What's he tryin' to suss
> out noo? Is he tryin' to kid us on?" Aye, that's the way
> they think. You take it from me, Danny boy. I know.
> (big laugh).

A small proportion of the population were openly antipathetic
towards us and declined to have anything to do with Anne Marie
Bostyn or myself, behaviour that we did our best to mitigate.
Some of these individuals later indicated that they had come to
accept us, and in one case a man literally extended a hand of
friendship. In fact we were both happily surprised by the lack of
hostility we encountered. Though some certainly resented our
work it was only on occasional (usually drunk) moments that
this was expressed: "You ask too many questions . . . You're a
pryer . . ." .

Another pleasant surprise was that we were not disliked for
being English. Far more important as a divisive factor in Lowland
Scotland is religion. Though I could honestly state that I had no
particular religious faith, I felt it politic to disguise the fact I had
been brought up as a Roman Catholic.

Sharing one's findings with those studied

Though our study was never intended as an action-research
project, we felt obliged to share our findings with people in

Cauldmoss and consult them about our conclusions. There were several reasons for this. First, if our interpretation of Cauldmoss culture really was as important as we presumed, then surely it ought to have been of interest to Cauldmoss inhabitants themselves, not just to fellow academics. Second, it seemed a basic right that people should have access to what was written about them, particularly since they had been generous with their time and assistance. It also seemed important that they should have 'a right to reply'. Entering a discourse with one's informants about one's interpretation of their lives before they are generalised in print is, of course, also extremely valuable to one's analysis.

We quickly learnt some of the hazards of disseminating one's findings amongst those studied when we distributed a copy of an ethnographic paper, *From Coal to Dole*, written for a university seminar and heavily edited to exclude references to locally recognisable people.

Responses were instructive and can be roughly grouped in three categories: most people concentrated on the quotes and liked these enormously, being surprised to find themselves presented in their vernacular, but they skipped much of the intervening text; a few read it all through carefully and approved of our interpretation of Cauldmoss, saying it was "down to earth", but some were appalled at our description: "That's not Cauldmoss!" . . . "Where's the nice side of Cauldmoss?". These people had clearly been expecting a rosy description of community life and felt we had betrayed their hospitality and co-operation by writing about fiddling the electric meters and stealing coal. Our focus on the unemployed in this paper, and our cautious qualifications when describing illegal activities, were both overlooked. One woman took us to task for talking to "the wrong folk" and her distress at how we had presented her village graphically revealed both how unaware she was of the way other inhabitants lived, and her own image of Cauldmoss which she had hoped to find confirmed in our paper. The reactions from *From Coal to Dole* demonstrated some of the problems (and advantages) in disseminating one's material amongst those studied. In retrospect I think a short synopsis of one's findings for one's informants to read would probably be more suitable, even though this would be less candid.

There are several ethical problems which are almost inevitable in conventional anthropological research: maintaining a relativist stance, deceiving one's informants to some extent whilst conducting one's research, objectifying them when writing up, and so on. These difficulties seem to be felt far more accutely when conducting research in Britain rather than abroad, which betrays the kind of relationship on which these methods were based. These issues have been considered elsewhere (Wight 1987: Ch. 2), but one matter which warrants further discussion will be considered in Chapter Eight.

PRESENTATION

'Cauldmoss' is, of course, a pseudonym, and in describing the village some insignificant details will be changed to protect its identity. Likewise, none of the villagers are referred to by their real names.

Clearly our ethnographic data, which comprised the bulk of my material, could not be audio tape recorded, and only a few semi-structured interviews were recorded due to lack of support for transcribing. Consequently, in contrast to better funded research projects, there are regrettably few quotations to substantiate and enliven the text. Speech presented in double inverted commas is a quotation from an informant, while quotes from the literature or technical social science terms are distinguished by single inverted commas. The 'ethnographic present' has been rejected as inappropriate to a study located at a very specific historical time: the first major recession since the Second World War in which 'full' employment had been abandoned as a key objective of government economic policy. In any case, the use of the ethnographic present has long been criticised both for accentuating boundaries by giving them a temporal dimension (e.g. Fabian 1983) and for being intrinsically conservative (e.g. Willis 1977). Unless otherwise stated this ethnography refers to 1984, but this is not intended to suggest that things have necessarily changed in the last decade.

2

Cauldmoss

The beliefs and practices which constituted the culture of
Cauldmoss can be presented as a collection of social categories
and boundaries. These marked out the villagers' world, providing a system of meaning by which they made sense of their
experience. The crucial categories were constantly reproduced
through people's daily interaction. The most important divisions
were binary: between female and male, private and public, cleanliness and dirt, respectable and non-respectable, "belonging" to
the village and being "an incomer", Protestant and Catholic,
working and not working. Other distinctions were graded, such
as those of age or kinship.

In practice, of course, even the daily ritualised observances of
these boundaries could not disguise the fact that the divisions
were not absolute: there were people who had married into the
village fifty years before and had become "one of us", Catholics
who had "turned" (converted) and people doing temporary
work while registered as unemployed. Furthermore, the norms
that were defined in terms of these boundaries did not inevitably
determine individual action but depended on more or less constant observance to be reproduced.

Cauldmoss lies between the Firths of Forth and Clyde, about 700
feet above sea level on a wide fairly flat expanse largely covered
in peat and "moss" (moorland). From the highest points in the
vicinity one can see the hills which bound the central Lowlands –
the Ochils, the Pentlands, the Campsie Fells and the first peaks

of the Trossachs – but more immediately one is surrounded by a mixture of moss and poor pasture, with very few trees other than decaying shelterbelts. These are made up of pines and wind-swept beeches that demonstrate how exposed the area is, a factor which, combined with the acid soil, severely limits agriculture and restricts cultivation to a small area of relatively fertile land. Beneath the subsoil of clay and course sand lies millstone grit and coal, the latter giving rise to another feature of the landscape: open-cast mines and abandoned bings [slag heaps].

The village is concentrated around the intersection of a few minor roads which connect it to other villages and the local town. Of the population of 1,500 (1981 Census) 73 per cent lived in council houses, most of which comprised a central scheme or estate built after the Second World War. The importance for spending patterns of such a high proportion of council tenants will be discussed in Chapter Seven. There was also a line of 1930s council housing – the first built in the village – which stretched out on one of the approach roads; Anne Marie Bostyn and I lived at the further end of this row. Beyond these council houses and along the other approach roads there was a little ribbon develop-ment of small private houses, mainly bungalows, and the other private householders lived within the central part of the village. A few private houses dated from the nineteenth century, but the vast majority of buildings in Cauldmoss have been built since the last world war. Sheltered accomodation for thirty old people was built by a housing association in the late 1970s, and other people lived on small farms, about two dozen of which lay within two miles of Cauldmoss.

In the middle of the village there were four grocery shops, one of which was very small and one (originally the co-operative store) considerably larger than the others. At the time, there were also three pubs and three club buildings, a bookmaker's, a post office, a fish and chip shop, a chemist and a bank, a car-parts store and two hairdressers which were only open part time. Several mobile shops augmented the shopping facilities, and Cauldmoss also had a community centre, health clinic, nursery school and primary school. From the age of eleven children travelled by bus to secondary schools in the local town. The Church of Scotland kirk was prominent on one side of the village, while the modern Catholic chapel and that of the Church of Christ were less con-spicuous.

In 1984, the only public transport serving Cauldmoss was a bus service from the local town, which ran at least once an hour and cost 85p each way. Half the households in the village had a car; the local town is accessible in twenty minutes and one of the two main cities in Scotland (Glasgow and Edinburgh) can be reached in under an hour. The nearest railway station is beyond the local town.

In 1981 there were slightly over 1,300 adults in Cauldmoss with equal numbers of women and men (1981 Census). Our first questionnaire survey in 1982 found that the unemployment rate for males over 16 was 37 per cent. Conversely the proportion of females over 16 and under 60 who were *in employment* was 48 per cent, a quarter of whom worked part time. According to the 1981 Census the main industries in which people were employed were distribution and catering (27.4 per cent), manufacturing (20.5 per cent) and 'other services' (31.5 per cent). Most of these jobs were in the local conurbation; there was little employment within the village itself, except for that provided by eight small businesses and some part time employment (mainly for women) in the retail outlets mentioned above. The small firms consisted of a grocer, two haulage firms, a builder, an exploratory drilling firm and three local coal merchants.

HISTORY

Until the 1830s Cauldmoss Parish had no real village within it, only several groups of houses and isolated farms. The only employment was in agriculture or related trades, and for several centuries prior to the nineteenth the population was probably stable at about 500.

In 1838 a branch railway was built across the parish and the construction work revealed several seams of good coal, heralding the sudden transformation of Cauldmoss into the bustling centre of a thriving coal industry. By 1854 there were nine main collieries in the parish and mining work continued to expand until the 1890s. The population swelled with a mobile labour force habituated to following employment opportunities wherever they emerged in southern Scotland, and mining settlements sprang up around the pits while a village began to grow around the church. The population figures for Cauldmoss Parish until the 1930s, like those of Shotts (Heughan 1953: 3) and Ashton (Dennis *et al.* 1956: 12), illustrate how working class demography was determined by the vagaries of industries to which

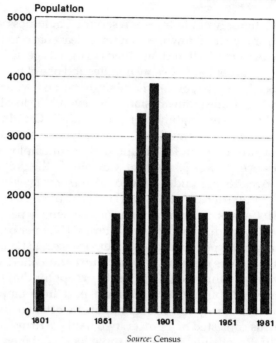

Source: Census
FIGURE 2.1   Population of Cauldmoss 1801–1981.

human labour was merely another variable input (Figure 2.1).

Although the industry expanded until the end of the century, the miners were extremely poorly paid and were housed by the coal owners in cramped, damp quarters, often of only one room. In 1857 they were paid just over a penny per ton of coal they dug (about two and a half pennies a day), when household coal cost thirty pennies a ton. Strikes were organised throughout the second half of the century and had some success in raising wages, but lockouts, blacklegs, the truck system and the Desertion of Service law greatly impeded the miners' progress (see Page Arnot's history: 1955).

By the turn of the century more pits were being closed than opened as owners were reluctant to invest further capital once the most readily accessible reserves had been exhausted. Some of the older people in Cauldmoss in the 1980s still blamed the coal owners for the decline of the industry, and modern open-cast operations all around the village support their claim that there is still plenty of "the best coal in Scotland" under the ground. Many outlying hamlets were deserted by 1910 as the workforce moved on to employment elsewhere, and by 1928 the four main seams in the parish were abandoned. However, mining continued to be one of the villagers' principal occupations for several decades as workers were bussed up to ten miles to neighbouring pits. By the time these were closed in the first half of the 1980s, due to a combination of disinvestment and the 1984–5 Miners' Strike, only three miners were left in the village to take the redundancy pay. A few small mines (without shafts) were worked around Cauldmoss until the 1970s and shifting open-cast sites have a striking impact on the landscape to this day. However, in contrast to their visual presence they provide employment for only one or two villagers.

Since the exploitation of coal started in the 1840s there have been other subsidiary industries at various times in Cauldmoss. These included a gas works from 1855 to 1940, two woollen mills and, from the beginning of this century, the exploitation of the peat moors for moss litter, horticultural and fuel peat. In the nineteenth century there were several brickworks in the parish and the industry was re-established in 1937, employing a few dozen local people. However, it closed again in the 1970s due to a decline in the building trade.

There has been a church in Cauldmoss since the Middle Ages, but the existing parish kirk was built in 1810. At the Disruption in 1843 the minister in Cauldmoss did not break away from the church, but nevertheless a Free Church was established and a new church built. When the two denominations were united in 1929 both buildings continued to be used until 1946 when the Free Kirk became a church hall.

During the second half of the nineteenth century both churches had large congregations, and Sunday schools were held in several of the outlying mining settlements. There was also a Methodist chapel, the Church of Christ, a Roman Catholic chapel built in 1885 and an active band of the Salvation Army. These institutions dwindled with the village population and by the 1980s only the Church of Christ and Catholic chapels remained as alternatives to the kirk. The three remaining denominations will be discussed in greater detail below.

Attendance at Church of Scotland activities can be partially traced from the *Church of Scotland Yearbook* which started in 1929. There was a gradual decline in participation after the Second World War, but when a much-loved, long-established minister was succeeded in 1969 there was a dramatic fall in attendance at church services, Sunday School and Bible Class. In the 1980s only about fifty of the 400 communicants attended services, which included only six of the twelve elders.

At the beginning of the nineteenth century the extreme poor depended on the Kirk Session for relief: the number receiving assistance fluctuated from three or four to over a dozen. In 1845 Parochial Boards were established to administer poor relief under the Poor Law (Scotland) Act, and money was raised by a levy on local households. However, members of the Kirk Session sat on these Boards and so ecclesiastical views on work and idleness continued to influence who was sent to the poorhouse and how much relief they were due. The new legislation coincided with the growth of Cauldmoss and by 1866 there were twenty-nine poor on the roll, some of whom would be sent to the poorhouse in the local town if there was room. It is important to note, however, that figures for those on relief are a considerable understatement of the extent of poverty, since there were great disincentives to claiming help (not least the way the regulations broke up families) and many were not eligible anyway. 'The Act was a failure, because it was vitiated by the old Scottish principle that the only qualification for relief must be disability added to destitution.' (Mitchinson 1970: 388) In 1904 responsibility for poor relief was moved from Parochial Boards to Parish Councils, but in 1929 these were abolished, to be replaced by District Councils. The Poor Law came to an end and the poor had to rely on National Assistance which was funded by both the central and local government.

The first permanent school in Cauldmoss was built in the middle of the last century and became the Public School after the 1872 Education Act. The Free Church and Catholic Church also set up schools which lasted until the first quarter of this century. In the 1930s the Public School was extended to create capacity for 600 children, but in the 1960s it was modernised and restricted to primary children. Since then those over 11 years old have travelled to a high school in the local town.

LOCALS AND INCOMERS

Excluding incomers

Apart from gender, the most widely articulated classification Cauldmoss inhabitants had of themselves was that of being "locals" or "incomers". In the course of our stay in the village we were frequently reminded of our status as "outsiders", and when a local told Anne Marie Bostyn that she was "one of us" in contrast to the other incomers on our street it was evidently an important statement of acceptance. Frequently people would tell us "I'm an interloper . . . " or "I'll never be a Cauldmosser, I know that", although they had moved to Cauldmoss over fifty years before in their early childhood. From our acquaintance with other Lowland villages it would appear that this parochialism was not peculiar to Cauldmoss (cf. Heughan on Shotts 1956: 12).

The first questionnaire survey found that nearly three-fifths of villagers had been born in Cauldmoss. Sixty per cent of council tenants were in this category with opposite proportions amongst private house residents. However, not everyone born outwith the village was regarded as an outsider. Those identified as "incomers" consisted of two principal groups: the "problem cases" who were moved into municipal houses by the local council and the majority of private house dwellers. The latter were criticised for being aloof and supposedly making no effort to get involved in local affairs. Most of these "strangers" had fairly widespread social networks which largely omitted Cauldmoss, and for this reason they do not come within the main focus of this book. The incoming spouses of indigenous villagers were not so clearly identified but were generally regarded as honorary locals, although they themselves rarely felt fully accepted. The first survey showed how Cauldmoss had become less endogamous since the Second World War. For married council tenants whose places of birth were known, a third of those over 60 were born in Cauldmoss and had married someone from the village, but only a tenth of those under 30 fitted this description. None of those in private houses had endogamous marriages.

The "foreigners" who moved into council houses had more immediate contact with those born locally than did the private house residents, and they provoked more intense differentiation. In the early 1980s they were concentrated on two particular streets and were often referred to in general as "wasters, problem cases" or, more often, "battered wives". The latter was a derogatory term (used mainly by men) since it was assumed that these women had moved there to avoid enormous rent arrears, not oppressive husbands. In fact the newcomers included single women, single men, couples and two-parent families, as well as the separated mothers who were assumed to be "battered wives". Some of these mothers had boyfriends with them and all had children. One of the streets with incomers was on the edge of the scheme and the other, more renowned street, was the line of old council housing where we lived, which had come to be known as "the Gorbals of Cauldmoss".

A council housing officer denied suggestions, widely believed by locals, that difficult tenants were "dumped" in Cauldmoss to remove them from the local town. He explained that when three successive people on the housing waiting list refused an empty house it became available for the Homeless Persons Officer to fill it with his/her clients: the problem of "ghettoisation" occurred because local people refused to live next door to a "problem" family. However, some indigenous villagers argued that if the council had kept the "Gorbals houses" in good repair local people would have been encouraged to stay there.

Incomers were frequently blamed for any deviant behaviour in Cauldmoss, and their children felt particularly marginalised, participating far less than locals in village activities like the youth clubs. Reproducing the community boundary meant that visiting youths from neighbouring villages were as likely to be fought as chatted with, and outsiders who got local jobs were deeply resented. Contributing to villagers' parochialism was their inexperience of other regions of Britain: many had never been out of Scotland and for older men most of their travel experiences dated from the Second World War.

How inhabitants viewed Cauldmoss

Many inhabitants saw Cauldmoss as a community, although the term itself was not often used. People talked of the place as a village, and most older people considered "ye're better living in a wee village than a city". To outsiders the village was presented as homogenous and so interrelated that some inhabitants suggested it was almost one big family, but as the next chapter will show, this ideology of unity was rarely invoked amongst villagers themselves. Natives seemed to fear that the newcomers were undermining the 'integrity' of the village. In fact the agreed condemnation of many of these incomers meant that their presence united indigenes more than divided them. The corporate identity of villagers and their inherited sense of belonging is a clear example of Lee and Newby's 'sense of commonality among a group of people', which warrants describing Cauldmoss as a 'community' in the sense that it constituted a particular type of relationship (Lee and Newby 1983: 57).

Cauldmoss inhabitants generally regarded the village as a friendly, co-operative place, but they also drew on images of it as an ex-mining settlement, as wild (in terms of both the weather and lawlessness) and as tight-knit, isolated and rife with gossip. Identification with coalmining, unruly behaviour and the elements all appealed to a particular notion of masculinity, to which I will return shortly.

Most locals were conscious of their mining legacy and even the young sometimes described themselves as mining folk, while the oldest generation, most of whom were miners or miners' wives, constantly referred to the industry when discussing their past. Older women shared the occupational identity of their husbands, saying "we miners were . . . ", and this generation were still proud of the village's reputation for hard work in the pits. The story goes that even in Canada at the end of the last century advertisements read: 'Miners wanted. Only Cauldmoss men need apply'.

Many features of mining culture survived the end of the 'occupational community' (cf. Bulmer (ed.) 1975, in particular Salaman), for the population remained after the pits closed. Several activities in the village probably stemmed from its mining origins: the keeping of whippets and pigeons, the popularity of outdoor pursuits and men passing their non-working time standing at the centre of the village. Though predominantly older men engaged in these things, some young lads followed the same patterns. Perhaps the most important legacy of mining culture that persisted was the norm for spending, which will be considered in detail in Chapter Five.

The village had a reputation for hard drinking, fighting and general lawlessness ever since miners from outlying settlements travelled in to the Cauldmoss pubs and dances at the weekends. Mass street fights and prostitutes soliciting around the pubs were frequently described in characterisations of old Cauldmoss, though by the 1980s the images used to portray its unruly character were taken more explicitly from the Wild West. Other images from the television were also drawn on, such as Bleasdale's *Boys from the Black Stuff* which had temporary currency. The graffiti 'Hazzard County' over a road sign on the approach to Cauldmoss was considered very apt, Hazzard

County being the fictional location of an American television series (*The Dukes of Hazzard*) about daredevil hillbillies.

Many men in Cauldmoss also revelled in their reputation as "fly". Taking advantage of people naive to Cauldmoss guile was often considered fair game, as when lads justified "jumping" [out of] a taxi when it arrived from the local town, arguing that the driver had been stupid not to have demanded cash before starting for the village. When a primary schoolboy was offered ten pence to sing a song on an outing he was advised: "Get the money first! Come on, Jim, you're fae Cauldmoss!".

Inhabitants frequently described Cauldmoss as subject to terrible weather. Constant gales, blizzards cutting the village off for days, and even snow in July were cited. Though the weather conditions were usually exaggerated (as elsewhere) it is noteworthy that when the road from the local town *was* blocked by drifting snow one winter's afternoon most men stoically walked more than half a dozen miles home, rather than stay in emergency accommodation.

Many younger people in Cauldmoss felt it was a backwater with very few facilities, although in comparison with neighbouring villages it was actually well endowed, and they were also more likely to find the close-knit relationships of the community restrictive. When these factors were combined with the unruly reputation and the supposed council policy of dumping unwanted tenants, many inhabitants were self-effacing about their village: "it's wasted, this place . . . all battered wives now . . . " or, more graphically, "it's the arsehole of Scotland".

Gala Day

The most formal expression of Cauldmoss's corporate identity was the Gala Day. Unlike the other main annual events in the village – the Orange March, Bonfire Night, Christmas and Hogmanay – it focused exclusively on Cauldmoss and had no other rationale. The Gala Day was started by the Cauldmoss Co-operative Society in 1905 and had been held annually ever since, apart from a period of a few years in the late 1970s.

Money was raised for the Gala throughout the year (principally with prize bingos), and funds were boosted during the week preceding the Gala Saturday by running extremely popular quizzes and competitions in the clubs and community centre.

The focus of the Gala was the procession around the village, made up of bagpipers and a brass band (both from outside Cauldmoss), young girls in fairy costumes, highly decorated floats packed with more young children, sometimes a troup of majorettes, and at the centre the Gala Queen (chosen at random from the primary school) attended by ladies-in-waiting and courtiers, riding in a white Rolls Royce or, in more extravagant years, on a coach led by horses. Another car or carriage carried last year's Gala Queen and her ladies-in-waiting, and behind them marched a group of halberdiers. In front of this royal party walked the mythical saint of Cauldmoss's history, dressed like a medieval monk. Participants assembled at the school with a great deal of confusion and waiting, during which time a large crowd gathered, photos were taken and the Crazy Gang (adults in ridiculous costumes such as gorilla suits or in drag) accosted people for money, including any unsuspecting strangers driving through the village. Eventually the procession set off in amateur-ish chaos: majorettes dropped batons, young boys burst most of the balloons and children cried as their float separated them from their spectating parents. At the War Memorial the Gala Queen laid a wreath and a respectful tune was played, though most people carried on chatting, after which it proceeded around the scheme and on to the recreation park where a stage had been assembled. While the brass band played ceremonial accompani-ments a compere welcomed each child with a special role on to the stage, culminating with the new Gala Queen. There was an exchange of robes and crowns between the old and new queen and a lot of bowing and curtseying between them and their entourage. Each of the main actors made a little speech and the ceremony concluded with the band playing 'God Save the Queen', to which nobody paid much attention.

Following the procession there were displays, ice-cream vans and stalls, and any activities the organisers could arrange to make it a fête. On rainy days the crowning ceremony was held in the community centre.

Enormous effort was made to decorate the village for this occasion, in particular the houses and gardens lining the route of the procession. Where each of the main participating children lived elaborately painted hardboard cut-outs decorated the gar-den, on some childish theme such as cowboys and indians or Snow White and the Seven Dwarves, and somewhere the child's name and role was displayed, such as "Margaret: Chief Lady-in-

Waiting". With the pendants and flags, the decorated gardens and the exotic costumes of the main actors (many of which were hired), it was a colourful pageant. Nearly all villagers came out to watch, most of them in their smart clothes.

Everyone recognised that Gala Day was above all an event for the children. They constituted most of the procession, the decorations were focused on them, they were often bought new clothes for the event, and at the end of the ceremony each child was given "a bag" of sandwiches, chocolate biscuits and sweets. Generosity and co-operation in assisting with the Gala Day was validated by reference to "the weans": "anything I can do for the weans . . . I'm doing it for the Gala Day".

The concern with equal participation by all villagers, the reference to village origins in the form of its saint, the acknowledgement of villagers who died in the two world wars, and the generosity of spectators in giving around £150 to the Crazy Gang's collection, all suggest that the Gala Day was a glorification of Cauldmoss as a community, in the folk sense of common interests and fellowship. Though the children were the first priority, it was a day of festivities for their parents as well. Several men started drinking in the morning and watched the procession from the pavement outside the pubs, many families had a special meal in the afternoon, it was a day for relatives to come to visit the village and in the evening there were Gala Day dances, usually a traditional one (with band) and a disco. The ethos of the occasion was well expressed one year when a highly proficient Cauldmoss gambler with racing contacts, who was living in England at the time, rang his brother-in-law in the village with a tip for a race on the Gala Day morning. Over a dozen men bet on the winning horse, providing hundreds of pounds with which to celebrate the Gala Day.

Village funerals

Another expression of community relationships came with the death of someone born in the village. As important as having a suitably costly funeral (to be discussed later) was that a large number of people should turn up to witness it. Even a limited acquaintance with the deceased gave one a slight obligation to attend the funeral, and close relatives never resented such attendance as presuming too much familiarity: instead the minister thanked everyone on behalf of the family for "paying your last

respects". Whether or not there was "a good turn up" for a funeral
was of greater interest than the details of the hearse or coffin, and
for many older people attending the burials of their friends and
acquaintances was their main contact with the church. As Rees
described in Wales, the funeral of someone who belonged to the
village was a ritual which renewed the community's unity: 'the
bond between an individual and the general body of neighbours
is perhaps never so fully manifested.' (Rees 1950: 96)

Durkheim and integration

By now it will be clear that Cauldmoss had many of the characteristics Durkheim described as 'mechanical solidarity' (1964),
where cohesion is based on the similarities between individuals
and the common moral sentiments binding them together. Since
Durkheim's theories, as well as their imprecision and inconsis-
tencies, are well known I will not rehearse them here, except to
note that two of his fundamental concepts, those of 'integration'
and 'collective representations', are particularly pertinent to understanding the social life of Cauldmoss.

The conformity of thought and behaviour in Cauldmoss and
the importance that was attached to social involvement (considered in relation to consumption in Chapter Five) both suggest
that Cauldmoss was a community bound by the solidarity
Durkheim analysed. The sanctions against those who excluded
themselves from village life were discussed by a "hippy" couple,
Gail (an incomer) and Jim (a local). "If you don't join in with
the group, if you're a bit of a loner, then they classify you as a
snob . . . ", Gail said. Her boyfriend had more vivid evidence of
how "no' being part o' the system" was seen as "quite a crime":

> When I came back to Cauldmoss I didnae get involved
> wi' the people in Cauldmoss, and because I didnae I
> got beated up twice. I didnae do *anythin'*, I just wasnae
> part o' them . . . I just wasnae into joining in because it
> just wasnae my thing. But that's quite bad, aye. They'll
> set aboot you for things like that. That happened to me
> an' Mav [his brother] twice. . . . They beat the shite out
> o' us . . . because they didnae know what I was doin',
> that's what it was. They want to know what you're up
> to, what makes you tick – an' they couldnae figure out
> what made me tick. An' they didnae like it an' it

frightened them. So they get frightened, so they retaliate. They beated us up.

The concentrated, often overlapping, networks of kin, neighbours and friends, which were intensified by the immobility of the population, provided abundant information for gossip. Cauldmoss was "clannish" and "what ye do is everybody's business". A young man bitterly complained that his aunt "kens the colour of your new carpet before it's delivered", and an old man, speaking in the relative privacy of his living room, summed up his perception of village life:

> Cauldmoss as far as I'm concerned, they know everybody's business unless their own, and they mind everybody's business unless their own. I'm surrounded here wi' people.

In these conditions, people tend to reach consensus on norms and exert a consistent informal pressure on each other to conform.

GENDER

As in other cultures, differences of gender are so fundamental to social existence in Cauldmoss that they are part of the taken-for-granted natural world, usually only commented on when conventions are breached. The categories of masculine and feminine are at the core of people's self-identity and practically all their social roles, from their relationships with their siblings as children to their roles in the economy, and they also provide one of the most important principles by which social space is organised. Gender is, as Martin argues (1981), one of the social categories mapped in greatest detail by cultural boundaries. Here I will describe the main ways in which gender distinctions are experienced in Cauldmoss: the sexual division of labour and recreation, the institutions of marriage and the family, masculine identity and the hierarchical relationship between women and men. Gender is a recurrent theme in this book, and it will form a central part of the analysis of employment and consumption in Chapters Four to Six.

Sexual division of labour

Nearly all domestic labour was the responsibility of women. Cooking, washing up, buying clothes and repairing them, knitting, doing the laundry and ironing, making beds, cleaning the house and windows were all female activities, as was decorating to a large extent. Women also had prime responsibility for budgetting the household income, but this important duty should not be equated with women exercising real control over the allocation of resources (Kerr and Charles 1986: 119) (discussed in Chapter Five). Budgetting did, however, give them the further task of doing practically all the shopping: it was rare to see a man in the Cauldmoss grocers buying anything other than cigarettes, a newspaper, sweets or alcohol. If a man was seen returning with a full shopping bag this would often be commented on by other men in a manner that ostensibly did not challenge his masculine esteem: it was pretended that he was thought to have "a carry out" (of alcohol), and jokes were made about the ensuing party. Within the house wiring up plugs, basic repair work, some decorating, bringing in the coal and making the fire were the only male duties. Outside the house mowing the lawn, digging the garden and growing vegetables were male activities, as were looking after pet birds or dogs, cleaning the car and repairing it.

Though the segregation of activities was most entrenched amongst old people, in 1984 the young still maintained most of the traditional roles. Female responsibility for domestic work was so established that many men thought it natural to sit in an armchair and watch their wife cleaning around them, and then demand rather than request a cup of coffee. The division of labour was also maintained beyond the house: after parties in the community centre it was the women who swept and mopped up, even in the gents' toilets. On top of domestic production women were, of course, almost exclusively responsible for child care, whether washing and feeding babies or entertaining children.

Of course there was some variation in the degree to which these activities were gender specific, both between the different tasks and between different households. It is possible to identify those activities that were most central to the woman's sphere (cf. Morris 1985): changing nappies and bathing children, washing and ironing clothes, cleaning the house and planning the weekly shopping. Husbands only exceptionally gave their wives substantial help with these tasks, even when they were unemployed and their wives had jobs. When they did lend a hand they were more ready to do female tasks in the house (such as hoovering) than to display their role flexibility publicly (for example by cleaning the windows, hanging out the washing or pushing a pram).

Men's discretion in carrying out 'female' tasks led the few men who went for "the messages" [the shopping] to be called "the carrier bag brigade" by the (female) shop assistants, since they carried a plastic bag in their pockets which they only brought out inside the shop, thus disguising their purpose until they arrived. The main contribution men did make to regular shopping was on weekly expeditions to the local town, but even then their role was usually limited to driving and child care (cf. Kerr and Charles 1986: 118). It is significant that men's co-operation in the female sphere was generally referred to as "helping".

Women were also highly constrained from taking on the few male activities around the house, but this was often experienced as a physical or mental incapacity (e.g. in mowing the lawn or fixing the car) rather than an aversion to transgressing gender roles. The results of our first questionnaire survey on the categorising of activities by gender (Wight 1987) were in keeping with Bott (1957) and Harris (1969) who emphasise how the extent of spouses' homosociality shapes role segregation. Those men with greatest role flexibility were usually those least involved with close-knit male friends, such as husbands who were recent incomers to Cauldmoss. The relationship between a person's kinship links and her/his adoption of gender roles will be discussed in the next section. A further factor was class: in general the inhabitants of the private houses were more flexible in their gender roles than council tenants.

The division of labour within the house was closely associated with the allocation of roles in the wider economy. Men were still considered the prime wage earners and servicing them was generally considered a natural role for women. Few questioned that they should get up before their husbands in order to make the man's breakfast and sandwiches, even though this might mean rising at five and going back to bed once he had left for work. When asked why her husband did not make his own breakfast such a woman said: "Oh no! He's hopeless!" The inevitability of these roles was probably even less questioned by men themselves. When they return home from their jobs men consider they deserve a "proper" meal of meat and two vegetables (cf. Murcott 1982).

Many women in Cauldmoss born before the mid-1920s either

having jobs, apart from being in service as maids before getting
married, or under exceptional circumstances like the Second
World War. One woman of sixty-five remembered leaving the
munitions factory in 1945:

> You missed all the company. I wouldnae say I missed
> the work though . . . I suppose I was quite happy wi'
> out working . . . I didnae really miss work . . . I knew
> not to go. *He* was the breadwinner . . . *He* was goin' to
> do it – and he did! . . . It was just one o' those things.

When she found a job her husband was adamant that she should
not do it, threatening to quit working himself at the end of the
week. She did not take the job: "It was just one o' those things",
she repeated.

Younger women were generally keen to have a job. By the
1970s they had come to expect the greater opportunities for
female employment that had developed during the 1940s
(Heughan 1953: 11), though unemployment in the early 1980s
undermined this. Frequently women's main stated motive for
employment was the change of environment and company, but
the wage was also an important consideration for many: "I've
always worked – sometimes you get fed up with it, but you
couldn't live without the wages." Having some income independent of one's husband was also important for many women.

Although nearly all young women leaving school sought employment they rarely questioned their primary role as mothers
and wives, and were often happy to abandon their jobs when
their first child was imminent. While it had become acceptable
for women to participate in the labour market, this was on the
assumption that their domestic roles were not compromised nor
men's primary position as wage earners threatened. Wives were
obliged to fulfil all their usual domestic duties even when in full
time employment. Several women (both young and old) expressed the view that female employment exacerbated the problem of
unemployment and that women ought to be excluded from the
labour market.

Leisure

Women and men's leisure activities were as segregated as their
domestic and paid work. The main exceptions to this homosociality

were watching television and reading at home (which involved the minimum of interaction), and going out together at the weekend, normally on a Saturday evening, or sometimes on a car trip. When asked how they spent their free time (second survey) female council tenants most frequently reported (apart from television and reading) knitting, visiting friends, going to bingo and shopping as favoured activities, while men listed gardening, walking, playing bowls, and going to the Masons . This division was less marked amongst private house residents. Nearly all hobbies were associated with one or other gender: men kept pigeons and dogs, went fishing, and played football, while women did crosswords, baked, made jam, went to keep-fit classes, helped with play groups and so on. The lists of women's activities show how their 'leisure' was often combined with domestic production, making it problematic to talk of 'women's leisure' at all (Talbot 1979). Baking, for instance, was an activity whose demise was much regretted by older men who regarded it as an important criterion of a good wife. Our first survey found that women did not have a consistent way of describing those pursuits which are both recreational and productive; they were each variously described as "work", "necessity" or "pleasure".

As a result of the sexual division of labour much of women's recreational contact with their friends and acquaintances was integrated into their domestic duties. During the day they would slip round to a friend's house between household tasks, or have a chat when they met up while shopping or fetching their children from school. In the evenings women sometimes congregated in a friend's living room, usually where a woman had young children to mind. Despite child care duties and restricted access to public places women "went out" slightly more often than men each week (second survey), but it was less likely to be spontaneous and was usually to a formal institution: the Women's Rural Institute, a church social, the Eastern Star (the separate women's section of the Masonic Lodge) or the bingo. Apart from the church socials and evenings out with their husbands, all the women's social events were attended predominantly by other women. Sexual motives were assumed (by both women and men) if individuals of one sex joined the opposite sex in their activities, which constrained wives to keep to formally designated women's activities. Thus when wives went drinking at the clubs it was either with their husbands at the weekend or on a specially instituted "ladies' night". Women's presence in the male domain of pubs will be discussed in Chapter Six.

The ideology of marriage and the family

Although the economic interdependence of wives and husbands has eroded since the Second World War (Beechey 1977), within Cauldmoss marriage remained an ideal, and though it was harder to live up to, people kept trying.

In 1984 most youngsters in Cauldmoss still aspired to get married, despite an increasing rate of divorce, and two-thirds of the population lived in couples (first survey). Most of the remaining third were widowed, divorced or separated, and they usually cohabited or, occasionally, remarried within a short time. Cohabiting outwith wedlock was only condemned by the oldest villagers. Having children was still essential in completing the transition to adulthood in the early 1980s, and young adults were even more eager to reach this stage than in the past, whereas getting a job was no longer necessary in starting the transition. The age of family formation seemed to have declined over two generations, the proportion of council tenants who had their first child before the age of 25 being 25 per cent for those over 60 and 47 per cent for those under 30.

Children's continuous observation of gender roles within their families made them seem natural rather than cultural phenomena, but parents also actively developed gender identities in their offspring. Mothers often dressed up their daughters in elaborately feminine clothes, which earned the admiration of other women, while little boys were encouraged to eat more than their sisters in order to grow up as big men, and were urged to be competitive with each other, most importantly in playing football. Children were socialised into homosociality with their earliest participation in the community centre. The preferences of 5- to 9-year-olds for different games according to their sex (football for boys, rounders and touchball for girls) was reinforced by having a male leader supervising the boys and a female in charge of the girls. Older girls were keen to do disco dancing and train as majorettes while boys played pool, space invaders and football, hung about on the streets or stayed at home, sometimes to use home computers.

I have emphasised how central gender categories and the

ideology of the family were to the culture of Cauldmoss because they underlay the meanings employment and consumption had in the village. To a large extent it was one's identity as a woman, man, child or parent that shaped how one spent money and the meanings that goods had, as we will see in future chapters. Similarly the value attached to hard work and earning large wages was intricately connected with men's roles as "breadwinners". Another aspect of familial ideology important to the main theme of this study is that the ideal family has a stabilising and conservative influence. As Barrett notes, it 'provides a uniquely effective mechanism for securing continuity over a period of time.' (Barrett 1980: 212)

Masculinity

The concepts of gender in Cauldmoss were largely defined in terms of familial ideology, femininity being characterised by the themes of romantic love, motherhood, self-sacrifice (deference), responsiveness, nurturing and responsibility for the household finances, and masculinity by protection, financial support and control. As already explained (Chapter One), this book is primarily focused on men; here I wish to outline some of the important elements of masculinity in Cauldmoss. The issue of financial support will be considered in Chapter Four.

Central to the concept of masculinity in Cauldmoss was the expectation that men "be strong". Although men's physical strength was recognised to vary considerably, deficiency was meant to be compensated for by emotional strength. It was never appropriate for men to cry, and since only the most extreme emotion prompted them to "greet" in public it usually aroused considerable sympathy from both women and men. A young lad who shared a prison cell with a drunken driver sympathetically related how his cell mate had cried all weekend because he could not be with his wife who was giving birth. "I felt ashamed for him", the lad said. Conversely, being prepared to fight was directly related to manhood. When a man condemned one of the pub landlords for being "chicken" in avoiding a fight with him over some disagreement, he concluded his drunken tirade with the statement: "A man *is* a man."

Part of the obligation to "be strong" was the norm that men should protect their female relatives. This was most salient to the more pugnacious young, and brothers were expected to protect or avenge their sisters or fight together in mutual support. As with most hostility there were far more threats than actual violence, but the honour of Mediterranean style vendettas was invoked.

Being tough was synonymous with being manly, a term even used to describe villages. Being gullible, on the other hand, was perceived to undermine one's masculine credentials. When someone joked about how "soft-natured" he was in buying people drinks, another man told him not to be ridiculous: "you'll be a man all your life." Examples like this of men confirming each other's masculinity were common, and were consistent with the tendency already noted for men to conform to their gender roles more in male company. 'For it is amongst other men that patriarchal masculinity is celebrated and constructed and it is within this bonding that men also experience their vulnerabilities.' (Hey 1986: 69).

Young men were expected to become sexually active in their mid-teens and were admired as "studs" by both sexes if reputed to have had a high number of sexual partners. However, two-timing was generally condemned and once a man was married or in a steady relationship further sexual relationships were not approved of, though sometimes condoned. One of the main criteria by which men categorised women was by perceived physical attractiveness, and men boasted with each other about being the first to seduce and "screw" a pretty woman. "Screwing" typified how sex was usually described in terms of physical action on (sic) a passive object. However, as with fighting talk, this intra-male discourse was acknowledged to be largely fantasy, though it did reproduce a predatory model of male sexuality. As one might expect, this emphasis on the heterosexual role of men was combined with the expression of profound homophobia.

In striking contrast to the acceptance of several (serial) sexual partners for men, sexual morality was far more restrictive for women. This double standard has been the subject of much analysis (e.g. McRobbie and Garber 1976; Smart and Smart 1978; Cowie and Lees 1987). One of many illustrations from Cauldmoss was the warning a man gave me that a woman who had just left the bar had "the pox". He vigorously condemned her as a whore (demonstrated by the disease) and particularly blamed her for infecting his friend who was now suffering through her wantonness.

Patriarchal ideology

In describing the explicit delineation of the categories of female
and male in Cauldmoss and the meaning of gender I have only
hinted at a difference in power or prestige between the sexes. In
fact this hierarchical difference was thoroughly institutionalised
both economically and ideologically. Indeed, in contrast with the
more subtle sexism of middle class society, the description of
male chauvinism in Cauldmoss at times appears to be an exaggerated parody.

Though when questioned, most villagers of both sexes claimed
that men and women *are* equal, just different, men's behaviour
frequently implied their superiority while that of women often
demonstrated their deference. Women were often assumed to be
ignorant of politics, economic affairs, geography and other
worldly matters, and what they did know about was usually
defined by men as trivia. Everyday language tended to deny
women's existence independent from men, in the use of "wife"
as a generic term for any adult woman, and phrases like "man
and wife". The term "hen", widely used by both sexes to address
women, had no male equivalent. Though it was a friendly pet
name the figurative use of "hen" for woman in other contexts was
always negative ('hen-pecked', 'an old hen' etc.) (Mills 1991).
Within the home it was common for older husbands to order their
wives about, to do this or fetch that, and some took pride in their
chauvinism: "She wouldn't know what to do if I didn't tell her."
The gender hierarchy was also illustrated by children being told
to substitute for their mothers, as when a man got his young son
to make coffee and toast for him since his wife was already in
bed.

Although we had little indication of the incidence of domestic
violence in Cauldmoss, it was possible to get an idea of how
Cauldmoss men judged it. A young man described how conservative villagers were about wives being hit:

> People see it as being bad, but they don't see it as being
> *too* bad because it's a way o' life: it's always been that
> way. There's always been someone skelping their wife.
> Because it's always been there it's easier to accept.

Even some younger men considered domestic violence partially
excusable, as if it were exercising one's right over property. When

three unmarried lads gossiped about another villager who had "skelped" his girlfriend and, being drunk, had given her a kicking, one of them said a smack across the jaw is to be expected but not a kicking, while his friend laughed as if it was unimportant. However, the fact that this incident was worthy of gossip indicated that hitting one's partner was not considered respectable behaviour. The assumption that incomers who claimed to be "battered wives" were fraudulent (discussed above) contributed to the belittling and concealment of the issue.

The hierarchy between genders was to such an extent 'common-sense' knowledge amongst both sexes in Cauldmoss that women generally regarded it as natural. They often accepted that they knew nothing about "serious" matters and overall men "know that much more anyway" because their work and travel broadened their experience. Even some younger women who, in public, appeared to have a more egalitarian relationship with their spouses did not protest at being treated in a subordinate way at home. The sexual division of labour was rarely questioned and women took it for granted that men would stand idly by while they were busy at some "female" task. These domestic jobs were usually described as a "necessity" or "pleasure" (first survey), and when questioned about child care women frequently said they "dinnae think it's work".

Very few women commented on the portrayal of themselves as objects, which was how their husbands saw them each day in the *Sun* or *Daily Record*, and they accepted as normal images such as the pin-up girls on Tennents lager cans.

The demarcation of gender categories pervaded every area of villagers' experience and determined much of their behaviour, their view of the world and concept of themselves. It is therefore understandable that women resisted foreign political ideas that undermined these fundamental categories which had been learnt and reinforced from infancy. We never heard the word feminism in Cauldmoss and "women's libbers" or "that 'burn-your-bra' lot" were generally regarded by both sexes as ridiculous eccentrics. However, some women explicitly rejected their views: "I dinnae believe in equal rights for women – that's a lot of shit really," said a twenty-three year old housewife. Many women felt that feminist censure of pin-ups, page three girls, and overtly sexist jokes spoilt what was simply "good fun". Lack of interest in, if not hostility towards, feminist thinking illustrated the importance of gender identity in Cauldmoss culture and the threat that a critique of femininity and masculinity posed. Although the problem of why woman 'is often well pleased with her role as the Other' (de Beauvoir 1972: 21) has long been discussed, the feminist explanation for women's consent and collusion is far from resolved (Barrett 1980: 251).

This presentation of gender relationships is oversimplified in omitting changes between generations and in ignoring women's authority in their own domain. The villagers' values were changing, partly as a result of the weaker economic rationale for marriage already mentioned which meant women were less dependent on their husbands. The differences in marital relationships between the generations was commented on by both older and younger women, and both thought younger men were usually more flexible in their domestic roles than their fathers. Older women approved of their daughters' generation divorcing rather than putting up with oppressive husbands.

The rigid gendered division of labour made men reliant on women, as well as the reverse. Several young men got their own homes and relished this assertion of independence and adulthood, yet they returned to their mothers each evening for tea and took her their washing every week. Other young bachelors did not seriously contemplate establishing their own homes until they were engaged, daunted by the prospect of cooking, cleaning and washing. When married men lost their wives they often returned to their mother's home, or lived so close that she (or a sister) could do much of the house work. The home is essentially female territory and, as Martin argues (1984), men must learn to evade the woman's authority. However the power that this gives women is problematic: order can turn 'into tyranny and nurture into moral blackmail. Masculine resentment then rebounds on women to make them feel guilty, worthless and doubly rejected' (Martin 1984: 34). The control that comes with responsibility for the household budget is also equivocal, as we shall see in Chapter Five.

Another complicating factor in the hierarchical relationship between men and women is that, according to the different criteria of social differentiation to be described in the following chapter, women were expected to maintain more demanding standards of respectability than their husbands. While being fly, never going to church, or enjoying "bevvy sessions" in the old hotel boosted masculine esteem, the same men who boasted of these qualities took great pride in the honesty, cautious budgetting and respectability of their wives.

In spite of these qualifications it is clear that there was an overt ideology of male superiority in the culture of Cauldmoss. Certain aspects of this ideology were peculiar to the class position of most people in the village. Women's economic dependence on men and ideological inferiority mutually reinforce each other, and amongst the working-class men's subservient role in the economy further exacerbates women's dependence (Beechey 1977). Women's position was further weakened by the specifically masculine and positive meaning attached to manual labour in traditional working-class culture.

Willis argues that one response of male labourers to their subordinate social position is to inverse the ideological order so that they prefer manual labour to 'feminine' mental work, thus supporting their occupational status with patriarchal values (Willis 1977: 149; see also Bourdieu 1984: 384). This is only possible because manual labour is associated with masculinity, as it was in Cauldmoss, though mental work was not associated with femininity in the village. Clearly, relying on the masculinity of one's work for one's self respect strengthened the division between the sexes and men's sense of superiority as males. Of course women generally did a considerable amount of manual work themselves, but because it was mainly domestic labour and not perceived as strenuous it was often not recognised by men.

KINSHIP

Kinship and membership of Cauldmoss

Within Cauldmoss kinship provided the most important basis for social organisation after gender. An individual's social world was founded on her/his family: social position, moral values, friends, role models, identity with a particular area and occupation were all shaped by kinship. It was a concept frequently referred to by villagers, who often mentioned that they were "connected" to apparently unfamiliar people, and emphasised that Cauldmoss was extraordinarily interrelated (cf. Shotts as described by Heughan 1953: 12). Some estimated that two thirds of the population in the early 1980s was related to each other in some way, and consequently: "If ye speak ill o' yun, ye speak ill o' all".

Full membership of village society required that the other inhabitants knew who one's parents were and how one was connected to everyone else, thus a person's social identity was largely inherited from her/his family. Only those who had a parent who lived in Cauldmoss and who were themselves born there could claim to be true villagers, and, as we saw earlier, the distinction between "locals" and "incomers" was one of the most widely articulated in Cauldmoss. Local women were referred to by their maiden names after marriage, and though their children had their fathers' surnames, when young they were often described in relation to their mother, for instance "Yvonne McGee, Mag Brodie's wee lassie". This illustrates the tracing of bilateral kin ties and inheritance of identity.

Kinship also influenced people's mental maps. For many, practically the only time they travelled beyond their region was to visit their relatives, whether they were in another part of Scotland, in England or on the continent, either for a holiday or to try and find work through them.

Kinship gave a sense of time as well as social place, and indeed a knowledge of how the biographies of one's fellow villagers were interwoven was an important aspect of village membership, as Emmett noted in North Wales (1982: 207). Association with the past was maintained by naming children after their parents or grandparents, principally by giving them the same Christian name. When there was no intervening generation between namesakes, which was often the case, it was difficult to distinguish relatives, and diminutives had to be consistently used. Thus a father was "Jimmy" and his son "James", or one "Thomas" and the other "Tam".

It was one's ancestors' participation in the village that gave one the right to say "I *belong* to Cauldmoss", which suggests that were it not for them having lived out their lives in the village the place would have had no current social existence. In this sense Cauldmoss belonged to the locals just as much as they belonged to it. Given the importance of family connections with the past it is noteworthy that few people traced their ancestry back beyond a few generations. This is characteristic of bilateral kinship and may be due to the limits of memory.

There was considerable similarity in families' involvement in village institutions over successive generations, particularly in their participation in the various churches, the Scouts, and the Orange Lodge, while it was almost impossible to enter the Freemasons or Eastern Star unless one's parents were members. Similarly the main law-breakers in Cauldmoss had parents with histories of offending themselves, or they were seen as anti-social in some other respect, such as being alcoholics (cf. Kolvin *et al.* 1990; Brown and Madge 1982).

Participation in institutions and moral character were two of the criteria that contributed to respectability in the village (to be discussed in the following chapter), so when they were combined with the inheritance of wealth (where it existed) it follows that social standing was largely inherited. More particularly certain families had a reputation for some unusual behaviour, such as a fiery temper or great generosity, which was assumed to be genetically inherited and thus identifiable in grandchildren or cousins.

Though extended families very rarely stayed in one household, kin often lived in close proximity to each other, which increased the importance of collateral relatives in transmitting values. Frequently one of the main motives tenants had to move council house was to live nearer their kin. In 1984 on one road there were three sisters and a brother in four separate households, along with their assorted spouses and children, while a grandfather had a daughter and granddaughter living nearby and four grandchildren from another child staying in various houses further on down the street. This residential pattern allowed women to do the domestic work of close male relatives while maintaining separate households.

Obligations to close kin

Although an individual's social existence was largely formed around her/his kinship links, the category of kin to whom there were obligatory duties was very small. Commitments that everyone acknowledged were restricted to one's children and one's parents, mothers being at the core of these obligations. They always risked the accusation that "they are no' caring for their weans" and many older women thought babysitting was wrong on principle. Most young men who did not move out of Cauldmoss either continued living in their parents' house or relied on their mother's domestic work (cooking, washing and cleaning) until they started cohabiting with a female partner.

Adults' obligations towards their family of origin increased with the age of the parents, and as one would expect, economic factors could become especially important once the parents had retired. The greatest duty was towards the mother, particularly if her spouse had died (or left her). This took a ritual form at Hogmanay when the mother was normally the first person visited after midnight, and also, though less commonly, on Mothering Sunday when her children returned to her. The exceptional examples of a mother abnegating her responsibilities to her child or *vice versa* aroused such moral censure that they illustrated the rule.

It was notable how men in Cauldmoss readily acknowledged their devotion to, and dependence on, their mothers, in marked contrast to the "hard" image of masculinity described earlier. The most violent skinhead in the village turned down a residential Youth Opportunities Programme after coming out of borstal, saying "Don't you think I've been away fae me mother long enough?". The association of virility and emotional attachment to one's mother might have been connected with the clear demarcation of sex roles which inhibited fathers from child care. Chodorow (1978) argues that the greater the infant boy's initial emotional identification with his mother the more disruptive is the transition to identify with the father and the more emphatic the boy's later denial of the need for, or feelings of, other intimacies, emphasising the machismo elements of masculinity (cf. Ryan 1985).

Although kinship connections were clearly identified by most villagers it is striking that there were no kin groupings which the elementary family necessarily aligned with in Cauldmoss (as Parsons observed for Western society in general: 1943: 184-5). Individuals' wide networks of relations were a resource they could use, but to whom they had few definite obligations beyond their first degree kin. The relationships which were maintained follow no logical structural pattern, except that they were more likely to be connected via females (whether consanguine or affinal) than via males. In general it was fairly arbitrary, and usually instrumental, which relatives were most important to an individual.

The substance of kinship for women

Bott's proposition (Bott 1957: 60), that the kinship network (especially for women) is associated with the degree of segregation in the role relationship of husband and wife was confirmed in Cauldmoss. However, whereas Bott implied that the kinship network is the independent factor, it could be argued from Cauldmoss that the division of domestic labour itself influences the level of involvement of wider kin. The rigid delineation of spheres of activity meant that if a man was left without a wife other female relations carried out her domestic chores. Furthermore the normal absence of men throughout the day (at least until the unemployment of the 1980s) meant women were far more dependent on their female relatives for company and assistance in domestic work than on their husbands.

The help female relatives gave each other in their domestic production was one of the reasons why kinship was generally more important to women than men. The scope for kin support was enormous, from lending a hoover to babysitting, though in fact domestic production was very rarely a communal activity, except perhaps in joint shopping trips to local towns. Kinship was also more important for women for affective reasons, and Bott's argument that women are much more likely to maintain kin links than men was borne out in Cauldmoss. Many aspects of men's lives gave them more autonomy than women, for instance being more likely to travel through their work and less constrained to go out in the evenings, and they were therefore less dependent than women on their existing network of kin to provide social contacts.

Kinship and employment

Personal contacts had always been important for finding work in Cauldmoss, and this was accentuated in the early 1980s by high unemployment, since fewer jobs were formally advertised and "work on the side" was gained exclusively by word of mouth. Through kin loyalty, and because social contacts were largely built around kinship networks anyway, relatives played a crucial role in finding jobs in the early 1980s. It was probably the most important form of economic aid provided by kin, more common between men than women simply because more were in employment. It had long been the practice in many industries that a son followed his father's occupation: an elderly man who used to work in the iron foundries said: "It was a case of doing what your father did. I was spoke for long before I was 14 – if your father could work, then you were guaranteed a job." Such recruitment

still operated in 1984, particularly in the local businesses and
open-cast mines, and several teenagers talked of going into the
firms where their fathers worked when they were old enough.
Men not only helped their sons find work, but also went to
considerable lengths to help their sons-in-law, thus furthering
their daughters' economic wellbeing. Since marriage or engagement was no longer a necessary demonstration of long-term
commitment, fathers sometimes assisted their daughters' steady
boyfriends as well. With "work on the side" lack of official
advertising and the need for discretion made relatives of existing
employees the easiest to recruit. At a different level economic
co-operation occurred between related small businessmen, such
as builders helping each other gain contracts, or between related
farmers during the harvest.

Contrary to Parson's analysis of the isolated nuclear family in
modern industrial society, large regions still exist with little
skilled, specialist work and so little need for mobility and little
economic differentiation between individuals within a class
(Harris 1983: 68). In 1984 Cauldmoss, and most of the Scottish
central belt, was still such an area, where the factors which would
lead the family to function as an isolated unit did not exist. Thus
kinship still played a vital economic role in job recruitment,
though whether this will endure through future changes in the
labour market is questionable.

Mobility of the population

The role of kin in finding unskilled or semi-skilled work is one
reason why extended family ties might be of greater significance
among the working class (cf. Klein 1965, vol. 1, section 1).
Another factor in Cauldmoss was the geographic immobility of
the population which made it all the more interrelated. Both
outsiders and inhabitants remarked on how few people left the
village when they grew up, and many of those who did leave
for employment or to get married later returned. It is difficult
to identify the relative importance of two potential influences
on mobility in Cauldmoss: the disincentives to move when
receiving the social and economic support of a closely knit
group of relatives (Barker 1972), and the scarcity of mobile
career patterns or job opportunities elsewhere in Britain.
Though people said they would not leave Cauldmoss because
"everyone you know is here, ken, all your family, ken," it seems

that the labour market was in fact the prime influence on mobility, especially for men with families. Had better opportunities for jobs existed elsewhere people would almost certainly have travelled to them, and when the demand for unskilled labour rose in southern England in the second half of the 1980s several young men went to work there. However, there was a general preference to be a migrant worker rather than move one's family for an insecure job, and this was what workers in the oil industry had done in the 1970s.

On the other hand, local cultural values inevitably influenced economic decisions. The reluctance to leave Cauldmoss, especially amongst young single people, was partly due to the assumption that others, even in big cities, had the same attitudes towards strangers as those held in Cauldmoss (described above). People from Cauldmoss in a strange town would not only be without familiar company or kinship support, but would themselves be treated as "incomers".

RELIGION

Religious affiliation provided a further important distinction by which the inhabitants of Cauldmoss defined themselves. Of the various criteria for classification in Cauldmoss culture discussed here, differentiation by religion is the only one that Martin does not mention in her analysis of traditional working-class culture in Lancashire (1981). This illustrates important regional variation in the minutely coded categories that characterise working-class culture, variations largely determined by historical factors. There were two distinct principles by which people were differentiated according to religion: either by denomination or by participation in church activities. The first was widely operated, comprehensively dichotomising the village, and it is this criterion that I will discuss here. Participating in church activities was only one of several factors by which Cauldmoss inhabitants distinguished different levels of respectability; it was rarely attributed much importance in itself, except perhaps by a small minority who were devout Christians.

Denominational allegiance

According to the first survey approximately 47 per cent of Cauldmoss identified themselves with the Church of Scotland, 5 per cent with the Roman Catholic church and 3 per cent with the

Church of Christ. Forty-three per cent said they were not associated with any church. Catholic children usually went to a
Catholic primary school and later a Catholic secondary school,
both of which were in the local town. This established explicit
religious segregation from the age of five, since each day while
most children walked to the local school, Catholics had to catch
the bus to the town and returned home at least an hour later than
Protestant children.

The particular religious form that social differentiation takes
in the traditional working-class culture of central Scotland has to
be understood as a legacy of nineteenth-century industrialisation.

> The Irish would accept low wages rather than stay at
> home to starve. In the central decades of the nineteenth
> century several hundred thousand of them entered
> Scotland. They created a new phenomenon in Scotland,
> the secular expression of cultural and economic rivalry
> that picked on religious difference as its nominal cause.
> The Irish enhanced poverty and overcrowding and
> contributed to the social evils that arose from these
> features, drunkenness and crime, to such an extent that
> Protestant antagonism to this influx was able to dis-
> guise itself as a concern for law and order.
>
>   (Mitchison 1970: 381)

The large scale Irish immigration came at the time when
Cauldmoss was rapidly expanding as a centre for coalmining,
and part of the 'economic rivalry' referred to above was the
undercutting of wage rates. Pit owners could play Catholic work
forces off against Protestant ones, sometimes breaking strikes by
importing Irish workers. In some parts of central Scotland this
has left adjoining villages largely composed of opposite denominations. When this material antagonism was added to the
general association of Catholicism with the horrors of industrialisation (Bruce 1985) it is not surprising that great
bitterness arose between the two groups. The bigotry that developed still survives well over a century later, long after its
economic origins have been forgotten.

An Orange Lodge was established in Cauldmoss around 1850,
but by 1911 it had ceased operating, presumably as a consequence

of the dramatic fall in village population. There was a temporary revival of the Lodge in 1936, at a time when two anti-Catholic parties, the 'Protestant Action' and 'Scottish Protestant League', were taking about 40 per cent of the local election votes in the Scottish Lowlands, but it was only in the 1960s that the Lodge again reopened, using the church hall. In the 1980s the separate meetings for men and women were held in the Masonic Lodge, and the small but dedicated membership was dominated by one particular family who "belonged" to Cauldmoss but was living in nearby villages. The Lodge's flute band became too small to survive and the players joined larger bands in the vicinity. Their motivation for participating in the regular rehearsals and travelling to parades all over central Scotland (and occasionally Northern Ireland – the most prized experience) seemed to be primarily their enjoyment of solidarity and belonging: "you meet your ain kind . . . Protestants".

The principal annual events of the Orange Order in Cauldmoss were the 'Juvenile's March' in June and the main Orange March in July, for which a band from a nearby lodge came to the village. The Cauldmoss Orange Lodge was small compared with others in the area, but this did not necessarily reflect greater tolerance in the village and the Orange March always attracted a large sympathetic audience. The description that follows is based on the 1983 march, but it has changed little in the last decade.

On the nearest Saturday to 12 July two coach loads of Orangemen, the flute band and a few women arrived at the pub on the edge of Cauldmoss at 7.30 a.m. They assembled with the local Orange Lodge members to form a procession headed by a woman carrying a purple felt cushion representing the bible and crown. Behind her came a man with a baton and flag bearers, then the pipers and drummers in blue and red uniforms followed by dark-suited men carrying the banners, and behind them a long line of smartly dressed men and women with orange sashes. St Andrew's flags and Union Jacks were carried, while the very elaborate and colourful banners portrayed a founding member of Cauldmoss Orange Lodge, William III in various victorious settings and a picture of Queen Victoria with a semi-naked black man kneeling before her. The bright procession marched along all the outer streets of the scheme with the band playing continuously until it reached the furthest edge of the council housing, the only pause in the noisy piping and drumming being when they passed the war memorial where the banners were dropped and two minutes' silence observed. After the march the Orangemen returned to their coaches and joined other marches around central Scotland, including a big rally of several bands in a nearby town. In the evening they returned to Cauldmoss, tired and less disciplined, and marched back along a shortened route in the opposite direction, passing the Catholic chapel and finishing up at the pub on the edge of the village.

A few dozen people were up to see the procession assemble in the morning, and as it proceeded around the village the accompanying spectators swelled to about a hundred while many others watched from their doors and windows. In the evening a much larger crowd came out to watch, so that the street and pavements were full with the band, their followers, older folk in smart clothes, young lads in T-shirts waving Rangers scarves or Union Jacks, parents holding their children on their shoulders and police cars preceding and following the march. It was a colourful spectacle winding through the grey scheme and most of the audience, particularly the women, viewed it as a pageant rather than an assertion of Protestant supremacy. One woman who was admiring how smart the marchers were – "what an angel young Joe looks, that dressed" – and regretted that there were not more of them, then commented on their pausing beside the Catholic chapel to beat the drums louder: "it's no fair, really, is it Daniel?".

Many of the more committed male followers, however, were very clear about the partisan rationale of the march. At the approach to the chapel it slowed down, there was a crescendo of intimidatory drumming, and the young men cheered as the baton was thrown increasingly high into the air. Almost every year the chapel was vandalised on the night before or after the march, though the damage had become fairly minimal compared with the incident a decade earlier when it was burnt down. The parish priest thought this "was a blessing in disguise" because it turned many Protestants in Cauldmoss against the Orange Lodge. Also around the 12 July graffiti in blue often appeared around the village, such as 'UVF' (Ulster Volunteer Force) or '1690' (the Battle of the Boyne), mainly the work of two or three youths. The march always ended with the band playing 'God Save the Queen' at which the audience stopped chatting, many men stood to attention and several people sang the words. This respect was in marked contrast to the casual atmosphere when 'The Queen' was played on other occasions, such as at the Gala Day ceremony.

Throughout the year anti-Catholic bigotry was expressed spasmodically, nearly always by men and usually when they were drunk. Orange sentiments clearly ran in certain families. An old man commented:

> it's bred in them from the day they sook their mother's breast. There you are. And before you're a right Orangeman it's got to be bred into you . . . I don't think it'll ever change. They're breedin' the thing in to hate the Catholics, but then on the other side it's getting bred in too, thick an' heavy. It's quiet in Cauldmoss noo, there's a battle now and again, right enough, but I don't think anything'll ever cure it.

Generally the rivalry was manifested in songs and jokes: 'Q: What's the quickest way to hospital? A: Drive to [name of Catholic village] and sing "The Sash".' In a fine example of a group deriving its sense of identity by contrast with others (Cohen 1985: 116), rather as the pueblos of Andalusia do (Pitt-Rivers 1971: 8), many men in Cauldmoss could recite a litany of local villages which they classified as more or less Catholic or Protestant. Orangemen generally considered things were worse in the west than the east, Glasgow being mainly Irish. Cauldmoss, of course, was "a Protestant village, a Protestant *stronghold*". Occasionally antagonism actually led to fights, but villagers remembered this happening far more in the past, when large families of Catholics would start a fight by simply walking into "Billie's", the most Protestant pub (cf. Shotts in Heughan 1953: 13). One or two men in the village had connections with the UVF in Ulster. The content of religious beliefs was not relevant to the sectarianism, except in providing identifying symbols for either side, and some suggested that even the political history had been largely forgotten by the protagonists. I had a revealing conversation by accident with four Protestant teenagers when they asked which religion I believed in and I turned the question back on them, asking how I would know. None could identify any differences between Catholic and Protestant beliefs, despite having just fantasised about smashing the Pope's skull like rotten wood, and after a long silence one of them sang a Rangers song. Then another lad said you could easily tell Catholics from Protestants in Cauldmoss

because the Catholics were "two faced fuckin' bastards", they all
stuck together and drank with each other in the pubs.

The Masons

Freemasonry provided one of the most extreme examples of
category demarcation in the culture of Cauldmoss, in its rigorous
exclusion of non-members, elaborate hierarchy and segregation
of the sexes, and it is striking how popular it was amongst
villagers. A Masonic lodge was established in Cauldmoss in 1868
and a Masonic Hall built in 1901. In 1950 a branch of the Eastern
Star was started for the Mason's wives and daughters and in 1984
both organisations were still flourishing. Masonry in Cauldmoss
had none of the elitist aspects it has in England, though it was no
longer the case that someone in every household in the village
was a Mason ("if no' the father, then the son", as used to be
claimed). Any man could join so long as he was accepted by the
Lodge, the first principle being that "he believes in a supreme
being – in God", and the second that he gave allegiance to the
Queen. The membership was fairly representative of the male
Cauldmoss population, including both unemployed and self-
employed men, but it tended to be the "nicer" folk who regularly
attended meetings – a much smaller number than the total membership. Women could only join the Eastern Star if their father or
husband was a Mason, and they had about fourteen 'visitations'
(meetings) a year.

Although Catholics were not formally disqualified from joining the Masons, a former Grand Master in Cauldmoss was clear
that they would have found it very difficult to join locally. There
was a considerable overlap of membership between the Masons
and the Orange Lodge (which met in the Masonic Hall), but
there were some Orangemen who were "too extreme" for the
Masons.

The Masonic Lodge and Eastern Star raised money for charities
and for a benevolent fund for their own members, but the main
activities appeared to be ceremonial and social, as far as their
secrecy allowed one to surmise. As for mutual help in important
areas like job recruitment, Masons implied that membership of
the Lodge was analogous to being part of the regular clientele of
a pub: having access to an informal information network about
the labour market, whether as an employee or employer. The
Masonic Hall also functioned as a working man's club, and the

social events held there were open to anyone, though few Catholics ever attended.

The rigidly structured hierarchy, the secrecy and the ritual of the two Masonic organisations were certainly great attractions for people in Cauldmoss. A woman in the Eastern Star told me with relish how there were many different levels through which you could progress, but you never knew what the teachings were at the next stage until you entered it, as was the case with the secrets of the masons of Solomon (upon which the organisation is based). Her husband added that only previous masters in the Masons got to choose the new master for the year, "otherwise what would be the point of having masters?". This nicely illustrated a tautology common to several secret societies: one of the main rationales of the exclusive group is to exclude others, and the ultimate secret of the society may be that there is no secret (Goffman 1971: 76).

Martin's omission of religious differentiation does not undermine the applicability of her thesis to Cauldmoss, for bigotry between Protestants and Catholics is analogous to the racial prejudice that historical circumstances have made the predominant form of boundary maintenance in other parts of Britain. As Martin would have predicted, when Asians did come to the village in 1982 they experienced greatest prejudice from those villagers most concerned to maintain boundaries in other areas of their lives, most particularly between themselves and Catholics.

3

Respectability

The principles by which social classes can be differentiated constitute one of the most enduring sociological debates, but whether one considers occupational position in the labour market, wealth and inheritance, or cultural capital central in defining class, the vast majority of Cauldmoss inhabitants would be categorised as working class.

The 1981 Census classified the population according to the social class of the head of each household (generally taken to be male), based on his/her present or previous occupation. The figures were only based on the 10 per cent sample, which means that their accuracy for the whole population was reduced. In 1981 36 per cent of Cauldmoss households were headed by people who were retired or had never been economically active. Table 3.1 describes how the remaining households were classified:

TABLE 3.1 Social classes in Cauldmoss by head of household.

	Social classes	Percentage
Unskilled workers	V	16
Partly skilled workers	IV	9
Skilled manual workers	IIIM	44
Skilled non-manual workers	IIIN	5
Intermediate workers	II	16
Professional workers	I	5
Members of the armed forces and those who inadequately described their occupation		5

Source: 1981 Census.

From these figures it is clear that the vast majority of families in Cauldmoss were what is generally termed "working class", and only 26 per cent could be described as "middle class". (See my introductory comment about the use of the term 'class').

One of the striking features of Scottish class structure is that, with council house tenure far more prevalent than in England, housing tenure corresponds closely to the traditional divide between non-manual and manual occupations. In Cauldmoss 73 per cent of the population lived in council housing in 1981. Practically all the small businessmen and farmers of the village were owner occupiers, as were most of those in managerial and other non-manual jobs. There were some manual workers who lived in private housing, primarily lorry drivers and men in the building trade, but they were nearly all self-employed. The distinctiveness of owner occupied households in terms of head of household's occupation was accentuated by considerably higher employment rates amongst private house women (69 per cent of those between 16 and 60 had some kind of employment compared with 28 per cent in council houses) and considerably lower male unemployment rates (14 per cent as opposed to around 42 per cent amongst council house men), using figures from our first survey in 1982. There was virtually no privately rented accommodation in Cauldmoss in the early 1980s.

The potential for income generation and, more importantly, capital accumulation from home ownership has led to a long-running dispute over the theoretical validity of identifying 'housing classes', in the Weberian sense (Rex and Moore 1967; Saunders 1978; Hamnett 1989). This ethnography is not intended to contribute to that debate: my simple point is that if housing tenure *is* considered a criterion of class division, then Cauldmoss was still predominantly working class. I am, however, concerned to analyse the significance of housing in terms of social status, and will return to the subject shortly.

The aspect of cultural capital (Bourdieu 1984) in Cauldmoss that probably had greatest economic importance was information about the labour market and personal contact with employers. While this was crucial to finding employment, and will be discussed at length in subsequent chapters, at best it tended to reproduce one's material conditions. Minimal formal education and ignorance or rejection of middle class taste (Bourdieu 1984) ensured that for the majority of people in

Cauldmoss their cultural capital was of restricted value and more likely to hamper than assist upward social mobility.

Locating Cauldmoss in the class structure is essential to understand the salience and substance of social status in the village. My argument is that social status and class are closely interrelated in contemporary British society, and that one's position according to one dimension of stratification is perpetuated by one's position in the other. A fundamental contrast between the two concepts is that whereas classes are generally considered objective categories that exist irrespective of the actors' consciousness, the status hierarchy is meaningless unless the major status distinctions are recognised by the population. Having outlined the 'objective' position of Cauldmoss inhabitants in the class structure, the bulk of this chapter analyses the actors' own criteria for social stratification.

INFLUENCES OF CLASS POSITION ON CULTURE

Lack of class consciousness

It is striking that few people in Cauldmoss ever used class terms to differentiate themselves. Instead most described themselves as "working people" or "working folk", and males continually referred to themselves as "working men" rather than "working class". To some extent there was an ideology of homogeneity in the village, with people asserting that everyone in Cauldmoss was the same, "all working folk", which was an aspect of the community feeling described in Chapter Two. In fact after stating this similarity between villagers people often went on to identify distinct groups amongst the workers.

Very few classified others according to their occupation, except for those who were identified as small businessmen or farmers. They were sometimes referred to derogatorily as "snobbish", or the kind that "think they're better than everyone else", and their relative wealth was resented. However, most people acknowledged that these folk had worked hard for their money, and many ordinary villagers were on familiar terms with them, greeting them in the street by their Christian names. These entrepreneurs and farmers were rarely described as middle class, and when asked to classify the different groups in the village only one person mentioned this division between the self-employed or "business folk" and the others. No one described different groupings in the village in terms of skilled and unskilled workers.

A subordinate culture

One of the most important features of working-class existence is the limited control over many of the fundamental aspects of life, in particular the nature of employment and, for council tenants, lack of control over housing. To a large extent working-class culture can be analysed as a response to this subordinate position. Hoggart captured this excellently:

> When people feel that they cannot do much about the main elements in their situation, feel it not necessarily with despair or disappointment or resentment but simply as a fact of life, they adopt attitudes towards that situation which allow them to have a liveable life under its shadow, a life without a constant and pressing sense of the larger situation. The attitudes remove the main elements in the situation to the realm of natural laws, the given . . . material from which a living has to be carved.

(Hoggart 1957: 92)

Marxist sociologists have also accepted this idea of a subordinate culture (e.g. Willis 1977: 3; Critcher 1979: 38; Campbell 1984: 5). There were several aspects of Cauldmoss life which could be understood in relation to this concept. The conservatism already discussed was reinforced by the fact that much of the villagers' lifestyle was taken for granted as natural: the choices that were perceived concerning diet, clothing, leisure activities and so on were very limited, and the way people organised their lives was usually extremely regular, with set times for meals, shopping, redecorating, and so on.

Resignation to a life of intrinsically alienating employment or housework, or a combination of the two, informed most teenagers' attitudes to schooling. Cauldmoss children seemed to enjoy primary school but showed less enthusiasm for the secondary school and usually left at 16 with no qualifications. Of the first survey sample 83 per cent had stopped their formal education at the minimum school leaving age. Amongst council tenants the figure was 89 per cent and amongst those in privately owned houses 63 per cent. There was little difference between the ages that girls and boys had left school, but younger council tenants seemed to have had still less formal education than their parents: all of those under 30 had finished school at the minimum possible age. Willis has described the self-fulfilling assumption of the manual working class that sons will follow in their fathers' kinds of jobs, making formal education largely irrelevant and leading pupils to leave at the minimum age (Willis 1977). In the first half of the 1980s most Cauldmoss pupils preferred to leave school at 16 and apply for their £16.50 Supplementary Benefit than stay on to retake 'CSE's and 'O' Levels, in which case their mothers would have only received £6.50 Child Benefit. (Since 1988 people under 18 have no longer been eligible for Social Security benefits). Better qualifications would have improved their chances of finding employment, but since these were virtually nil anyway – in December 1983 there was one vacancy advertised in the local Job Centre for over 400 school leavers – the attractions of receiving more benefit in their own right, attaining the adult status conveyed by this and being free from school, predominated. The teachers at Cauldmoss Primary acknowledged that education had always been intended to socialise children for employment, and that this must now be questioned: "We've really got to teach them for leisure", the headmistress said. However her concept of what that would entail was vague and unimaginative: – "give them games: badminton, pool . . . " – and in fact the curriculum and discipline of the school seemed to reaffirm the old values intended to shape good employees. There was no suggestion that the traditional passive role of the manual working class would, or should, change, and little encouragement for them to assume more control over their lives.

Several other features of Cauldmoss life could be related to the inhabitants' subordinate role in the wider society, such as their deference towards administrative institutions, particularly amongst women. A more general consequence of the way people made sense of their lack of control over their lives was their concentration on the immediate and personal.

An immediate personal world

People in Cauldmoss lived in a very personal world where the really important concerns were the details of individuals' lives, whether the main life course events or the minutiae of everyday affairs, not abstract ideas, theories or politics. The vast majority of the conversations that fill our field notebooks are about local individuals and their activities, immediate concerns of the day or past events in the village: so and so getting a new dog, a cousin getting arrested for a burglary, how much a cassette recorder could be bought for or how so and so earned his nickname. Working class life is, in Hoggart's words, characterised by 'the intimate, the sensory, the detailed, and the personal' (Hoggart 1957: 104). The main themes of a woman's conversation are:

> among the great themes of existence – marriage, children, relations with others, sex. Much the same is naturally true of men's ... they are exercising their strong traditional urge to make life intensely human, to humanise it in spite of everything and so to make it, not simply bearable, but positively interesting.

> (Hoggart 1957: 105)

The preoccupation with personally known individuals reinforced the tremendous importance of kinship in Cauldmoss life.

This concern with the personal was amply illustrated by the popularity of the tabloid papers, in particular the *Daily Record* (about 320 copies sold in Cauldmoss) and the *Sun* (about 100 copies sold). In these, abstract ideas and overt politics were minimal, and the main references to famous people, whether pop stars, politicians or royalty, were about their personal lives. But celebrities were not essential: the readers could be just as absorbed by stories about ordinary people, so long as they were sufficiently intimate and involved one of the main elemental themes, like the bridegroom who died of a heart attack at the age of 21. For many people in Cauldmoss, particularly the men, these papers were their only reading; as Seabrook forcefully argues (1986 and 1987b) they should be taken seriously as bearers of ideology. The *Sun* is the most explicit in its veneration of money as the supreme good and its disgracing of people as venal and violent: 'The main ideological thrust ... is to demonstrate that the system that delivers the goods is not the same as the one that delivers the evils.' (Seabrook 1987b: 17). The basic philosophy 'is that life is something out of which it is the highest duty of each individual to squeeze as much money, sex and fun as may be had.' (Seabrook 1986: 25). I will return to this attitude to money in a later chapter.

Politics

The most immediate, most intensely experienced world was that of daily affairs, gossip, and social status in the village: political consciousness in national or ideological terms was very limited. Again this can be related to the working class being in a dependent position: 'it is a subordinate class, and being a socialist means surrendering a culture of subordination for self-determination.' (Campbell 1984: 5).

The Cauldmoss electorate had voted Labour at both national and local elections for decades, a tradition generally associated with Cauldmoss being "a guid mining village". However, in the early 1980s the local Labour branch was moribund. In the previous thirty years party membership had dropped from about twenty to three in the village, one of whom was the local district councillor who never attended party meetings and who privately condemned many of Labour's policies. He had not had his position contested for over a decade and, though he was frequently criticised by villagers for anything that could be construed as his responsibility, the surgeries he held in Cauldmoss were poorly attended. Indeed, the state of local politics seemed to fit Smout's characterisation of the Scottish Labour Party thirty years earlier as having: 'nothing whatever to do with participatory democracy, enthusiasm for socialism or hope for the future.' (Smout 1987: 274)

Conventionally trade union activity provided the most obvious form for employees to pursue their class interests, combining practical political action with self-interest, but very few people in Cauldmoss were actively involved in their trade unions. By the early 1980s far fewer of those in employment belonged to unions than a decade earlier, since a higher proportion of the work force were in part time jobs, women's jobs or in small businesses. One of the few officials in Cauldmoss, a shop steward for the Transport and General Workers Union, was laid off when a major foundry closed in 1982. Most people in the village still considered trade unions important in protecting the worker, but they often commented that they had become too powerful and politicised in the past, implying some support for the Conservative government's industrial relations legislation.

A few local people assisted the Conservative Party's electioneering, but they disguised their allegiance in the village and only helped canvassing in neighbouring areas. There were no Scottish Nationalist, Liberal or Social Democrat activists evident in Cauldmoss.

The lack of interest in national politics in Cauldmoss was exemplified by the 1983 general election which was scarcely commented on, and no posters or stickers were displayed anywhere in the village. When the local Labour MP visited to canvass votes during Gala Day he was virtually ignored in favour of the procession. The few political conversations that did occur during the election campaign were in terms of personalities, usually confirming the speakers' longing to be rid of "Maggie Hatchet". One woman described how she had an horrific fascination for watching Margaret Thatcher on television:

> when I see her scrawny neck . . . I hate her, so I do, I really hate her . . . but I like to watch her, ken, to hate her the mair; aye, I do.

There was no serious discussion of the alternative policies offered by the political parties, even on issues close to home such as unemployment, and the use of election addresses (from all parties) as firelighters was a standing joke.

The 1984–5 miners' strike provides another important illustration of political attitudes in Cauldmoss. There was implicit sympathy for the miners and a general wish for Thatcher to be defeated, but there was also considerable criticism of Arthur Scargill and the miners' tactics. There was no active support for the National Union of Mineworkers, even through fund raising, and no one joined the pickets at a pit only fifteen miles away. This was remarkable when contrasted with the kind of response striking miners got from such culturally distant areas as London. Furthermore, when coal was being driven into Ravenscraig steel works after the railwaymen supported the NUM, lorry drivers in Cauldmoss told me that they would be prepared to drive through the pickets themselves if they got a contract to supply Ravenscraig. During a recession one has to take whatever work is available, they argued: the rationale of financial gain excluded values of solidarity that might have been transmitted from a previous era when Cauldmoss had been an occupational community.

The political views that were expressed in Cauldmoss were generally parochial and conservative, and most people were keen patriots and monarchists. Thatcher's stand over the Falklands conflict won general support and several men relished the military engagement. There was an insatiable curiosity for the personal details of royal lives, and undying loyalty to the Queen was often stated (often associated with allegiance to Protestantism, mentioned in the previous chapter). Perhaps because of the concentrated attention on the everyday life of the monarch she seemed to be regarded as a warm, friendly, down to earth sort of family woman, sympathetic to the concerns of ordinary folk, in striking contrast to the Prime Minister. During a conversation in the pub several men agreed that the Queen *hates* Maggie Thatcher, and they portrayed the monarch as very paternalistic: "*she* doesnae want to see people idle". One man said that, after all, she did not choose her job and she would probably prefer not to have it. *He* certainly would not want it. The deferential political outlook in Cauldmoss was suggested in the Gala Day procession: although tenuous links with mythical saints were resorted to to give the village pageant some historical depth, there was no reference at all to the history of coal mining but instead the event focused on a queen in a white Rolls Royce accompanied by numerous symbols of high rank.

This tendency, illustrated above, to accept as given the structural factors constraining one's life and to focus on that area of one's experience that at least appeared subject to one's influence, explains the salience of social status to those who assumed that their working-class position was ascribed.

SOCIAL STATUS: THEORETICAL CONSIDERATIONS

The theoretical marginalisation of social status

Studies of working class culture throughout this century have emphasised the importance of respectability (see Goldthorpe and Lockwood 1963: 141). Ethnographers confirm each other's findings on the importance of status distinctions in working-class localities, and Pahl even asserts that 'status-consciousness has always been more important than class-consciousness', (Pahl 1984: 89). However, with some key exceptions (for example Marshall 1953; Lockwood 1958; Parkin 1979; Barbalet 1986; Turner 1988), British sociologists have, in general, shown little interest in the issue of status. This is probably due in part to, first, their bias towards tangible, quantifiable data and macro studies of society, and second, the predominance of analyses framed in Marxist terms with 'the theoretical postulate that all significant social relationships may ultimately be understood in terms of a class analysis', (Newby 1983: 5).

> Marxism lacks a clear conception of the interrelationship between class and status structures. This is because the analysis of the institutionalisation of status has no place in its theory of social integration. The entire problem of status is lost sight of in highly general and essentially functionalist conceptions of ideological domination.
>
> (Lockwood 1981: 448)

Since Frankenberg's discussion of status, in what turned out to be a conclusion to the tradition of community studies (Frankenberg 1966: 259–64), there has been little consideration of the concept until the recent revival of detailed ethnographic research.

Status groups, prestige and esteem

To analyse social status in Cauldmoss necessitates a clarification of terms. My starting point is, predictably, Weber:

> In contrast to classes, *status groups* are normally communities ... we wish to designate as 'status situation' every typical component of the life fate of men that is determined by a specific, positive or negative, social estimation of *honor*. This honor may be connected with any quality shared by a plurality, and, of course, it can be knit to a class situation: class distinctions are linked in the most varied ways with status distinctions.
>
> (Weber 1948: 186–7)

Several problems have been identified with Weber's concept of status, the principal ones being the relationship between status and class and the factors governing the distribution of status honour (in particular whether status privilege is the outcome of conflict). Other authors, most recently Turner (1988), have summarised the development of 'status' by neo-Weberians; here I will simply point to certain useful conceptual distinctions.

Davis (1942) distinguished between 'prestige' and 'esteem', a distinction that Parkin returned to (1971) using the terms 'status of position' and 'status of person'. Prestige or status of position is the social honour attributed to a particular location in a social system irrespective of the individual occupying that location. Obvious examples from Cauldmoss were the prestige of a physician, a minister, a professor, or a member of parliament. Esteem or status of person is the social honour attributed to a particular individual by virtue of her/his performance in one or more social roles. It is usually based on personal interactions with others and is therefore of greatest importance amongst groups of people whose social relationships are closely interknit. One of the most widespread dichotomies based on esteem in Britain is that between respectable and non-respectable, the specific criteria for this distinction varying considerably according to class, ethnicity, age, gender and so on.

For both Davis and Parkin there is no necessary connection between prestige and esteem, and Parkin argues that while esteem is relevant to the analysis of small groups it is irrelevant to the formal properties of the system of social inequalities. Indeed, the conflation of the two conceptually distinct notions of status is, he claims, one of the great weaknesses of neo-Weberians. In presenting the ethnographic data that follow I intend to challenge this position.

The role of lifestyle in status distinctions

Turner argues that 'social groups distinguish themselves from competitors by their "superior" dispositions, bodily gestures, speech, and deportment' (Turner 1988: 67). This cultural dimension of social status Turner calls 'lifestyle', following Weber:

> In content, status honor is normally expressed by the fact that above all else a specific *style of life* can be expected from all those who wish to belong to the circle.

(Weber 1948: 187–91)

Recently the English translation of Weber's *Class, Status, Party* has been criticised for ignoring his distinction between two separate elements of *Lebensstil* (lifestyles) (Abel and Cockerham 1993). These are *Lebensführung* (life conduct), which refers to chosen behaviour, and *Lebenschancen* (life chances), which refers to the social conditions that structure choice of behaviour. Thus Weber did not regard lifestyles simply as volitional, but the outcome of the interplay between agency and structure: 'the possibility of status-specific life conduct is of course in part economically conditioned' (Weber 1922: 537, quoted by Abel and Cockerham 1993). We will see in this ethnography that life conduct is also very much conditioned by cultural factors.

To return to the earlier distinction between esteem and prestige, if the social honour accorded to particular life conduct or cultural practices, such as dress, diet, domestic furnishing or etiquette, is attributed to an individual on the basis of her personal performance then it is defined as esteem. If social honour is accorded to an individual because of her prior membership of a social group, then it is defined as prestige. Since the collective adherence to a specific lifestyle which leads to the development of status groups depends on numerous individuals' life conduct, it follows that the prestige of a status group is, in large part, dependent on the esteem of many individual actors. To give a topical example, the prestige of the royal family is inevitably affected by the life conduct of its members. On a more humble level, in Cauldmoss the prestige of general practitioners as a whole was undermined by the low esteem in which the local doctor was held, due to his cavalier treatment of patients. Thus both informal and formal social controls often exist to discourage individuals from bringing their profession/collectivity into disrepute.

The necessity of conforming to a particular lifestyle as a qualification of status in Cauldmoss will be documented in subsequent chapters, and the relative importance of different aspects of lifestyle for different generations will be discussed. It is worth stressing that for Weberians lifestyle is only important in social stratification if it is linked to a collectivity, typically one in competition with other social groups.

Following Turner (1988), I have avoided suggesting that either economic class or social status has causal primacy. However, the main status group in Cauldmoss, the respectable working class, was by definition a fraction of an economic class, and the significance of status distinctions to the inhabitants of Cauldmoss was largely attributable to two consequences of their class location. First, the interknit social relationships of the village (described in the previous chapter) resulted from geographic immobility which was a feature of class position. Second, the concern with the personal and immediate, which made individual reputation such a crucial aspect of villagers' lives, was characteristic of a subordinate culture that had developed in response to lack of control over the main elements of one's life, that is, in response to a subordinate class position.

CAULDMOSS AS A 'STATUS COMMUNITY'

Having discussed various conceptual terms relating to social status I will apply them to the social life of Cauldmoss. The village could be regarded as a 'status community' (Turner 1988) in the sense of a solidaristic collectivity, and the importance of being perceived to "belong" to this group or not has been described in the previous chapter. Membership of Cauldmoss automatically granted one access to support networks within the village and shared leisure activities (in particular the bingo, pubs and clubs), and many people felt it should also entitle one to local council housing. In fact, the local authority's points system for housing allocation did not take place of birth or childhood residence into account, and "outsiders" were allocated local houses. In any case, in 1984 there was sufficient council housing to meet local demand: it was only houses in specific streets that had scarcity value. Although it was widely claimed that personal friendship with the local councillor influenced one's chances of getting a desirable house, and many local people considered this would be legitimate, there were no established cases of such conduct overriding local authority bureaucracy.

How the social honour of belonging to Cauldmoss related to that of belonging to the respectable working class is difficult to interpret. It seems that different principles applied for different social strata. The respectable status of working class incomers was far more vulnerable to village opinion than that of those born in Cauldmoss, and they had to conform to the conventions of a respectable lifestyle more assiduously than those whose reputations had been established over decades. Conversely, middle class incomers (such as ourselves) seemed to be granted greater latitude in conforming to local cultural conventions than indigenous middle class residents. It was as if to express (and retain) their membership of the village that the locally born middle class had to conform to village conventions, which obscured the differences in economic class, while for middle class incomers this class distinction was acknowledged and it was recognised that rather different criteria of respectability applied. Of course in our anomalous position as "students" we were allowed far more leeway than most incomers, and the broad generalisations made above must be modified by recognising individuals' personalities which could, for instance, make someone generally popular despite his behaviour being wildly out of order.

BEING "NICE": THE RESPECTABLE WORKING CLASS

The boundaries around respectability

The 'respectable working class' was the principal status group manifest in Cauldmoss, though this was not a term used by villagers who rarely identified explicitly with a class or used the word respectable.

For working-class people in Cauldmoss being respectable was experienced primarily through the maintenance of boundaries between "nice folk" and "the wasters" ("the bad lot" or "the bad element"). The salience of this distinction between 'respectable' and "rough" working class in the 1980s demonstrates continuity in working-class history: thirty years ago the ubiquity of these two status categories was noted in the ethnographies of the 1950s (Goldthorpe and Lockwood 1963: 141). Their evident importance in working-class culture makes it remarkable how little attention they have received from modern sociologists.

Boundary maintenance on the 'upper' side of the respectable working-class category was not as pervasive and ritualised as it was between the respectable and rough. This was largely due to the fact that there was little regular social contact with middle class people. Although being middle class was deemed more prestigious than being working class, there were important controls on aspirations to move out of the respectable working class. For instance, the only indigenous term for middle class people was "snobs". Normative constraints on social aspiration were expressed in appropriate styles of consumption, which will be considered in Chapter Seven.

Although Cauldmoss inhabitants frequently referred to the division between the "nice folk" and the "wasters", there were in fact gradations of respectability within both groups and differences between villagers in how they classified individuals. To an

extent one's position in the hierarchy of respectability was relative. The great majority of villagers perceived themselves to be
"nice", distanced themselves from the "wasters" and regarded
anyone who was condescending or unfriendly to them as "snobs".
Whatever a person's subjective self-ranking, however, there was
usually considerable consensus in the village about a person's
status. Thus, amongst the "bad lot" were several who shared the
moral codes and norms of respectable villagers and struggled to
conform to them, thereby retaining their own self-respect. But
they were nevertheless viewed by most inhabitants as being in a
different category from "nice folk", even if it was through no fault
of their own (e.g. their husband had abandoned them). Whatever
their moral behaviour and aspirations, if they could not afford
the material lifestyle essential for respectability, they would be
judged as less than "decent". Others generally classified as "the
bad element" attached little importance to, or even rejected, the
norms of respectability. They shared the majority view of themselves as outwith the moral community, though they would not
describe themselves in pejorative terms such as "wasters".

At an empirical level the respectable working class in
Cauldmoss were distinguished by eight main criteria (see Figure
3.1). These can be divided between the 'objective' characteristics
of housing and occupation of head of household and six elements
of lifestyle. The criteria of social stratification considered most
important by sociologists – occupation and housing – were of less
daily concern to villagers than aspects of social life often deemed
irrelevant by macro sociologists, such as material lifestyle and,
above all, moral reputation. I will describe the components of
working-class respectablilty in rough order of their increasing
importance to local people.

'Objective' criteria: occupation and housing
Occupation was rarely a criterion for classifying other villagers,
as we have seen from the discussion of social class. Only small
businessmen and farmers were occasionally distinguished as a
group distinct from others in employment. Although being a
skilled worker "with a trade" (that is, having served an appren-
ticeship) was respected, no one considered that skilled workers
constituted a separate status category. Nor did one's current
circumstance of being in or out of employment define one's social
status; the important distinction in this respect was whether

unemployed men were perceived to be actively seeking work or not, which reduces the prestige of employment status to moral reputation.

Housing was more frequently used to differentiate villagers than occupation. However, there was not a simple social division between the 27 per cent who lived in private houses and the council house tenants. Private house residents were split between incomers and locals or the spouses of locals (amongst 38 per cent of the couples in private houses at least one spouse was originally from the village: first survey). Many of the local owner occupiers and their spouses participated in social activities attended predominantly by council tenants, several had relatives living on the scheme and a few had the same kind of jobs as those in council houses. In contrast most homeowning incomers had minimal social involvement with Cauldmoss. They were often strongly prejudiced against the villagers and frequently voiced derogatory generalisations, such as all the local people being "hangers-on" or "wasters".

It was noted above, when considering social class, that housing tenure was associated with occupational strata and marked differences in male and female employment rates. Given these income differentials on top of evident differences in wealth, it was surprising that council tenants did not regard private house residents in general as a distinct group. Frequent social contacts with locally born private house dwellers discouraged such a classification, and though the relative affluence of homeowners was sometimes resented, criticism of them tended to focus on incomer owner occupiers' lack of involvement in village life. Very few people described those in private houses as "middle class". The meaning of home ownership and the different patterns of spending between council and private house dwellers will be mentioned in Chapter Seven.

Differentiation of villagers by housing was confused by the extent of their integration into village life at both ends of the status scale. Within the council housing of Cauldmoss different areas were rated as more or less desirable, though strong consensus existed only at the ends of the spectrum, with two streets in particular being widely denigrated, one of which was the "Gorbals of Cauldmoss". Since hard-to-let housing was quickly occupied by incomers who were often clients of the Homeless Persons Officer (as described in the previous chapter), the less desirable streets were further stigmatised by the presence of "the problem cases", perpetuating their ghettoisation.

Even within such a small place as Cauldmoss fictitious descriptions of these roads gained currency amongst folk living a few hundred yards away: some women talked of how "half the windows are boarded up, no glass in them at all", when at that time none of the houses were in that state. Proximity to one's relatives was usually the overriding consideration when moving house, but getting out of undesirable streets and into "nicer" ones was also a common objective. Though there was considerable architectural variation within the scheme (for instance in materials – between brick, breeze block and steel – and design – four in a block, semi-detached or low rise flats) the most important factor determining the social status of different streets was the residents, and it only took three or four "wasters" to move into a road for it to be seen as less appealing by others.

Lifestyle

An individual's lifestyle was more important in establishing her or his respectability in Cauldmoss than housing or occupation. Lifestyle has greater sociological significance than merely being a matter of personal esteem, I argued above, since the esteem of many individuals is necessary for the prestige of a status group. The term 'lifestyle' subsumes numerous cultural practices. Those by which villagers attributed respectability to each other can be grouped into six main categories, all of which are interrelated (Figure 3.1). They are: material lifestyle, work, participation in leisure institutions, churchgoing, sexual behaviour and child care.

In each of these areas standards of respectable behaviour were gender specific, and, with the exception of work, the norms were far more pervasive and demanding for women than for men. To a large extent women were the guardians of their families' respectability (cf. Pahl 1984: 108), but as others have noted, this designation can be used to justify restricting their behaviour (Hey 1986: 35). This was most evident in respect to sexuality: as already mentioned, while men were half expected to have several sexual partners, a woman's 'promiscuity', and in particular extra-marital sex, was thought to threaten both her honour and that of the whole family. The close-knit relationships and immobility of people in Cauldmoss made sexual reputations particularly important. On a more mundane level, women's daily chores to keep their houses clean and tidy were physical expressions of their industriousness and commitment to a correct order. Furthermore

> The housewife is guardian not only of the necessities but also of all the elements of consumption through which the class identity or the life-style of the family is defined and displayed.

(Martin 1984: 32)

Thus to some extent husbands established their status vicariously through the consumption of their wives, a point I will return to later.

Work and material lifestyle are the subjects of Chapters Four and Five respectively. They will not be discussed here, except to outline my argument that reputation as a "worker" and the maintenance of a respectable standard of material consumption were intrinsic to moral repute, and to point to generational differences in how respectability was perceived. Sexual behaviour has been discussed briefly in Chapter Two, and the norms of child care were so specific to women that they are beyond the immediate focus of this book. Suffice to say it was in relation to sexual behaviour and child care that status stratification was most explicitly moralistic, for instance mothers perceived to rely over-frequently on babysitters (even when they were relatives) risked being excluded from the moral community.

Participation in certain leisure institutions was seen as an important indication of one's social status (or aspirations), while helping in their administration was considered prestigious. The Bowling Club, the Rural Institute and the Churchwomen's Guild all tended to be seen as "stuck-up", "clannish" or "snobbish" by those who did not attend them, although the first two institutions included many members from the scheme. By contrast the old hotel was a pub with a bad reputation that was avoided by the "nicer folk" in the village. The respectability of different locations for drinking will be described in Chapter Six, and collective leisure activities, such as bingo, described in Chapter Seven.

Going to church was not generally considered necessary to being "nice", which presumably it had been in the past, but attendance at either kirk or chapel certainly established one was not one of "the wasters". For a certain peer group in Cauldmoss kirk attendance was essential for social respectability while for others it was one of several criteria by which "snobs" could be identified. This parallels the findings of an earlier study of church membership in a similar area (Sissons 1973). Only a minority of the congregation were noted for having different moral standards from the non-church goers in the village, or expressed deeper religious belief. The majority of people in Cauldmoss saw churchgoing as something pleasurable, almost a leisure activity, and members of the congregation talked to each other about how they "enjoyed" a service.

A new minister had managed to expand his congregation to about fifty regulars by 1984, two-thirds of whom were women (similar to other Lowland parishes: Willis and Turner 1980: 27) although the elders were all male. The Women's Guild had a membership of about twenty, and around ten children attended Sunday School. The Church of Scotland's influence in Cauldmoss was greater than the small congregation would suggest. Many non-attenders approved of churchgoing and generally subscribed to the kirk's teachings. Most villagers were familiar with the minister either through his involvement in secular institutions, like the school and the Scouts, or his home visits, and he was widely liked in contrast to the previous incumbent. The personalities of different Cauldmoss ministers were a topic of perennial interest to most villagers.

The Church of Scotland had a very active social calendar, organising concerts, dances, whist drives, coffee mornings and so on, in aid of various church appeals. They were held in the church hall or the school and were attended by a much wider group than the regular congregation, though still all "nice folk" (and some who were regarded as "snobs" by others), still predominantly women, and mainly middle aged or over.

Attendance at the Catholic chapel was generally regarded (by those other than Orangemen) as respectable as going to the kirk, but the motives probably had less to do with social standing given the Catholic doctrine on observing mass. About a tenth of the village were Roman Catholics, and the local priest said he had ninety-six people "on the books" about fifty of whom attended mass (a far higher proportion attending than in the Church of Scotland). In contrast to the kirk the Catholics organised few secular activities, the main one being an annual prize bingo which all regular bingo-goers of whatever religious persuasion attended.

The Church of Christ had a congregation of about twenty-four, almost entirely made up of three extended families. Of the active churchgoers in Cauldmoss this group was the one most clearly identified as "snobbish". An old man, who called them "Apostolics", described their social position in the village:

> the Apostolics is a clique too . . . are you in it? – I thought you looked like one . . . they are a crowd that keeps by theyselves. Mind you, they talk polite to ye, oh yes, an' I don't really think they'd do you a bad turn. But I know they turn up their noses at certain people in Cauldmoss, they talk a lot about the poor people in Cauldmoss.

Participation in the Church of Christ involved far more commitment than attending either the kirk or the Catholic chapel. There were unaccompanied hymns and spontaneous prayers during the services, and members tended to be seen as "holy Joes" in the village. This could have been connected with the sobriety, lack of swearing and respect for the secular law which characterised many of the congregation and used to be a hallmark of this sect (Hudson 1948: 205). No teenagers attended services in the early 1980s and the Church of Christ had no secular social activities.

Moral repute

The certification of respectability in Cauldmoss was moral repute, moral judgements constituting one of the commonest ways in which villagers categorised each other. "Nice folk", who were usually "good workers" or simply "good people", were distinguished from "the bad element", who were also described as "wasters", "a bad lot" or "dross". The central role of orientation to work in this dichotomy will be considered further in the following chapter.

The main criteria in Cauldmoss for being "nice" were: being disciplined in one's work, which involved good timekeeping in employment and certain standards of housework and child care; being well groomed, one's personal appearance being as much a sign of self-respect as a clean and tidy house; being able to manage one's resources wisely; showing some restraint in one's drinking or gambling without being mean or puritanical, and

maintaining a particular level of consumption. To deny aspiration to this material lifestyle was tantamount to denying the value
of a moral way of life.

Although within Cauldmoss a villager's social standing was
usually known from his/her personal reputation, amongst non-
villagers (and many of the incomers) social standing was
deduced primarily from manifestations of material lifestyle:
clothes, car, leisure pursuits and so on. Whether meeting people
in the local town or on holiday in Spain, a respectable level of
consumption was a surrogate for less evident elements of respectable working class status, such as working hard all one's life or
living in a clean, tidy, well furnished house. Thus material lifestyle was of crucial importance in providing the link between
esteem and prestige, between someone's honour attributed on
the basis of their personal reputation and honour attributed
because of their position within a status group.

The main grounds for moral condemnation were bad child
care, laziness and vandalism. Amongst those born in Cauldmoss
different families had acquired particular reputations, and although individuals were sometimes distinguished from their
kin, more usually people were assumed to inherit their moral
qualities, as we saw when considering the importance of kinship
(Chapter Two). Once categorised as of "the bad lot" it could take
years of consistently respectable behaviour to improve one's
esteem, while deviant behaviour by someone from a "nice" family
would not affect his or her reputation irredeemably unless
frequently repeated.

The distinction between local people and incomers, described
in the previous chapter, was given particular resonance by the
association of council house incomers with "the wasters". Unless
they were the partners of indigenous villagers, incoming council
tenants were usually housed in one of the two stigmatised streets
and were assumed to be morally reprehensible. The "problem
cases" were blamed for a litany of deviant behaviour: alcoholism,
vandalism, theft, prostitution, glue sniffing, neglecting their children, avoiding rent, and so on. A few blatant examples of such
deviancy served to tar all incomers in "the Gorbals houses" with
the same brush. In fact none of these activities were exclusive to
the "problem cases", but they were often accused of bringing this
anti-social behaviour into the village.

The criteria by which people in Cauldmoss evaluated the social status of their fellow villagers, and in particular differentiated between the respectable and non-respectable working class, can be summarised diagramatically (Figure 3.1). Each column represents a scale of social standing according to a different criterion. An individual could be at different levels on different scales, though there was a tendency for her/his position to be fairly consistent across the diagram. I have tried to show that often there were not smooth gradations between the extremes but, rather, abrupt transitions, which were clearly perceived by people in Cauldmoss, for instance between the "Gorbals houses" and the nice part of the scheme.

Scarce resources

Given the notion of universal entitlement in a democratic state it is not immediately obvious what the scarce resources were to which membership of 'the respectable working-class' might give one access. In terms of legal entitlement it might be argued that the welfare benefits to which one was eligible as a result of paying National Insurance Stamps were a reward of working-class respectability, though they were not restricted to the working class and only relate to one specific element of respectability: regular *formal* employment. However, many people in Cauldmoss did distinguish between those villagers whom they felt deserved their welfare benefits and those that did not, the principal criterion of perceived eligibility being the person's previous commitment to his/her employment (to be discussed more fully in Chapter Four). In 1980 eligibility for unemployment benefit was reduced from two years to one year and in 1982 it stopped being earnings related, which meant contributory benefits came to differ little from non-contributory benefits, a blurring of distinctions that angered many older people in Cauldmoss.

A less formal entitlement which membership of the respectable working class was assumed to give was permanent employment. Those who had worked all their lives and were conscientious timekeepers felt they had "the *right* to work", partly as a just reward for the years of disciplined labour they had already given and partly because this was a prerogative of the respectable working class. Fulfilling the daily obligations of a respectable lifestyle qualified one to be in full employment, in contrast to the wasters whose dissipated way of life meant they had to expect spells of unemployment. This was part of the

MATERIAL LIFESTYLE	WORK	CHILD CARE	SEXUAL REPUTATION	LEISURE INSTITUTIONS	CHURCH GOING	HOUSING	OCCUPATION
"SNOBS" privatised spending expensive new car several holidays per year designer clothes	"good workers" *women with tidy clean houses*	family outings *mothers rarely get babysitters*	"faithful" men	Church Guild Bowling Club – – – – – *active organisers*	Church of Christ elders and regular church goers	expensive private houses landscaped garden aloof owner-occupiers modest private houses	small businessmen professionals managerial jobs "pen pushers" – – – – farmers
new car			"faithful" women *(italic)*		attend church several times each year	"nice" part of the scheme tidy garden	self-employed skilled workers
"NICE FOLK" warm room generous spending butcher meat *jewellery* smart clothes annual holiday		regular school attendance		*Rural Institute* Community Centre *prize bingo* "Nancy's" pub Masonic club			
old car	unemployed with reputation as workers		promiscuous men	social club *cash bingo* "Billie's" pub the bookies	rarely attend church		unskilled workers
– – – –			"unfaithful" men – – – – –				
"WASTERS" spam eke out single drink	*women with dirty houses* "work shy" unemployed not seeking work	truanting	*"promiscuous" women*	the old hotel	never in church	other streets with incomers and "wasters" neglected garden	criminals
patched clothes not reciprocating gifts unlit fire	private schooling	*neglectful mothers* abusing fathers	*"unfaithful" women* *"prostitutes"*			"Gorbals houses"	

italics = predominantly or exclusively relates to women

FIGURE 3.1 Principal criteria by which respectability was assessed in Cauldmoss.

natural order of these two status categories. Whereas the Labour Movement had repeatedly reinforced this expectation and 'full' employment had been a principal goal of national economic policy since the Second World War, during the early 1980s Thatcher's government explicitly challenged people's entitlement to jobs. This gave villagers' conventional condemnation of the Conservatives unusual virulence, not least because Tory policies denied the respectable working class one of the most important privileges that distinguished them from the wasters. Martin has observed how the traditional working-class culture of boundaries and categories can influence political life:

> Even the trade unions operated at least in part on the basis of these established status priorities, as indeed they still do, through the defence of wage differentials and the pursuit of a not entirely new instrumental militancy. A great deal of working class history is misread if we mistake *category* identity for *class* solidarity.

> (Martin 1981: 68)

In Cauldmoss, however, a more important privilege of respectable status than contributory benefits and 'the right to work' was the right to associate with other "nice folk" in the village. Although in this fraction of the working class control over material resources was limited, social relationships consisting of conversation, shared leisure, exchanged commodities and mutual respect could be granted or withheld. In terms of social wellbeing, the dignity of belonging to the moral community was a scarce resource in Cauldmoss, only earned by fulfilling the obligations of respectability discussed above. Furthermore, membership of this status group could have a material dimension in that most employment was gained through personal contacts.

Generational differences

This analysis of social status in Cauldmoss has not, so far, distinguished how different age groups perceived status categories. The significance of belonging to Cauldmoss, a 'status community' in itself, was as great to young people as it was to older generations. However, the relative importance attached to different elements of working-class respectability varied considerably between generations. Whether these differences result from a person's stage in the life course, or whether they reflect change over time cannot be established without a longitudinal study. It is only possible to reflect on how these separate, but not incompatible, interpretations might relate to other features of social life in Cauldmoss and consider the relevant findings from studies elsewhere in Britain.

For heuristic purposes it is useful to distinguish three age groups: those under 30, those between 30 and 60, and those over 60. Being within the status category the respectable working class, that is, being "nice", was of greatest importance to the oldest people in the village. They were most careful to do things in the "nice" way and most resistant to changes in the ritualised distinctions between the respectable and non-respectable. Moral repute was most salient to the oldest generation for they had accumulated the greatest store of memories by which to judge other villagers and had spent the longest period establishing and maintaining their own reputations. The employment ethic (to be described in the next chapter) dominated their notion of respectability, largely because they themselves had generally had to work extremely hard when they were young and had made a virtue of this necessity (cf. Williams 1990).

The old were not only most concerned to maintain the boundary between "nice folk" and "the bad element" but also to maintain the boundary on the 'upper' side of working-class respectability. They had no aspiration to higher social status but strove to keep to their appropriate place in the hierarchy. While it was necessary continually to defend one's status it would have challenged the proper order of things to try and improve it. Older people were most likely to condemn others for what they perceived to be social aspirations, branding them as "snobs", which sometimes led to conflicting ideals when their own children "did well". The way in which these ideals led to contradictory consumption patterns will be addressed in Chapter Seven.

In contrast with the old, those under about 30 were less concerned with moral repute, although they subscribed to the condemnation of "the wasters" on moral grounds. The young had not experienced regular long term employment and some had never had any jobs other than on Manpower Services Commission schemes. Few expressed an employment ethic. They were, however, very concerned with their material lifestyle and had much greater consumer aspirations than older generations, largely unconstrained by possible accusations of being "snobs".

The contrast between old and young generations characterised above can be readily understood as a feature of people's stage in the life course. When young, villagers were not yet able to establish their reputation as hard workers, good parents or dutiful wives. What reputation they had was likely to be based on their opposition to the conventions of adult respectability, simply because of the rebelliousness of young people. While the importance of reputation was minimised, material lifestyle had greater significance. Young people's reference groups were much wider than the village, since they went to school in the local town, would go drinking and dancing there, and were concerned to impress potential spouses. Until they were established in a particular occupation, which, given the unemployment of the early 1980s, was often delayed well into their 20s, many were not committed to living in Cauldmoss and therefore not primarily concerned with the opinions of fellow villagers.

Older people who already had children and were working locally (or their spouses were) expected to continue living in Cauldmoss for much of their lives. Their comparative reference groups increasingly comprised relatives and neighbours within the village. The longer they lived in Cauldmoss the more they were evaluated according to their performance as workers, parents, housewives and so on, and the more knowledge they accumulated about other villagers' competence in performing these roles. Personal reputation gradually took a more important place in their perception of respectability while material lifestyle diminished in significance.

The generational differences in the evaluation of social status might alternatively be interpreted as an historical development. They might result from different ideologies that have arisen at separate stages in the development of our industrial economy, an employment ethic being associated with the economy's early demand for labour which was replaced by a consumption ethic when the economy needed greater consumer spending. The argument that there had been a secular change might be supported by old people's accounts of their hard work and frugality in their youth. However, such reminiscences are notoriously unreliable and it is more useful to consider the relevant sociological literature.

The values which were held by older people in Cauldmoss have much in common with the 'traditional workers' that Lockwood characterised in his much debated typology of ideal types of working-class images of society (Lockwood 1966). Older people's concerns with maintaining the boundaries around the status category of respectable working class incorporate both the status hierarchy of Lockwood's deferential traditional worker and the 'us : them' distinction of the proletarian traditional worker (in that the 'them' were too remote to form a significant reference group and so the stratification was bounded by the limits of 'us'). On the other hand the less restricted status values held by younger people correspond partially to the 'privatised' worker's 'pecuniary' model of society, in which 'consumer durables are of primary significance in mediating his status with his neighbours.' (Lockwood 1966: 258).

Several studies suggest that 'privatised' workers have become numerically predominant in the working class since the 1960s, and this has been linked to general developments in Western societies which make stratification more fluid:

> All forms of subcultural particularism – those based on region, ethnicity etc., as well as those based on class – are broken down, on the one hand, by the need for greater geographical as well as social mobility within the labour force and, on the other, by the growing influence of mass consumption and mass communications.

> (Goldthorpe 1985: 127)

Goldthorpe might wish to modify this overview given the resurgence of regionalism and ethnicity in Europe during the 1990s, but the factors he identifies to explain the eroding of traditional status categories applied to the young in Cauldmoss in 1984. This theme will be explored further in Chapter Seven.

4

Employment

INTRODUCTION

The significance of work, and in particular employment, in the culture of Cauldmoss has already been referred to. This chapter briefly describes how villagers were employed in 1984 and then analyses the meaning of employment to Cauldmoss men. It is important to emphasise that these findings are based on research within the village and not in men's workplaces. This is therefore a description of what employment meant in the residential context, one involving women and families, and the values transmitted in the workplace are only considered in so far as they affected village life. A considerable literature already exists on workers' orientation to their employment as it is revealed in their place of work (see for example Zweig 1961; Goldthorpe *et al.* 1968, 1969 and 1970; Beynon 1973; Dubin 1976). As previously explained, in this chapter I will ignore the 37 per cent of economically active men in Cauldmoss who were unemployed in 1984 and will concentrate on the cultural values that had arisen from a time of 'full' employment. In Chapters Five and Six I will argue that these beliefs underlay many of the more general values in Cauldmoss, in particular those that informed consumption patterns. Chapter Seven will consider how the culture of 'full' employment was modified by unemployment.

DEFINITIONS OF WORK

A social anthropological account cannot treat 'work', 'leisure', or any of the other central categories relating to economic life axiomatically, as if these are discrete areas with unambiguous meanings (Cohen 1979: 265). Wallman argues that anthropologists should tackle the cross-cultural semantic diversity of 'work' by identifying the different dimensions it has, and then studying how they are interrelated (Wallman 1979: 3). One of the original aims of the Cauldmoss research project was to explore the semantic domain of 'work' in a culture whose members describe themselves as 'working people' (Turner 1981). In order to compile a lexicon of terms relating to work and leisure, the first survey asked respondents to clarify forty-five different activities as 'work or something else' and the responses were subsumed under twenty codes (a detailed report on this questionnaire can be found in the appendix of Turner, Bostyn and Wight 1984). The indigenous terms most commonly used to describe the activities were "work", "pleasure", "leisure" and "a necessity". There were no significant differences between the responses of different age groups.

> It was found that those activities which the vast majority agreed were "work" were all paid employment, for example coal mining, cooking school meals and selling insurance. An analysis of indigenous definitions for the terms "work" and "job" revealed that these describe an activity which is done in return for money (the most common definition), or which involves effort of some kind, or which is unenjoyable, or which is something that *has* to be done. Often all four criteria were given, and it seems that the hallmark of true work is that it is an alienating experience.
>
> By looking at how different terms were explained by informants, it is clear that the terms "occupation" and "profession" describe a job done by intelligent, skilled people. "Hard work" usually implied considerable physical effort, but it could also mean a mentally demanding job, or one that involves coercion or dislike, which reinforces the meaning of "work" already stated . . .

The results suggest that there are two semantic possi-
bilities for the word 'work': 'work' and REAL 'work', the
former being inclusive of the latter. A nice illustration
of this came when someone was asked if, when he dug
the garden, he saw that as work. "No", he said firmly,
"with the garden you're working for yourself". It
seems that only paid employment is regarded as REAL
'work', and though it is not often articulated, an important facet of real 'work' is that it occurs in a specific
workplace which is not the home.

Those activities for which 'work' constituted the largest
number of replies, but where it was not a majority
verdict, were mainly household tasks, such as repairing a car, or doing the washing up. These tasks tended
to be described by others as 'necessity' or 'unenjoyable' – the 'work' involved in them seems to be of a
different nature from that involved in formal jobs.

(Turner, Bostyn and Wight 1984: 65–6)

THE WORKFORCE AND WHERE THEY WERE EMPLOYED

The first and second surveys showed the proportions of the
Cauldmoss population in different economic categories, omitting housewives and the retired (Table 4.1).
    The data from the first survey, administered in 1982, differ
from the 1981 Census data because of slight discrepancies in the
definition of economic categories, the inevitable limitations of a
10 per cent rather than 100 per cent Census sample, and the
changes in the local economy over that period.
    The main changes between the 1971 Census findings and those
of the 1981 Census were an increase in the proportion of those
economically active seeking work (from 6.4 per cent to 15.4 per
cent), a reduction of those in full time employment (from 83 per
cent to 72 per cent of the economically active), and a significant
rise in the proportion of married women in the labour force (from
31 per cent to 44 per cent). Despite the greater number of married
women in the labour market, however, in the age groups of 16 to
19 and 55 to 60 there were *fewer* women describing themselves as
economically active in 1981 than 1971. The increase in those
seeking work, the higher proportion of part-time jobs and the

TABLE 4.1 Employment status of those over 16 years of age, from 1982 and 1985 surveys.

Numbers and percentages of column total

	Summer 1982								End of 1985							
	Under 30		30-49		Over 50		TOTAL		Under 30		30-49		Over 50		TOTAL	
Male council house residents:																
Full or part time employed	11	55%	13	57%	10	50%	34	54%	8	47%	17	71%	7	41%	32	55%
Seeking work	8	40%	8	35%	4	20%	20	32%	8	47%	6	25%	2	12%	16	28%
Invalidity	-		2	8%	3	15%	5	8%	1	6%	1	4%	-		3	3%
TOTAL ♂ COUNCIL HOUSE RESIDENTS	20		23		20		63		17		24		17		58	
% male unemployment		42%		43%		41%		42%		53%		29%		22%		36%
Male private house residents:																
Full or part time employed	2	100%	4	100%	6	67%	12	80%	6	67%	4	67%	8	73%	18	69%
Seeking work	-		-		2	22%	2	13%	-		2	33%	1	9%	3	12%
Invalidity	-		-		-		-		1	11%	-		-		1	4%
TOTAL ♂ PRIVATE HOUSE RESIDENTS	2		4		9		15		9		6		11		26	
% male unemployment		0%		0%		25%		14%		14%		33%		11%		18%
Female council house residents:																
Full or part time employed	9	43%	10	42%	2	14%	21	35%	5	24%	10	63%	2	10%	17	30%
Seeking work	-		-		-		-		2	10%	-		-		2	3%
Invalidity	-		-		-		-		-		-		-		-	
TOTAL ♀ COUNCIL HOUSE RESIDENTS	21		24		14		59		21		16		21		58	
% women 16-60 in employment		43%		42%		67%		43%		24%		63%		25%		38%
Female private house residents:																
Full or part time employed	3	100%	5	63%	1	33%	9	64%	1	33%	7	63%	3	50%	11	55%
Seeking work	-		-		-		-		1	33%	1	9%	-		2	10%
Invalidity	-		-		-		-		-		-		-		-	
TOTAL ♀ PRIVATE HOUSE RESIDENTS	3		8		3		14		3		11		6		20	
% women 16-60 in employment		100%		63%		50%		69%		33%		64%		60%		58%

TABLE 4.1 (continued.)

Numbers and percentages of column total

	Summer 1982				End of 1985			
	Under 30	30-49	Over 50	TOTAL	Under 30	30-49	Over 50	TOTAL
All men:								
Full or part time employed	13 59%	17 63%	16 55%	46 59%	14 54%	21 70%	15 54%	50 60%
Seeking work	8 36%	8 30%	6 21%	22 28%	8 31%	8 27%	3 11%	19 23%
Invalidity	–	2 7%	3 10%	5 6%	2 8%	1 3%	–	3 4%
TOTAL MEN	22	27	29	78	26	30	28	84
% male unemployment	38%	37%	36%	37%	42%	30%	17%	31%
All women:								
Full or part time employed	12 50%	15 47%	3 18%	30 42%	6 25%	17 63%	5 19%	28 36%
Seeking work	–	–	–	–	3 13%	1 4%	–	4 5%
Invalidity	–	–	–	–	–	–	–	–
TOTAL WOMEN	24	32	17	73	24	27	27	78
% women 16–60 in employment	50%	47%	60%	49%	25%	63%	38%	44%
OVERALL TOTAL:								
Full or part time employed	25 54%	32 54%	19 41%	76 51%	20 40%	38 66%	20 36%	78 48%
Seeking work	8 17%	8 14%	6 13%	22 15%	11 22%	9 16%	3 5%	23 14%
Invalidity	–	2 3%	3 7%	5 3%	2 4%	1 2%	–	3 2%
OVERALL TOTAL	46	59	46	151	50	57	55	162

$$\% \text{ male unemployment} = \frac{\text{seeking work} + \text{invalidity}}{\text{full time employment} + \text{part time employment} + \text{seeking work} + \text{invalidity}} \times 100$$

Source: First and second surveys.

increase in the number of women in the labour force seem to reflect general employment trends throughout Britain during the recession of the early 1980s.

The 1981 Census only provides a crude breakdown of which industries the Cauldmoss workforce were employed in. About a quarter worked in distribution and catering, a quarter in manufacturing, a quarter in 'other services' and a tenth in transport. Over 20 per cent of the workforce were employed outwith the local authority district in 1981, with a particularly large proportion of construction workers in this category. Many such men worked at one large building project after another all over central Scotland, for instance commuting daily to work on a shopping complex in Glasgow for four months, and then for a year on the gas processing plant at Mossmorran in Fife. Some form of joint transport was usually arranged, either in a works van or a worker's private car, and it was not uncommon for people to start out at 5.30 a.m. and return at 7 p.m. when working at a long distance. A few men stayed away from Cauldmoss for several weeks at a time when employed a long way off, though the main source of such jobs, in oil-related work around Aberdeen, had virtually disappeared by 1984. Several people worked in Glasgow or Edinburgh but the majority were employed in the local town (within the local authority district).

A small proportion of the workforce had jobs in Cauldmoss itself. Half a dozen local businesses employed men full time, the biggest (with thirteen employees) being a haulage firm, next largest a building firm and an exploratory drilling firm each with three or four men, and then three local coal merchants each employing one or two assistants. Several of the local farmers employed Cauldmoss lads on an irregular basis, but there were hardly any full time farmworkers' jobs, due to the small size of farms. There were several part-time jobs in the village for women but few full time. Part-time employment existed in the community centre, school and health clinic as caretakers and cleaners, and in the shops and post office as sales assistants.

The social classes of the Cauldmoss population, as defined by the Census, have been described in the previous chapter. The Census also provided data on the employment status of those with jobs. In 1981 nine-tenths were employees. A twentieth were self-employed with employees and a twentieth self-employed without employees, most of the latter probably being skilled tradesmen in the construction industry. In the early 1980s sub-contractors in the building trade increasingly demanded that workers should be formally self-employed, although still under their direction. This saved them from the legal responsibilities and costs of being employers and avoided paying wages when rain or slack demand prevented work. In such cases the worker was in much the same subordinate role as a formal employee, and although for tax and insurance purposes he was self-employed he did not regard himself, nor was regarded by his mates, as being "his own boss". Few people in Cauldmoss entertained the idea of setting up their own business. The main objections expressed were the insecurity of an irregular income and the lack of clearly defined working hours, which meant one might work all evening and which confounded the fundamental boundary between work and leisure.

FINDING EMPLOYMENT

In the discussion of kinship we have already seen how the information and influence of one's relatives was the most important means by which people found employment (Chapter Two). If one's job had not been found through kin networks it was usually through some other personal contacts: peer groups in the pubs, clubs or bingo, or friends at home, providing information about likely vacancies and suitable applicants. "It's no' *what* ye ken, it's *who* ye ken," was the phrase repeatedly used to summarise the situation, and apart from jobs on government schemes it was rare to hear of anyone getting work other than through personal networks. It was even said (by a local employer) that employees in the Job Centre informed their own friends of vacancies before advertising them publicly.

In theory the Job Centre in the local town, the official agency for finding work, should have informed those registered of the vacancies for which they were suitable. In practice there was no time to do this since staff were so overwhelmed by enquiries as soon as a notice was posted that it was usually a case of first come first served, which obviously militated against those in outlying villages. In fact the Job Centre seemed to operate more as an employment exchange, providing facilities for employers to pick the best recruits from the labour force and for those in jobs to swap them for better ones, than as an agency helping the unemployed find work. The jobs advertised in the centre were mainly for sales representatives willing to work entirely on a commission basis, for low paid clerical and cleaning staff (jobs usually taken by women), and for time-served, experienced tradesmen, especially in the construction industry.

Although training and experience were more important to employers than a person's residence, when there was nothing else to choose between applicants for unskilled or semi-skilled posts, most employers in the local town tended to discriminate against those from Cauldmoss. Contrary to the supposed reputation of local miners in the past, the Cauldmoss workforce was not highly regarded in the local conurbation. This was partly due to geographic factors, since employers feared that Cauldmoss workers would not be able to commute easily and in the winter were likely to be cut off by snow. But it was also connected with the reputation that the village had: an official at the local Job Centre said employers tended to see Cauldmoss as a troublesome place (citing articles in the local paper about offences committed there), and he knew of one person who refused to see an applicant on learning that he was from Cauldmoss.

EXPLICIT REASONS FOR EMPLOYMENT

In the early 1980s the vast majority of men and most unmarried women in Cauldmoss wanted to be employed for a full working week, while many women with older children sought part-time work. The importance of regular employment in people's lives was very clear, both for the old and young. In this section I will discuss people's stated aims for doing paid work and in subsequent sections will show how employment was also motivated by less explicitly articulated beliefs.

Money

Since employment for money was at the core of the Cauldmoss concept of work it follows that money was the first thing people stated they sought from their jobs. Their immediate conscious motive to do paid work was to earn a living: to accumulate enough to put a deposit down for a car, to meet the weekly bills, to afford "to go out" more than once in the week, or whatever. Even in industrial society, however, economic objectives are not in an autonomous sphere but 'hemmed in by the social prescription of means and ends' (Wallman 1979: 4). The "necessities of life" for which money was sought were not inevitable but socially constructed, which is the subject of the next chapter.

The emphasis on remuneration from their employment was linked with workers' identification with their wages. An equation was made between someone's wage and his or her worth. Thus men on good overtime took great pride in, for instance, "clearing £180 a week", or bringing home £300 on a Friday and handing their wives £120 in cash. While the "big earners" in the village were generally respected – their esteem confirmed by expensive consumption – those known to receive low pay were rather pitied. For most people the amount they earned was more important for their self-esteem than their occupational identity. The measurement of a man's worth by his wage was evidently an old and widespread attitude in coal mining communities (Jahoda 1987: 6; Dennis *et al.* 1956: 74).

There is a paradox in this equivalence of wage with worth. On the one hand it was a clear example of how capitalist economic values are internalised to shape one's self-identity, as others have previously observed: 'The bourgeoisie, wherever it has got the upper hand, . . . has resolved personal worth into exchange value' (Marx and Engels 1967: 82). Yet because workers were understandably loath to accept lower wages (and worth) in different economic circumstances, the equation ignores the market mechanism of wage determination. This was not completely foreign to Cauldmoss villagers (they were well aware that unemployment allowed employers to reduce the quality of their working conditions), but workers' perceptions of what their time and skills were worth incorporated much more than the supply and demand for labour. They were related more to the training required to do the job, the customary amount paid and differentials with other jobs. In particular the time served as an apprentice, usually for very low pay, was thought to validate a good wage later on, and a City and Guilds certificate supposedly guaranteed one's worth.

It was taken as axiomatic that one sought to maximise one's pay as the first priority in seeking work, and almost any hardship or disruption was considered if the wage was right. For instance, some construction workers in Cauldmoss seriously contemplated working on the Falkland Islands for a year when they learnt it would pay £30,000 per annum. There were several elements which determined the minimum wage acceptable, including financial circumstances (particularly responsibilities to others), awareness of the current labour market and previous earnings. Several men said they thought one should not have to work for less than £150 per week after tax. Very few were prepared to work for less than they would receive in benefits (to be discussed in Chapter Eight), and the minimum acceptable margin between this and one's net income was typically between £10 and £20. Though women tolerated far lower pay than men, and it was not important to their gender identity in the way it was for men (see below), they too had minimum acceptable levels. One woman was berated by her aunt for doing the doctor's cleaning for £8 a week (some years previously): "Even the nig nogs wouldn't work for that! You're worse than the darkies!". To accept a reduction in wages was considered belittling. For instance, an unemployed skilled worker who had previously earned £200 a week "clear" (take home pay) for a long time refused to consider jobs paying less than £180 a week, even though he said he had not known how to spend his wages while in work.

Achieving an approved level of consumption for one's family and equating one's earnings with one's personal worth both gave a moral dimension to employment, but the monetary implications were more complicated than this. Whenever motivation for a job was discussed the financial arguments were inevitably deemed paramount, but in practice people's actions did not always accord with this legitimising rationale. Twice men belittled enquiries as to why they worked, stating adamantly that it was simply to earn money: as soon as they found they were gaining no more than the dole they would stop. But their wives then told me that their husbands could never stop working, whatever they were paid: "It's built into you, work." It would seem that in our capitalist society non-financial motives for employment, assuming the worker was conscious of them, were thought to have little validity.

> Those which are acceptable explanations in our society are the ones which relate the economic implications of certain kinds of action to the notion of individual property rights . . . In other words, what counts as an explanation must be economically rational.

> (Henry 1978: 118)

A structure to one's time

Two non-monetary but valued aspects of paid work were a temporal structure and the changed environment, though men were more likely to articulate these benefits in relation to the frustration of unemployment than as conscious reasons for doing a job. Women did cite the change of environment as a reason for paid work. There seemed to be a general desire for the discipline and time structure of employment, revealed by the common wish for a forty hour working week, the absence of which was said to be one of the main disadvantages of self-employment. Even if they could earn a good wage in only twenty hours, men said they would look for another job to fill the day, and when on holiday workers in Cauldmoss sometimes complained by the second week that "It's too long; you get fed up." The need for temporal order has long been emphasised by social psychologists:

> In modern industrialised societies the experience of time is shaped by public institutions . . . but when this structure is removed . . . its absence presents a major psychological burden.

> (Jahoda 1982: 22)

It was the time structure of employment which gave meaning and value to that period away from work; essentially there was no leisure without employment. Leisure hours complemented working hours, they did not substitute for them, and part of the appeal of leisure was its relative scarcity. This theme is explored in detail by Bostyn (1990).

Changed environment

The change in environment provided by employment was valued because it allowed one to "get out the house" and relate to another social group. This was particularly significant in Cauldmoss where for most people paid work provided the only opportunity to have daily contact with others outside the village. This was especially valued by women, who were generally less mobile than men, and who often stated that meeting more people was as important to them as earning an independent income.

For men, going to work not only meant a change of environment but also allowed them to get out of the woman's domain during the day. The importance of this was clear from

unemployed married men's attempts to find occupations that
would keep them out of the house as long as possible. The
readiness of some men "on the bru" to take jobs for less money
than their social security payments was interpreted by male
acquaintances as an attempt to end matrimonial rows precipi-
tated by the husband's presence at home during the day.
Similarly the difficulties that couples often had in adjusting to the
husband's retirement were frequently related to the necessity of
re-negotiating gendered space.

The importance of the temporal and spatial aspects of employment suggest that the substance of paid work was less significant
than its form. For men the routine of employment seemed paramount: going out to work in the morning with their "piece"
(sandwich), coming back dirty, washing, having tea, and then
maybe going out to the pub; looking forward to the weekend
through the week, and the local trades fair (the annual holiday)
through the year. This rhythm provided order both at a daily and
annual level, the repetition, as Martin argues (1981), giving the
work/leisure differentiation a sacred dimension and a normative
quality.

ALIENATION

> The role of the worker is not to direct production, it is
> to put himself at the disposal of the employer for a
> certain period of time. As a consequence . . . the prod-
> uct of his labour is alienated from the immediate
> producer, the labourer . . . there is a sense in which
> every worker suffers 'monotony'. It is not the monot-
> ony of the operations he carries out, considered in their
> concrete aspect, so much as the tendency for his work
> to be directed and controlled entirely from outside
> himself.

> (Dennis *et al.* 1956: 27–8)

To give some meaning to one's time, to have a change of sur-
roundings and, above all, to earn money, were the three main
motives for employment articulated in Cauldmoss. Very few
people mentioned gaining satisfaction from the actual activity of
working, or from the product of their work. Employment was
generally assumed to be boring and though a few said you *should*

enjoy your work no one said they would swap more stimulating work for less money. Men remembered how in a different economic climate fifteen years before they had sometimes worked for three different firms in a week, switching jobs for as little as "three punce mair an hour" in order "to follow the cash". The moves were not made because of conditions or type of work, but for the overriding concern to maximise wages. These priorities might have been a legacy of people's mining background, since for generations work was relatively unskilled hard toil for which comparatively high wages were expected (Dennis *et al.* 1956: 174–5). A comparison with the meaning work has in a settlement with a tradition of skilled crafts would be instructive; contrasting attitudes have been found in a Scottish fishing village (Willis and Turner 1980).

Throughout the world most work on the shop floor is 'degraded and degrading' (Jahoda 1982: 41; Palm 1977; Haraszti 1977; Linhart 1976; Beynon 1973). In Cauldmoss employees' estrangement from their work was manifested in many different ways. Most people ritually changed out of their work clothes as soon as they returned home, whether or not they were dirty, and it was common to distance oneself from one's product. A sewing machinist at a Wranglers factory said she would never buy Wranglers jeans, nor would anyone else in the workforce, even though they could get them at reduced prices. As with alienated Ford car workers (Beynon 1973: 110), she acknowledged that the products from her factory were in fact probably no worse than those of other companies. There was a general feeling that employees "don't owe" their firms or employers anything, whether informing them promptly of illness, giving notice when leaving and so on, and the avoidance of work while in the workplace was widely condoned, if not admired.

Just as earnings were more important than occupation for esteem in Cauldmoss, so being seen to be in a job was more important than what one did within it: productivity was a negligible element of most people's identities as workers. A few men boasted of "skiving" on the job, even though they were jealous of their reputation as workers. A striking case was that of a Cauldmoss miner who derided his neighbours as "wasters", yet went on to describe how he fooled the Coal Board officials in their calculation of productivity rates so that he got large unearned bonus payments. Again the economic rationale rendered this acceptable. The local doctor was renowned for his willingness to "gie you a line" on almost any pretext, and getting out of work early or feigning sickness was not uncommon. However, those who sometimes boasted of avoiding work had to manage their reputations carefully by demonstrating their usual readiness to work.

Village identity as a coal mining community still lingered amongst a generation who had not worked in the pits themselves (see Chapter Two). Unlike mining, the jobs available in the early 1980s were neither lifelong nor had a 'firm profile' (Berger 1975: 166), and so were unlikely to replace the inherited occupational identity. As Brown concluded from his study of the Newcastle labour market, there was an increasingly remote chance of manual workers finding jobs with which they could identify (Brown 1985: 474).

A crucial exception to the predominant evaluation of employment in Cauldmoss, however, were the views of those time-served tradesmen who did have a strong occupational identity. But they did not include all skilled workers and their views were not widely expressed in village life. The analysis that follows focuses on the majority without such an occupational identity.

The expectation that employment was done primarily for money and was inevitably boring and unenjoyable made non-monetary rewards for work-like activity very strange to people in Cauldmoss. The few men who did do some "voluntary work", for instance helping at the community centre, usually hoped that it would contribute to their future career. The commitment of a few men to lead and coach village football teams was understood in relation to the company and sport involved, but to do an intrinsically tedious job simply because of one's beliefs, such as leafleting for the Labour Party, was incomprehensible to most people. When a man learnt that I was continuing my research work while on Unemployment Benefit, and furthermore that I actually paid to travel to the university each fortnight, he was incredulous: "You're a fuckin' nutcase!".

Although Cauldmoss women did not take on many voluntary activities, their involvement in the community centre, church socials and charity prize bingos was considered far less odd than if men had done these things. In part these tasks were regarded as an extension of their domestic duties, in particular helping with children and old people in the centre, but there was a further reason why more voluntary work was done by women. The equation of wages with personal worth was particularly import-ant for men, and their earning capacity was associated with their masculinity (discussed below). Suffice to say, a woman's identity was not undermined by doing work for free in the way that a man's was. The oddity of doing unpaid work had particular consequences for men's response to unemployment, to be con-sidered in Chapter Eight.

ADULTHOOD AND MASCULINITY

Paid work meant more to people in Cauldmoss than earning money, structuring one's time and changing one's environment. Although not often referred to explicitly, employment was also highly important as an expression of adulthood and masculinity.

Paid work was seen as the most significant transition to adult-hood, though in the early 1980s few school leavers were lucky enough to experience this. Older men remembered how they had longed to leave school at 14 or 15 in order to take any employ-ment, however arduous: "we couldn't leave the school quick enough", . . . "you were brought up to work". Paid work meant being old enough for someone to think one's labour was worth buying, and even an afternoon's work splitting logs for an odd-jobs man was eagerly sought by school leavers. Wages gave young people "an independence" from their parents, and though this was usually only expressed by paying "dig money" to their mothers, this financial autonomy had great significance. When young men started work they often assumed rather different relationships to the rest of their families, and were frequently waited on by their mothers as secondary "breadwinners".

The term "working men", which was by far the most common way males in Cauldmoss described themselves, is significant not only in its omission of class but also in the way the two central concepts of "work" and "men" were continually merged in ev-eryday speech. We have already seen how women's subservience in the working class is exacerbated by the association of physical labour with masculinity (Chapter Two). Far from being an eco-nomic inevitability, as Bourdieu implies (1984: 384), this connection is based on the ideological exclusion of women. Their employment is seen as secondary to that of the "breadwinner", and their manual domestic work is largely ignored. So physical

labour is suffused with masculine qualities and though intrinsically meaningless it is interpreted as an expression of manhood.

The construction of masculinity in Cauldmoss was largely
sustained by elements of employment thought to typify male
work. Men liked to discuss in the pub how arduous their work
was and the conditions they had to endure: "the hardest work in
the building trade – your hands are red raw". Oil-related employment around the Shetlands (which was virtually finished by the
early 1980s) still provided good anecdotes, such as being forced
to work in thermal suits or suffering the storms: "see where the
two seas meet – the Atlantic and the North Sea – fuckin' terrible".
Strength was often considered as virtually synonymous with
being a hard worker, and older men were proud of their sons on
these grounds: "doing the work of three brickies – he's a *worker* –
can't stand idle". To some extent the dirt, noise and monotony of
a job, and the strength and self-discipline needed to "hold it
down", were valued as challenges which, by being overcome,
established one's masculinity. As Willis argues (1977: 150), the
brutality of paid work is understood more through the masculine
toughness required in confronting the task than through the
nature of the system imposing it. Given the durability of values
in Cauldmoss, the association between work and masculinity
might have been strengthened by the legacy of coalmining. Since
Lawrence and Orwell, miners have epitomised the equation of
physical work and essential masculinity:

> The socialist movement in Britain has been swept off
> its feet by the magic of masculinity, muscle and ma-
> chinery. And in its star system, the accolades go to the
> miners – they've been through hell, fire, earth and
> water to become hardened into heroes. It is masculinity
> at its most macho that seems to fascinate men.

(Campbell 1984: 97)

The masculine attributes of physical work were extended to a
man's earnings by a simple association between harder work and
greater pay, and this was reinforced by the man's role of providing for his family.

> this idea, "I'm the man of the family". Whether you've
> got a family or not doesnae matter, you're supposed to
> be a macho man, like, go out and earn a wage, like, you

know. When you cannae do that it makes you less of a
man in other people's eyes.

Earlier we saw that the wage was seen as a measure of personal
worth, irrespective of gender, yet wages had far greater significance than this. The wage packet was 'the particular prize of
masculinity in work', both because the man was held to be the
breadwinner and because the wage was 'won in a masculine
mode', according to Willis. The implications of this are considerable: 'The wage packet as a kind of symbol of machismo dictates
the domestic culture and economy and tyrannises both men and
women.' (Willis 1977: 150).

The sacrifice of energy and comfort that men made in order to
earn a wage for their families gave them an emotional hold over
others in the household who were seen to have made less of a
sacrifice. These ideas were at the core of the normative prescription for men to be employed, to be discussed in the following
section. Furthermore the emphasis on men's role as breadwinners 'has subordinated all other dimensions of their workplace
politics to the politics of pay – their own pay' (Campbell 1984:
147). At the same time the masculine prestige earned by disciplining oneself to dirty, strenuous, monotonous employment meant
men did not consider the improvement of their working conditions an overriding priority. Instead the principal concern was
pay, and this economism

> is a function of the political priority of a trade union
> movement based on men's self-interest as breadwin-
> ners . . . and on individual families' self-sufficiency
> supposedly achieved through men's wage as the family
> wage.
>
> (Campbell 1984: 151)

THE WORK ETHIC

In one sense all the values associated with employment described
above could be regarded as constituents of a work ethic, in that
they give a moral dimension to employment. However, the term
'work ethic' is often used in a more specific way than this, to mean
the moral obligation to be committed to work (given greatest
theoretical weight by Weber in *The Protestant Ethic and the Spirit
of Capitalism* (1930)). Yet as Williams notes (1990: 223), different

elements of this commitment to work are emphasised in different cultural contexts, whether it is self-discipline and the pursuit of duty, the application of skill and high standards or the value of work as the source of basic personal worth outside the work place. In Cauldmoss the moral evaluation of "work" was, for men, nearly always related to employment, in keeping with the dominant meaning of "work".

Expressed moral attitudes regarding work

In the course of general conversations working hard was frequently commended, those who did not work were frequently condemned and assumptions were expressed that everyone (in particular men) would, or wanted to, work most of his or her adult life. For both sexes one of the greatest accolades was to be described as "a good worker", and the description of someone as a "*hard* worker" or as having "worked all their days" often implicitly subsumed all the other moral qualities of respectability. Wives were proud of their husbands' commitment to work – "John's never been a day off his work", or "my man's never been idle" – sometimes even admiring them for taking a job that paid less than they might have received on benefits, and men commended their colleagues with comments like: "they men *worked*", or, "he never missed a shift". Workers often took pride in their record of continual employment: "I've always got through to my work, even in snow" or despite illness (even a sprained wrist, in one case) they had not gone sick. As discussed earlier, this self-esteem was not related to much sense of loyalty to their employers but a commitment to a life of routine employment. "I've never been on the bru all my life. I've always *earned* my money . . . never lived on the state." The moral value of work was clearly expressed when villagers tried to establish the respectability of Cauldmoss: "The majority are decent, hard working folk."

The corollary of this praise for work was a widespread condemnation of those not employed. Frequently this was expressed in jokes or teasing, for example a family's banter when the oldest son got his first job since leaving school two years before: "He's never worked in his life!" said a brother scornfully, and his mother added "You won't know what's wrong wi' you!". Others were described as being "immune from work" or: 'as Rabbie Burns said, "never feared laziness" '. The accusation of laziness and being a "waster" was very common - "Ye do get that label if ye're no' workin' " - and many condemned half the unemployed for preferring to "sit in the hoose" and have the government keep them rather than find work. Some were far more extreme in their criticism. A young woman told me: "Quite a lot of them on the bru dinnae *want* to work. They're just fuckin' lazy!" and, at a loss as to what should be done with them, mentioned shooting them.

Despite the current shortage of jobs it was still regarded as axiomatic by most people in Cauldmoss that employment should be central to a man's life. Going out to work every day through the week, eleven months of the year, from the age of 16 to 65, was still considered the normal lot of working men. Mass unemployment was a temporary phase which perhaps a third of the work force were suffering, but there was no serious consideration that their fundamental destiny as workers was at an end. Even the young unemployed found it difficult to conceive of anything different. They were unanimous that benefits were too small, but rejected the suggestion that Supplementary Benefit should be set at £40 a week because then "nobody would work". A man in his 20s told me: "I reckon maist o' your young generation definitely want to work . . . no question about it. Because it's the only thing to do – it's the system. And ye can't beat the system."

Many people over about 40 considered that the worst aspect of mass unemployment was that teenagers had nothing to leave school for and had no experience of working. Sympathy for the young was mixed with concern at the lack of discipline that employment was thought to provide. "Aye, 'cos you're better workin' – to me – it'll ruin them: they get into mischief," said an old woman of her grandchildren. A father described the general effect of unemployment on the young: "See how fuckin' cheeky the weans are: weans are wasted. I'd have National Service back . . . would learn you something". His daughter only rose at eleven each morning because she had nothing to get up for, he argued. She should be given a job for her "bru money", like an apprentice hairdresser, so that she could learn a skill and *do* something for her money. This last opinion was widely held amongst older people:

> It's no' helpin' them . . . getting all that and no' doing anything for it. I don't think it's good for them at all – they're no' going to try to get away from it [getting

things for nothing]. I don't think it's going to help them
in later life.

An employment ethic

The activity of hard physical work was sometimes valued in its
own right (usually when it was related to masculine prowess),
but most of the time what was admired was people's subjection
to the rigours of employment. I want to argue that, for men, the
moral values surrounding work are best understood as an *employment* ethic, rather than a general work ethic. The essence of
this employment ethic was that a man disciplined himself to earn
money for himself or his family, and the extent of hardship
suffered to this end was an expression of his manhood (as described in the preceding section).

The concept of an employment ethic makes sense of the numerous references to the *form* of employment and little mention
of its *substance*. Thus men were praised for having "worked all
their days" and having "never missed a shift", but the productivity or quality of their work was hardly ever referred to. Being
industrious was not of much consequence in the village, and this
attribute was usually only discussed amongst work mates who
were working on a self-employed basis. Such people, for instance
men working on large building sites, clearly had a financial
interest to both work fast (to finish the job quickly) and well (to
get further work sub-contracted to them).

For most workers what was admired by their colleagues and,
more particularly, by others in Cauldmoss was their ability to
stand the demands of employment over a long period: one's
record of consistent punctuality, readiness to overcome minor
ailments and ability to work long hours overtime. This evaluation
of employment was reflected in older people's concern that the
young were not experiencing the discipline of a working life. In
short, what was admired about a "good worker" was his ability
to hold down a job, to use a telling phrase.

The work-related norms affecting the unemployed provide
further support for this interpretation of the employment ethic.
Those on the dole felt no obligation to be productive, and hard
manual work did not, in itself, confirm their status as respectable
rather than as wasters. Indeed, doing unpaid work was considered dubious rather than admirable. These values will be
discussed again in Chapter Eight.

An integral part of the employment ethic was earning money, as the attitudes of the unemployed indicate. The discipline of a working life, which had come to be valued in its own right, was really the means to an end: earning the wage to support first oneself as an independent adult and later one's family.

> Often there is an element of self-sacrifice in men's attitude to work – a slow spending of the self through the daily cycle of effort, comfort, food, sleep, effort. But this sacrifice brings the wage which keeps the home fires burning and, besides, 'the kids will have a better chance'. So there is dignity and meaning, even in sacrifice. It also gives a kind of emotional power – a hold over other members of the family who do not make the sacrifice.
>
> (Willis 1984: 13)

The association of regular employment with "fighting for your country", made by those old enough to have done both, suggests that the self-sacrifice of a lifetime's toil was perceived as not just for one's family but also more generally for the nation.

> I sees people running about the village who've *never* worked and never fought in the war, and they get a new suit every year off the public assistance . . . I never *minded* working in my life.

If the work ethic is better understood as an employment ethic, where does this leave women? Although this book is largely restricted to the male world of Cauldmoss, two points seem worth mentioning. First, the discipline of a regular job was valued for young women as well as young men, though the imperative to get a job was not so strong and women were expected to give up employment when they started a family. This suggests that the employment ethic was not just about masculinity. Second, when a woman got married her moral obligation to work was extended to cover practically all the domestic chores (described earlier) and child care. The same kind of moral censure was applied to women perceived to neglect their house work as to men who were thought of as work shy. Women were frequently apologetic about the state of their houses, as if always aware when visitors called that they could have worked harder,

and they had to balance the merits of domestic work and employment in order to maintain their respectability. When asked if she
minded no longer having a job a middle aged woman told me:

> Glad. Didnae want to work ... No' really, son. I was
> always busy in the house. Half those folk who go out
> to work dinnae bother about their house. But I like a
> clean house ...

This highlights an important gender difference: men's work was
overwhelmingly employment, in which the form was crucial, not
the substance, whereas women's housework was probably more
important than their employment, and was evaluated according
to productivity. This was related to the woman's role as guardian
of the family's respectability, but it is also consistent with an
interpretation of the employment ethic which views its underlying rationale to be support of the family. For women this
obligation involved domestic work as much as it did employment.

Just rewards: employment and reciprocity

The expectation that a life of hard work should be rewarded, and
the concomitant resentment felt against those who seemed to get
by without ever having really worked, were part of a belief that
one's sacrifice should not have been in vain. This notion was
reinforced by the fundamental principle of reciprocity, according
to which people lose their esteem when they receive something
for nothing. These ideas were often expressed in relation to the
authorities' decisions about entitlement to benefits, rebates,
houses and so on, decisions that were frequently viewed as
arbitrary or unjust (cf. Williams 1990).

The operation of the means test was considered particularly
iniquitous. Why should someone whose husband had worked
hard all his life and saved for their retirement have to pay the
council rent, when the neighbour who had hardly worked at all
was getting almost total rent rebate? Why should a self-employed
butcher who had had an accident be denied Supplementary
Benefit because he owned too much, despite the fact that "I've
never been off my work, paid stamps every week ... ", while
special benefits were available to others who had been idle all
their lives? Others were indignant that their children could not
get council houses, even though they themselves "have worked

all my days", yet families of "wasters" in which no one had ever done a serious job appeared to be allocated a house whenever one of the children applied.

Many of those in work were proud that they were *earning* their money, and they implied it was degrading to be "living off the state", "waiting for a giro to come through the door". Many also resented the size of benefits the unemployed received, in particular the occasional Single Payments (abolished in the 1986 Social Security Act). Those families which were identified as always having been idle, even when jobs were to be found, were begrudged practically all their benefits. The ethic that people ought to earn their money through employment was manifest in the apparently inconsistent attitudes towards defrauding the DHSS which were often expressed. Making illicit claims for special needs was regarded as cheating the state, while work done "on the side" was seen as a legitimate effort to earn a livelihood, so long as it did not become a permanent state of affairs.

The principle of reciprocity, in the simple sense that one should give something in return for what one gets, when combined with the employment ethic, explains why the take-up for contributory benefits was higher than the take-up for non-contributory benefits. Similarly less stigma was attached to receiving Unemployment Benefit than Supplementary Benefit, particularly amongst older claimants.

The economic context

It is important to stress that the employment ethic was part of a culture shaped by very specific economic conditions. This is illustrated by noting how far the ethic extended: the boss would never have been described as a good worker however industrious he was, any more than peers of the realm would have been described as work shy or wasters. We have seen that most people in Cauldmoss expected employment to be alienating, knowing they would have little control over their work and expecting it to be boring, repetitive, unenjoyable, and probably strenuous. It will already be apparent that the rigours of employment which a "good worker" had to subject himself to were exactly those most likely to alienate him. Given employees' powerlessness to control the conditions of their jobs, the employment ethic seemed to be a way in which they could make sense of their experience of work. The only aspect of their employment left within their influence, their endurance under the pressures of the job, was accorded great moral significance in a kind of internalised alienation. If employment could never be anything more than a means to the end of providing for oneself and one's family, and if it was always going to be an unpleasant experience, then at least a virtue could be made of necessity. Since for at least a century the people of Cauldmoss and their forebears had had to sell their labour in order to feed their families, it seems quite probable that the merit accorded to the second task was extended to the first, so that the same moral obligation came to apply to both.

It is unsurprising that having sacrificed themselves to employment for most of their lives, older people harboured a grudge against the young unemployed who seemed to be getting the rewards of work without suffering it (cf. Williams 1990: 225). The moral duty to support one's family had become so indistinguishable from the obligation to be employed that people of middle age or older sometimes valued disciplined employment even when it payed no more than the social security benefits for which they would have been eligible. In the early 1980s the material necessity of employment (not to mention the possibility) had been undermined, but for many its virtue still remained.

Differing evaluations of employment by age groups

Different economic circumstances prompt differing evaluations of employment, as well as exposing the variations between age groups. The preceding discussion may have suggested that beliefs about work in Cauldmoss were fairly homogenous, but in fact there were marked differences in people's commitment to the employment ethic. For convenience one can characterise the difference in attitudes between the old and the young, but it is important to stress that there was no clear division between age groups and considerable variation within them: the general trend was complicated by personal histories, family upbringing, individual psychology and so on. Nevertheless a contrast can be drawn between the way old and young people responded to the 'unemployment trap': the situation where the highest wage someone could hope to earn was little more than the welfare benefits to which their household was entitled. The causes of the unemployment trap and how people responded to it will be considered in detail in Chapter Eight; here I will simply mention them in regard to what we can learn about attitudes to employment.

The oldest generation in Cauldmoss, in general those over 60, had a deep commitment to an employment ethic. It appeared that remuneration was not the overriding value they attached (or had attached) to their jobs, and instead the non-material benefits such as the temporal ordering of their lives, the changed environment, masculine identity, moral worth and so on were more important. They were prone to condemn the younger generation because "they'll neither work nor want". Those between about 30 and 60 seemed to share the employment ethic of the older generation, though in a rather weaker form, but the wage was much more central to their concerns particularly since they often had a family to support. The young were less concerned with respectability and seemed to accord far less value to disciplined work. Though they did not seriously consider a future life without any employment, their reason for wanting jobs was overwhelmingly financial. Unless a job was likely to provide an opportunity for a future, better paid, career, in general the young were not prepared to take low paid, uninteresting work. They readily admitted that they would not work as hard as, or in the same conditions as, their fathers, but they still ascribed masculine attributes to manual labour. Though these generational differences were certainly related to stages in the life course, in my view they had more to do with social change, in particular the different experiences of the labour market which these age cohorts had had.

CONCLUSION

The central meaning of "work" in Cauldmoss was paid employment. Unsurprisingly the most explicit reason people had for getting jobs was to earn money, but they also valued the time structure and changed environment that employment brought. Paid work also had implicit meaning as an expression of one's adulthood and, particularly with strenuous manual work, one's masculinity. Nevertheless the vast majority viewed employment as something that could never be fulfilling: 'It is not the satisfaction of a need, but only a *means* for satisfying other needs' (Marx 1844: 85). One way in which men seemed to make sense of their alienating employment was to accord great moral significance to the one aspect of it which was within their influence: their ability to endure the rigours of the work. The employment ethic made a virtue out of necessity and reinforced the masculine value attached to paid work. Both were expressed in the equation of wages with worth. Since the wage was fundamental to people's understanding of employment, it is logical to proceed from this chapter to consider the main objective of employment: consumption.

5

Compulsory Consumption

In the previous chapter we saw that the overwhelming majority in Cauldmoss had no expectation that paid work would be other than arduous, monotonous and routine, offering no intrinsic satisfaction; their conscious motive to be employed was above all the remuneration. It was shown that the wage had considerable symbolic value in itself, but to understand the motivation to be employed more fully we must examine how the money earned was spent. This chapter will describe what was effectively a compulsory material lifestyle in Cauldmoss. The impetus for consumption will be analysed subsequently in Chapter Seven.

Although consumption plays such a central role in Western societies, and an increasingly important one elsewhere, sociological analysis of the subject has been extraordinarily limited when compared with the attention given to production. In part this is due to the common belief that the logic of economics – whether classical or historical materialist – largely determines our material existence, a view that has become increasingly widespread over the last 200 years. Since formal economists do not question what motivates demand, and since Marxists take 'use value' as given, this is where enquiry usually stops and it is assumed that goods are simply wanted as ends in themselves. Another reason for the minimal attention given to consumption is the 'deep-seated ethnocentricity' (Campbell 1987: 39) which takes the insatiability of wants for granted, as if it were normal or rational.

Although there has been considerable market research into consumer behaviour little attention has been focused on the values and attitudes which give rise to the dynamics of modern consumption.

Since this book concentrates on men this chapter begins with a discussion of their role in consumption: how was the wage allocated within households and could responsibility for spending be equated with control (cf. Edwards 1981)? I will then describe consumption in Cauldmoss, but any ethnography of material lifestyle will inevitably be partial. The household budget data had various weaknesses, mentioned in Chapter One, and so instead of analysing details of expenditure I have discerned various patterns underlying much of the consumption in Cauldmoss. Even treating material lifestyle thematically it is necessary to be selective: this chapter emphasises the obligatory nature of consumption in the village.

> no one is free to live on raw roots and fresh water . . .
> the minimum of imposed consumption, is the standard
> package. Beneath this level, you are an outcast. Is loss
> of status – or social non-existence – less upsetting than
> hunger?

> (Baudrillard 1981: 81)

Others might have adopted a more individualistic approach (e.g. Campbell 1987) or have focused more closely on one social variable (e.g. social class: Bourdieu 1984) or one area of consumption (food: Charles and Kerr 1988). Here I will discuss consumption patterns in terms of the requirement to conform to conventional standards and the constraints against inappropriate spending patterns. The themes explored will be illustrated in the following chapter which is a case study of one of the few commodities bought predominantly by men: alcohol.

ALLOCATION OF THE WAGE: CONTROL OR RESPONSIBILITY?

Forty-four couples participated in the second questionnaire survey and slightly over half reported that the woman was "in charge of the money in this household". A quarter said that neither partner was in charge, and about a sixth said that the husband was in charge (Table 5.1).

TABLE 5.1 Person said to be in charge of household money.

	Wife	Husband	"No one"	Total
Wives asked	17	4	2	23
Husbands asked	9	3	9	21
Couples wife employed	11	2	4	17
Couples (exc. retired) with wife not employed	10	4	7	21
Couples not retired (exc. unemployed)	19	3	6	28
Couples retired	5	1	0	6
Couples in council houses	21	5	5	31
Couples in private houses	5	2	6	13
TOTAL	26	7	11	44

Source: Second survey, Q. 13.

Respondents were also asked how they or their spouse divided the wage(s) between the two of them (for instance handing over a set amount each week or as their spouse needed it) and what aspects of household spending they discussed together. The answers allowed an approximate categorisation of households according to the woman's responsibility and control of household income (Table 5.2).

In about half the households the woman had considerable control as well as responsibility for household expenditure. In most of these homes there was a 'whole wage system', in which the whole of the husband's wage was handed to the wife and she made all the decisions on spending. She usually gave her husband a set amount of "spending money" or "pocket money" each week, but some gave their partners money "as he needs it".

TABLE 5.2 Households categorised by woman's responsibility and control over household income (approximate).

Person rep. in charge of money	Res'bility and signif. control	Shared decision making	Res'bility but little control	Little res., virtually no control
Wives	17	0	9	0
Husbands	0	0	0	7
"No one"	4	7	0	0
TOTAL	21	7	9	7

Source: Second survey.

Handing over the wage packet was an act of considerable symbolic significance for men, being the culmination of the sacrifice they had made for their family through employment, and a few husbands took great pride in passing it over unopened. Men were also aware that to a large extent their wives judged them on their ability to ensure security for the household by providing a steady weekly income (cf. Dennis *et al.* 1956: 187; Hoggart 1957: 58). A woman whose husband was unemployed told me:

> I always saw his wage packet. It's no a good man that doesnae show his wife the wage packet . . . that doesnae give his wife the money . . . they're the drinkers an' gamblers.

Table 5.1 shows that if the wife was employed it was more likely that she would be said to be in charge of income. The sense of responsibility wives had for their house and family meant they generally added their own (usually very low) wages to the housekeeping money: "My money goes into the house too. No such a thing, Danny, as keeping it aside for yourself!" Yet although they rarely reserved much of their wages for their personal enjoyment, many were keen to earn an independent income in order to strengthen their right to control the household budget.

It was remarkable that in nine of the eleven cases where no one was said to be in charge of the money it was the husband who was questioned. This suggests that men might have liked to imagine they participated in joint financial decisions, while women regarded this responsibility as their own. On the basis of wideranging discussions it seemed that seven of the forty-four couples shared decision making on most aspects of expenditure.

Amongst those couples where the husband retained some of his wage and only paid his wife housekeeping money the woman had to undertake major responsibilities with severely restricted control, even when she was "in charge". This was the arrangement in the majority of Ashton households (Dennis *et al.* 1956: 187–8), which had the advantage that the wife got a fixed amount whatever the vicissitudes of the miner's weekly earnings but the disadvantage that when on good wages much of it went on his personal amusement leaving nothing saved for a "bad patch". This allocation of the wage was conducive to a ready spending ethic amongst men, to be described in Chapter Seven. In Cauldmoss only about a quarter of the couples we questioned had this kind of arrangement, six of whom reported that the wife was in charge of the money and five the husband. In these latter households the women had least responsibility and virtually no control over the budget. In some families like this the wife never knew how much her husband was earning, and withholding this information was clearly a strategy of domestic power. One woman who was resigned not to know her husband's wage thought it was "sixty odds, according to *me*", when in fact it was £105 take home pay. The husband felt his financial responsibilities to his wife and three children were fulfilled when he handed over the "sixty odd": "She gets the housekeeping money. I dinnae bother after that . . . I like to make sure everythin's paid." Another woman thought it a joke when I asked if she gets handed the wage packet: "Christ, on Friday night I have to go looking for him to get the wages!"

Couples in private houses seemed to share financial responsibilities more frequently than those in council houses, which was in keeping with the less segregated gender roles normally associated with middle class culture. It might also have been a result of the different kind of economic concerns affecting private house dwellers: costs of repairs, extensions, and above all, the mortgage. These were the sort of "large matters" that were seen as the man's responsibility, or at least not solely the woman's, which did not exist in council houses.

In most households the wife had control over spending on food, cleaning and toiletry articles, decorating, furnishing, children's clothes and their spending money. Between a quarter and a half of all women either supervised their husbands' clothes purchases or actually bought the clothes on their own. The things that were frequently the man's responsibility, even when the woman had overall control of the money, were spending on the car, cigarettes, alcohol, particular pets the husband might have kept such as pigeons, and sometimes the major bills like the rent, electricity and coal. Responsibility was rarely clearly demarcated, however, and the husband might have to beg an extra £3 "spending money" off his wife before he could go to the club and buy her a drink.

In the majority of households, where the woman was responsible for the bulk of domestic expenditure, there was a striking lack of discussion between partners about how money should be spent. The only important exceptions were major financial decisions like holidays and cars. It seems as if neither partner thought there was much choice to be made, in part because of low incomes which did not allow for 'discretionary income' (a culturally determined concept), and in part due to the homogeneity of consumer values in Cauldmoss. The absence of discussion on spending was also related to the entrenched division of domestic labour and responsibilities between the sexes, and in particular women's roles as guardians of their families' respectability, as defined and displayed in their material lifestyle. It is unsurprising that husbands deferred to their wives' expertise in these matters, especially since too much interest might have seemed effeminate. Responses to the question 'Do you discuss household spending together?' were consistent: "No' really. No' really enough to discuss . . ." or jokingly: "Generally Martha's got it spent and we discuss how it's paid later", and again: "No' that much to discuss how to spend it . . . She gets the money and decides how to spend it – it's always been like that".

Yet the allocation of household income was not as simple as a sixteen year old suggested: "Mother, she does all the financial side of it. My father *works* for the money, my mother dishes it out, seems to be." Although the vast majority of married women had responsibility for their household's income, the main person they were reponsible *to* was their husband. This was evident from the importance husbands attached to their wives' ability to manage the budget, praising them as "good handlers", and wives' anxiety to fulfil their husbands' expectations. When the council mistakenly sent a woman notice of £80 rent arrears she was outraged, exclaiming: "I'll never let my husband say I wasnae payin' the rent!". Furthermore, on occasions when exceptional financial decisions had to be made, or when the established routine was changed, the husband was likely to be consulted. This suggests that regular confirmation of spending decisions was not necessary because an acceptable pattern had already been established.

Among married or cohabiting couples the woman spent about three quarters of the household income. However, even in those households (about half) where the woman had control over the budget it was likely that she made many consumer choices on the basis of her husband's wishes. In a study of food provision in northern English families, it has been shown that wives can internalise their husbands' preferences to such an extent that they can be unaware that what they buy and cook is largely shaped by their husbands' wishes.

So natural had this process of privileging the preferences of other family members become to women
that they frequently found it difficult to describe
their own food preferences and, in some cases,
would deny that they had any tastes at all . . . Thus
these women's responsibility for the purchase of food
did not endow them with the power to indulge their
own tastes but rather obliged them to subordinate
their food preferences to those of their husbands and
children.

(Kerr and Charles 1986: 124)

THEORIES OF MODERN CONSUMPTION: A CULTURAL APPROACH

Since the mid-1970s there has been greater theoretical interest in
consumerism, mainly from the perspective of postmodernist
theorising. Drawing on this work and earlier writings on consumption, it is possible to classify the various explanations of the
origin of consumer wants into four broad strands of thought. The
first approach locates the source of consumer demand in biological needs, while the second interprets consumption as a means
of expressing and establishing social relationships. The third
theoretical position, which can be labelled 'productionist', treats
modern consumption patterns as manipulable and subject to the
needs of capitalist production. The last group of explanations for
the origin of consumer wants, which will be referred to as
'hedonist' perspectives, are more individualist and they resort to
dreams and imaginative hedonism to understand modern consumption.

Although consumption is widely explained in terms of innate
human needs this approach can be quickly dismissed. Campbell
(1987) has illustrated how Galbraith in his analysis of *The Affluent
Society* (1979) and certain economic historians have an
'instinctivist' perspective that presupposes that wants are inher-
ent. Temporal variation in consumer behaviour is therefore
explained by social factors which either constrain or unleash
'latent demand', such as an inadequate supply of goods (constraining demand) or the relaxing of ideological inhibitions
(releasing demand). Evidently there are biological needs for such
things as food and shelter, but it is highly implausible to regard
the consumer's 'sharply defined conduct in pursuit of particular

products' (Campbell 1987: 44), conduct which is both highly diverse and changeable, as motivated by biological needs.

This ethnography will draw primarily on the second theoretical perspective mentioned above: interpreting consumption in terms of the continued reproduction of social relationships and divisions. Many authors following this approach are only concerned with social stratification, but others have a far more comprehensive Durkheimian view of commodities as important constituents of the cognitive order that is based upon social divisions. In the following pages I will summarise the main arguments used in this approach to consumption.

While this cultural interpretation of material lifestyle is considered most appropriate to the data from Cauldmoss, it is not theoretically incompatible with either 'productionist' or 'hedonistic' perspectives on consumption, so long as the exclusively individualistic aspects of the latter perspective are modified. Indeed, these theories will be used to explain the dynamism that pervades all aspects of consumption in the village, and they will be outlined in Chapter Seven. By providing some empirical detail of working class material culture, which is glaringly absent from most works that theorise on the subject, I hope to illustrate the utility of these differing approaches to understanding the consumption patterns in one specific working-class village.

Consumption constructing distinctions and a cognitive order

The perspective characterised above as 'cultural' emphasises consumers' own desires as social beings to distinguish themselves from others and express salient categories. It can be distinguished from a 'productionist' tradition, exemplified by Baudrillard (1981), which argues that concern with social differentiation results from the manipulation of the public by an elite in society.

Veblen (1899) was one of the first social theorists to analyse Western consumption in terms of its social and cultural significance, focusing on how goods come to take on meaning. Veblen was specifically concerned with 'the Leisure Class' of America, who used their new-found wealth to express their status through conspicuous consumption and leisure, the irony being that their self-conscious social pretensions clearly distinguished them from the 'authentic' leisured class that they aspired to join. Veblen argues that the values of the new leisure class, which defined good taste as distance from the world of work, were emulated by all levels of society.

Bourdieu (1984) develops Veblen's central idea that the significance of ordinary goods lies in their being expressions of taste. He extends his analysis much further than Veblen, however, to cover all sections of (French) society, though his empirical illustrations come predominantly from the middle class. Whereas Veblen presumed that all social strata imitated their superiors (a much criticised assumption: Campbell 1987), Bourdieu argues that different social groups have very different consumption patterns which are practised largely to distinguish themselves from other groups.

Bourdieu attributes the basic differences in taste between different social groups to class experiences. Working class tastes derive from the immediacy of their materially insecure environment, middle class tastes from the confidence that material necessities will always be met. In the upper middle class taste is increasingly split between the two fractions of the 'dominant class'. Those whose social position is based on economic capital tend towards the overt display of luxurious consumption analysed by Veblen, while those whose superior position rests on cultural capital value refined, cultivated pleasures that have to be learnt, such as abstract modern art or *nouvelle cuisine*. Objective conditions give rise to specific subcultures (termed 'habitus' by Bourdieu) which have different desires expressed in different tastes. These tastes classify other people but also classify the person making the distinctions: 'taste classifies and classifies the classifier' (Bourdieu 1984).

Although Bourdieu has a less culturally monolithic concept of society than Veblen, they share the same limitation of viewing consumption almost exclusively in terms of hierarchical distinction. Bourdieu is one of the few sociologists to give status distinctions any theoretical weight recently, but cultural practices are ultimately reduced to social class. The determinism of his argument is most evident when he briefly considers working class consumption as 'the choice of the necessary'. As critics have previously noted (Miller 1987; Jenkins 1992), it is extraordinary to argue that working class people do not make aesthetic choices in their daily lives.

The analysis of consumption as an expression of social distinctions does not always restrict the meaning of commodities to social stratification. Both Sahlins (1976) and Douglas and Isherwood (1979) consider that consumption plays an important role in establishing and communicating cognitive order, only one aspect of which is hierarchical stratification. Since one of the main deficiencies of Douglas and Isherwood's work is resolved in Sahlin's analysis I will discuss the two books in that order, rather than chronologically.

In *The World of Goods* (1979) Douglas and Isherwood argue, in a Durkheimian tradition, that goods are best understood as part of a system of communication, by means of which social order is constituted and social relationships expressed. In trying to return the rational individual of formal economics back to her social context and explain the economists' theory of demand, Douglas and Isherwood pursue an eclectic analysis which, I feel, is ultimately incoherent and unsuccessful (according to their own objectives set out in the introduction). However, in the course of the book many stimulating ideas are proposed, two of which are particularly pertinent here. The first theme is that goods help us make sense of our environment:

> To continue to think rationally, the individual needs an intelligible universe, and that intelligibility will need to have some visible markings. Abstract concepts are always hard to remember, unless they take on some physical appearance. In this book, goods are treated as . . . markers of rational categories.
>
> (Douglas and Isherwood 1979: 5)

Commodities are used to establish social identities and express how their owners interpret the world. Yet it is not clear why people should own goods individually for them to express 'rational categories'. They could be borrowed (a suit at a wedding or the hired Rolls Royce in the Gala Day), owned collectively (a football trophy or banners in an Orange march), or belong to no one (as with the water frequently used in rituals in traditional societies). Furthermore, though goods are usually used to mark abstract concepts any physical behaviour could be used, such as a kiss, a handshake, a salute, or the avoidance of a relative; goods as such are not intrinsically necessary.

The second pertinent theme is that consumption is part of an information system. This follows from the analysis of goods as 'markers of rational categories', and is very much in keeping with both Baudrillard and Bourdieu. But Douglas and Isherwood are not so much concerned with goods expressing information about the user as allowing the user to *gain* information. Information is seen as the crucial scarce resource that priveleged groups have access to, and patterns of appropriate consumption are the means by which these groups are closed to outsiders. However, the example given of consuming in order to gain information about employment seems tautologous (as the authors more or less recognise, ibid.: 181), for the employment is presumably wanted primarily to increase income and so consumer capacity.

In their emphasis on the overwhelming desire for cognitive order, Douglas and Isherwood imply that culture is independent of structural factors and pay no attention to the interests of capital. In *Culture and Practical Reason* (1976) Sahlins avoids such a denial of material factors, while sharing Douglas and Isherwood's critique of theories founded on economic or utilitarian determinism. Following Saussure and Baudrillard (whom he acknowledges, a practice that seems uncommon in this field), Sahlins attempts to draw 'bourgeois society into the kingdom of symbolic order' (ibid.: viii). The idea that use value is itself symbolic is fundamental:

> to give a cultural account of production, it is critical to note that the social meaning of an object that makes it useful to a certain category of persons is no more apparent from its physical properties than is the value it may be assigned in exchange . . . The reason Americans deem dogs inedible and cattle 'food' is no more perceptible to the senses than is the price of meat.

> (Sahlins: 169)

Using aspects of Americans' food and clothing as examples, Sahlins illustrates how it is the social meaning that lies behind use value which determines economic demand and so effects production. He describes the vast range of manufactured goods as an elaborate 'bourgeois totemism' which communicates the socially significant aspects of a person and occasion:

> In its economic dimension, this [symbolic] project consists of the reproduction of society in a system of objects not merely useful but meaningful; whose utility indeed

consists of a significance. The clothing system in particular replicates for Western society the functions of
the so-called totemism.

(Sahlins: 203)

For Sahlins the manufacturing of goods is essentially the production of symbolically significant differences, and he asserts the
primacy of the symbolic or cultural over material forces. However, he avoids a simple idealist position by arguing that material
factors do influence culture, largely through 'the power of an
industrial productivity' (ibid.: 217) to reformulate the symbolic
significance of products: the 'new differentiation of symbolic
value in pursuit of greater exchange-value'. He concludes that
changes in the system of symbolic values of a capitalist society
can come from both the cultural sphere and the economic sphere.
In short, 'the code works as an open set, responsive to events
which it both orchestrates and assimilates to produce expanded
versions of itself.' (ibid.: 184). Thus the system of signs can be
partially influenced by the public through truly indigenous
styles, such as the skinheads, the hippies or punks (see Cohen
1972; Hebdige 1979), but these new styles are usually quickly
appropriated by manufacturing industry which develops every
conceivable variation on the theme.

As his use of semiology suggests, Sahlins is primarily concerned with the underlying system behind the production and
consumption of goods (the *langue*) rather than the empirical
details of behaviour (*parole*). There is therefore little discussion of
which groups are differentiated by which commodities, and how
social class, age, gender or kinship are variously signified.

Another attempt to synthesise 'cultural' and 'productionist'
explanations for the dynamic of modern consumption is Miller's
book *Material Culture and Mass Consumption* (1987). He follows
Douglas and Isherwood's analysis of goods in terms of their
expressive and symbolic function, but criticises them because
'they entirely ignore the interests and power of commercial
institutions'. (Miller 1987: 146).

Miller's analysis develops from Hegelian philosophy, and his
overriding concern is with alienation. He argues that the scale of
production in modern society makes alienation from one's labour
almost inevitable, but not alienation in consumption. Focusing

on the period of time *after* a person has purchased or been allocated a commodity, Miller argues that consumption can be seen as a form of work.

> consumption as work may be defined as that which translates the object from an alienable to an inalienable condition; that is, from being a symbol of estrangement and price value to being an artefact invested with particular inseparable connotations.

(Miller 1987: 190)

Work in this sense does not usually mean physical labour to modify the object, though it can do. More commonly it refers to other ways in which the commodity is transformed by becoming intimately associated with a specific individual or social group. This can be done, for instance, through the length of time the good is possessed, its presentation as a gift, or its incorporation into a 'stylistic array' which is used to express the owner's place in relation to peers engaged in similar activities.

The process begins with the dramatic transformation in our orientation to commodities that occurs at the moment of purchasing a good. When shopping the consumer is faced by a vast alienated world of products divorced from their production: she cannot relate the tin of beans to the land, the people or the machines that produced it. However, the moment the good is purchased 'the specific nature of [the purchaser or intended user] is confirmed in the particularity of the selection, the relation between this object and others providing a dimension through which the particular social position of the intended individual is experienced.' (Miller 1987: 190) Different goods are more or less amenable to being 'recontextualised' by the consumer, just as different segments of the population are more or less able to appropriate commodities for their own ends.

A major problem with Miller's argument is his implication that appropriating commodities so that they generate particular social relations and group identities is somehow inevitably progressive. But such 'recontextualising' of products can reproduce social relationships that are restrictive and obligatory: escaping alienation does not necessarily avoid exploitation or compulsion. Numerous examples can be cited of commodities being integrated into the development of non-progressive social relationships. This ethnography, for instance, shows how goods can become standards of respectability so that individuals feel obliged to continue in exploitative relationships of employment in order to procure them.

CUSTOMARY CONSUMPTION AND RESPECTABILITY

One of the principal features of consumption in Cauldmoss was a concern to conform to certain standards of respectability and to the conventional way of village life, in short, to be "nice". I will describe this 'respectable level' for the main areas of expenditure, considering how this relates to the employment ethic, and outline the principal constituents of conventional consumption in Cauldmoss. Several of the social categories described in Chapter Two that were central to the culture of the village were expressed in the predominant material lifestyle. Furthermore, some of the key variables behind these categories, in particular kinship and gender, shaped patterns of spending, as we saw in the way the wage was allocated.

The living room

The living room in Cauldmoss was both the core of the home and its most public area. Unlike the much analysed phenomenon of the parlour in respectable English working class homes (Hoggart 1957; Martin 1981), there was spatial division of houses between a room reserved for public ceremonial occasions, which certified one's respectability, and a living area (the kitchen) for the regular use of the family and friends. In Cauldmoss the living room was both what its name implied, the place where practically all domestic activities went on, apart from cooking, washing dishes and washing clothes, and also the room into which visitors were welcomed. They generally passed in and out with little formality, and close friends sometimes entered from outdoors without knocking; only strangers and children were likely to be kept at the front door. In contrast the kitchen was only entered by the most familiar friends, and here there was fairly rigid gender segregation: female visitors might be invited or venture in, but men very rarely entered other people's kitchens, unless they were close relatives or there was no woman in the household. Bedrooms were entirely restricted to the residents except for very unusual occasions such as Hogmanay parties, a "show of presents" preceding a wedding or funerals.

In broad terms, there was a basic demarcation in Cauldmoss houses between the public living room and the rest of the house, whereas in the Lancashire houses described by Martin (1981) there was a tripartite division between the front room or parlour, reserved for special, formal occasions and guests, the back room/kitchen used by the family and close friends, and the bedrooms restricted to the residents. This spatial arrangement of houses might be interpreted as reflecting, metaphorically, the wider social structure. The greater subdivisions of Lancashire houses would suggest a more stratified society, approximating perhaps to Douglas's ideal type of 'grid identity', whereas the overlap of family domestic activity and public space in the living room of Cauldmoss houses reflected 'group' identity: such village solidarity that there was no need to restrict friends from one's living space or devote a whole room to certifying one's respectability.

Gregariousness and warmth were essential to a good living room in Cauldmoss in the early 1980s (cf. Hoggart 1957: 35), and the furnishing was always conducive to these complementary ends. A deep, soft three-piece suite was arranged to face the open coal fire and the television, both of which provided a focus of constantly moving light throughout the day. The fire was normally made up by the husband before work and lit in the morning, even in the summer, because it heated the water with a back boiler, while the television was usually switched on as soon as someone began using the room. With a thick fitted carpet and net curtains distancing one from the weather outside, everything combined to make the room snug. Many families burnt three or four sacks of coal per week in the winter, and perhaps two in the summer, for maintaining a really warm room was fundamental to the home and imperative for hospitality. Again, not much had changed since Hoggart's day: 'A good housewife knows that she must "keep a good fire", . . . a fire is shared and seen.' (ibid.: 37). Very few people in Cauldmoss wished to replace their open coal fires with some other form of heating. The young still envisaged a coal fire in the house of their choice, and even the old wanted to keep the coal: if they talked of central heating they meant it to be taken from the back boiler.

Another essential for a living room to conform was net curtains or blinds. This was not simply to ensure privacy, for far more material than was functionally necessary was used to provide an

elaborate show of draped fabric. The panes behind the net always
had to be sparkling clean, and the two together were so indicative
of the respectability of a household that a street was given a seal
of approval simply by the phrase "there are some *lovely* windows
along . . . street."

Only one person in our survey sample of sixty-two households
did not have a three-piece suite. They provide a particularly clear
example of the compulsion for renewal: many households would
replace them before there was any obvious sign of wear. Employed council tenants renewed their suites more frequently than
private householders (Second survey), and spent twice as much
on large household goods. An obvious explanation for the different rates of furniture renewal was the greater disposable income
of council tenants without mortgages to pay. There might also
have been different priorities for expenditure: keeping ahead of
the obsolescence of goods was a confirmation of one's affluence,
one's continuous application to paid work and being "a big
spender". The boost to one's self-esteem from purchasing a new
three-piece suite might not have been so important if one already
owned a house. In general the renewal of living room furniture
was restricted to replacing the three-piece suite in a similar, but
updated, style. A few households diverged from this convention,
however, and bought outstandingly luxuriant furniture. For instance, one much remarked upon family had a settee, armchairs,
foot stool and TV cabinet all embossed in simulated leather, an
example of the less restricted material lifestyles discussed in
Chapter Seven.

The living room walls always had some kind of ornaments,
usually prints which would preferably be under glass and
framed. Some kind of glass-fronted cabinet often stood with
miscellaneous mementoes that displayed a 'still life' (Martin
1981) of the family's achievements of respectability (mounted
photos of the wedding and of ideal family life, certificates, sport-
ing trophies, etc.) along with souvenirs of past holidays or sports
events. Small coffee tables were compulsory furnishing for a
normal living room, as was a rug in front of the fire of the deepest,
thickest material possible.

The television was a prerequisite, and less than a tenth of
households (mainly the old or unemployed) simply had a black
and white set (Second survey). A living room without any television was considered soulless, and the occupants either

absolutely poverty stricken or most peculiar. We came upon only one during our stay in Cauldmoss. Watching television was the most ubiquitous way of passing one's "free time", but this was not done in a concentrated manner. Although "the box" was on continuously, people would break off viewing to chat with someone in the room, do the ironing, welcome a visitor, get the children to bed or go out, and only a few programmes – notably soap-operas and football – actually had priority over people's social relationships. By far the most popular channel was Scottish Television, which constituted about three quarters of the total viewing time in Cauldmoss. BBC Scotland was the next most widely watched, followed closely by Channel 4. BBC 2 was virtually never viewed, except for sport.

Videos were rapidly adopted into Cauldmoss households when they first appeared in the early 1980s, and by 1984 just over half the employed council householders had a machine (Second survey). Only a quarter of private householders in employment had one while very few retired people did. Videos were wanted principally to watch video films, commonly hired from the local ice-cream van or village shop, rather than for recording television programmes. Many hired tapes did the rounds of Cauldmoss, and videos did not greatly increase the heterogeneity of films seen within the village.

Food

Food constituted about 30 per cent of the household budget and was one of the highest priorities in women's domestic spending. They rarely denied their husbands or children more food at meals or snacks of biscuits in between times. Again, little seemed to have changed over thirty years: ' "A good table" is equally important, and this still means a fully stocked table rather than one which presents a balanced diet.' (Hoggart 1957: 37)

"Tea" was the principal meal of the day, usually at a regular time between 5 o'clock and 5:30 p.m. when the husband returned from his employment, and generally the whole family ate together (except perhaps the wife who had prepared the meal) (Second survey). The main characteristics of tea were the central place of meat, the almost ubiquitous potato (often as chips and rarely simply boiled), highly processed food – increasingly frozen rather than tinned – the accompaniment by tea and white sliced bread and butter, and the conclusion with chocolate biscuits.

Meat or meat products were the essence of a proper meal (cf. Charles and Kerr 1988): other things were mere accessories, almost a subordinate category of food. Roast meat was still what was generally used to make "Sunday dinner" special, though it was often chicken rather than beef or pork, and in some households this main weekly meal was on Saturday (Second survey). Through the week a considerable amount of processed meat was eaten in pork pies, sausage meat, mince, pie filling, beefburgers and so on. Liver and kidneys were rarely eaten, and, probably because of a stigma of poverty, other entrails and rabbits were not eaten at all, while in contrast having access to "butcher meat" was considered synonymous with a satisfactory income. A poverty stricken family was described as "having no meat in the house."

Health education messages on diet, although generally known, had little resonance for people in Cauldmoss. A great deal of sugar was eaten, in processed foods, tea, coffee, and soft drinks, as well as sweets. Indeed, many children spent 25 to 50 pence a day on sweets, and if dissuaded from doing so by their parents it was for economic reasons. Women were concerned about the fattening effects of sugar because of their appearance rather than their health. Deep frying was one of the commonest forms of cooking (particularly for potatoes), the meat eaten often had a high fat content (e.g.sausage meat) and butter was preferred to margarine. The more commercialised 'health foods' such as packaged bran cereals and brown loaves were beginning to enter Cauldmoss homes in the early 1980s. In the local town one of the largest supermarkets, that most used by Cauldmoss women, experimented with weigh-your-own wholemeal pastas, flours and rice, but although the prices were comparable with those for the conventional foods, the experiment was withdrawn within a year through insufficient demand. In central Scotland it would appear that the lack of interest in wholefoods was more a consequence of working-class cultural values than economic limitations.

Clothing

Clothes formed one of the most public expressions of one's material lifestyle in Cauldmoss, along with front gardens and cars which were constantly exposed for public inspection. Clothing was also the area of consumption most subject to fashion, which demonstrates the social dimension of this phenomenon in contrast to its individualistic character propounded by Campbell (1987).

In Cauldmoss the young were most anxious to wear "trendy" clothes and the old least influenced by fashion. For teenagers new clothing was likely to be of greater priority than buying records, cassettes or drinks, and clothes were one of the most common Christmas presents given by parents.

To be respectable one's clothes had to look smart. For those over about 30, there were several different degrees of smartness. Nearly all men had special "working claes", even when their work was not particularly dirty (such as driving a van), but even these clothes were not usually ragged, overalls often being replaced if ripped. The significance of wearing distinctly non-work clothes away from one's job has already been considered (Chapter Four). Men generally wore ironed shirts and trousers, and when going out, for instance to the pub, a light jacket was often worn. A formal occasion, such as a meeting or weekend visit to a relative, might have been marked by a tie, while it was usual to wear suits to church. Nearly every man had at least one suit, but for weddings it was very common to hire grey tails (kilts were very rarely worn). The greatest conformity to formal dress was at funerals: all the men wore black suits and plain black ties, while the women went in black and white.

For women make up and jewellery were essential to be smartly dressed, and at formal events hats were often worn. For older women there was a clear distinction between "dress" occasions and everyday wear. Those over about 30 would only wear trousers to do housework and perhaps to pop down to the village shops, while they would always wear dresses or skirts when going out. Often their watches were reserved for such occasions. For young women (at least those in employment) this distinction had been eroded and increasingly they wore jewellery all the time. They rarely wore silver rather than gold, and would pay £70 or £90 for individual ornaments.

The strict functional categorisation of clothes (noted in other studies of the working class (Martin 1981)) was further emphasised by ritualistic washing between different activities. Thus people would habitually have a wash on returning from their job before changing into non-work clothes and when getting ready to go out in the evenings, in both cases irrespective of physical dirt.

The obligation to look respectable inhibited people from wearing any clothes that were worn, patched or darned, even if doing manual work. Jumble sales played no part in Cauldmoss life. They were never organised to raise funds, and if anyone used them in the local town they never mentioned it in the village.

The vast majority of young men in the village wore tight blue jeans, baggy bomber jackets, white socks and delicate pointed grey shoes, in keeping with the fashion for young working-class males throughout Lowland Scotland in the early 1980s. It was notable that very few lads in Cauldmoss followed the 'spectacular styles' (Willis 1985) of youth subcultures more common in England. This can be explained by either interpreting exotic youth cults as 'mediated responses to the presence in Britain of a sizeable black community' (Hebdige 1979: 73) or, in the specific case of skinhead subculture, as an attempt to cope with the supposed withering away of their parents' traditional working-class culture (Cohen 1972). Central Scotland lacked both stimuli for these cultural forms: there were virtually no people of Afro-Caribbean descent (though there were some Asians), and around Cauldmoss the traditional proletarian culture had only begun to be undermined by industrial changes and mobility.

Whatever the validity of these analyses, for Cauldmoss lads to wear the conventional clothing of young working-class males established their integration in the village. Their clothes were particularly significant in being contrasted with the few young men who did dress as punks, skinheads and hippies, all of whom seemed to have adopted these styles as overt rejections of solidarity with the community. The three punks were all incomers to the village, they had few friends in the community and could presumably establish some self-esteem by identifying with a much wider group outwith the parochial world of Cauldmoss. Two of the skinheads shared these characteristics, while two other lads who went through a skinhead phase before disappearing to borstal seemed to adopt the style to distinguish themselves from their fellow locals whom they despised. Thus these young men ascribed their own specific meanings to commodities in mediating more national trends.

The garden

Maintaining a tidy garden was almost the only domestic task that directly expressed men's disciplined application to work (see

Chapter Four). The 30 square yards or so that made up most front gardens was the most public area of their domain and great effort was made to keep it "nice". This meant, above all, under control: the grass was kept below an inch in height, the edges were trimmed and hedges clipped regularly, any flower beds were thoroughly weeded, and, if the area was covered in gravel, this was sprayed with herbicides. Horticultural expertise was not prized, though colourful flowers were admired.

The approach of Gala Day in late spring made the tidiness of front gardens particularly significant, with most people making a special effort to maintain or establish order by trimming, mowing, weeding and so on. If unable to do so, for instance because of continuous wet weather and mower breakdowns, some older people sensed the whole village would condemn them on a day of community ritual (see Chapter Two).

The constant concern to maintain the neatness of one's garden illustrates how aesthetics are socially determined, in this case shaped by the imperatives of social status: to demonstrate that one was "nice" and not a "waster". Many people whose gardens joined a pasture field carefully tidied their own ground and threw everything, from grass mowings to bedsteads, over the fence to lie within sight in "the park", while others barrowed their rubbish down a nearby lane and dumped it on a disused tree nursery. In doing so the actors were maintaining their respectability, and their oblivion to disguising the source of the rubbish suggests that neither they, nor their fellow villagers, thought they were creating an eyesore. This is a further example of the rigid cultural boundaries in Cauldmoss: discarded objects within one's garden were unsightly rubbish, but lying on the other side of the fence, in space not subject to being ordered, they were largely unnoticed. By contrast, middle class preoccupation with litter, which Margaret Thatcher exploited politically in the late 1980s, is probably an illustration of how middle-class aesthetic judgement reflects their broader socio-political perspective that makes most areas of life the proper subject of their opinion (cf. Bourdieu 1984: Ch. 8).

Solvency

One of the most important ways in which people tried to distinguish themselves from the non-respectable, the wasters, was to avoid any behaviour which might be seen as motivated by poverty. When questioned about how they would spend extra money (Second survey), several people carefully clarified that, although more money would be welcome, they were not impoverished:

> Just to have a wee bit extra . . . to buy for Christmas . . . to give that wee bit extra, but it's getting more and more difficult. Don't get me wrong: we don't *want* for anything. But we don't live in the lap of luxury.

The denial of impoverishment was intertwined with the assertion of the housewife's competence to manage the household income, however small it was. Thus many women were careful to clarify that even when economising, for instance while their husbands had been unemployed, the family had had enough to live on.

For most people one of the greatest threats to one's respectability was to fall into debt. The fear of this has haunted working-class (and middle-class) households for centuries, though definitions of debt vary considerably (cf. Hoggart 1957: 79).

In Cauldmoss buying clothing and household goods by post through catalogues (known as "clubs") was widespread, women often joining together to order goods through one person. Similarly many women had charge accounts at department stores in the local conurbation, for which either they made a regular payment at the shop or someone came to collect it at their house. Approximately half of all council households had either a catalogue or credit account (or both) (Second survey), and two-thirds did where the husband was employed. Typical weekly payments were between £2 and £5. "Provi cheques" (from Provident Personal Credit Ltd) were also used widely, cheques for around £20 being paid off in weekly instalments over twenty weeks. The local agent was a Cauldmoss man who worked at this part time, and it was in his interest to avoid a loan to anyone unlikely to be able to make the repayments. Cheques were usually used for clothing, shoes, Christmas presents, holidays or household utensils, and most customers used them on a rotating basis, re-borrowing when a previous cheque had been paid off. (A detailed study of how debtors generally perceive cheque trading as a valuable service has been made by Kent: 1980).

The vast majority of those who had a club, charge account or Provi cheque did not regard themselves as being in debt, which would only have been the case if they had failed to pay their weekly instalments. While ideally they would have prefered not to buy on credit, they did not regard doing so as a failure to manage, simply as a practical way of easing the situation. But they were well aware of the need to "control your credit urge" and borrow within one's means to repay, not to "go mental".

Older people were less likely to view credit in such a neutral way. Many over 60 regarded catalogue buying as being in debt, and were proud of the fact they had "*never* bought a thing on credit in my life!".

> I've never been one for a lot of debt. I want to feel that what I've got is my ain, what I've got left is my ain.

Such people had generally saved up to buy their own furniture before they had got married, and they felt that "If ye can't buy it, do without it." Williams has shown how this aversion to being beholden was a manifestation of 'the precision . . . given to the law of exchange', from which it followed 'that to receive without having given, or being able to give, was the most demeaning situation of all.' (Williams 1990: 227) Tables 5.3 and 5.4 below show the variation in values and behaviour of different generations.

The final demonstration of solvency in life was one's funeral. It was considered so important that some started saving for it from the age of 25, but with increasing age people became more anxious about their ability to afford a "proper" funeral. A 93 year old woman described her life as:

TABLE 5.3   Different age groups' opinions about buying on credit.

	Below 30	Age groups 30–59	Over 60
Disapprove in general	1	6	9
Morally disapprove	0	2	2
Financially bad	1	6	3
Ideally avoided, but necessary	0	8	1
Necessary	2	1	1
Neutral	3	3	1
Approve	4	8	0
TOTAL	11	34	17

Source: Second survey, Q. 16.

TABLE 5.4 Different age groups' practice in buying on credit.

	Below 30	Age groups 30–59	Over 60
Never had credit	1	5	7
Only once had credit	0	1	2
Currently has credit	7	16	3
Don't know	3	12	5
TOTAL	11	34	17

Source: Second survey, Q. 16.

just sitting here by the fire and hoping there'll be enough money to be put in the ground . . . The old folk all had good insurances so you could get buried without any worries, but now it's so dear you cannae be sure you will get a decent burial . . . It's a natural thing to do. To have enough to put you awa' under the ground. It's no just twenties an' thirties, it's into hundreds now to be put awa'.

It seemed as if funerals were regarded as the ultimate assessment of one's respectability in life. The attendance at one's burial defined one's social standing – whether one had earned respect from the community (see Chapter Two) – while the expense of it was a final demonstration of one's worthiness. This explains the shame of a pauper's grave: not just the inability to afford the concluding symbol of honourable status, but a lack of kith or kin to ratify that status.

Commitment to work

The central place of work, and, more specifically, employment, in the culture of Cauldmoss has been discussed in the last chapter. Another aspect of this was the importance attached to the differentiation of work and leisure which, as Martin notes (1981), usually receives elaborate emphasis in working-class culture. In the early 1980s many families in Cauldmoss still repeated the same fortnight's holiday each summer. Some spent either one or both weeks of the "trades" at Butlins in Ayr or Blackpool, while others stayed in their caravan permanently situated in a Scottish coastal resort or on a loch. Not everyone was so regular, however; some took package holidays abroad or visited relatives in other parts of Britain.

The significance of work in Cauldmoss had greatest impact on material lifestyles through the obligation to maintain respectable standards of consumption. These standards expressed one's commitment to work, which was an essential aspect of being "nice" and not a "waster". For women this meant work in general, and so their moral worth was doubly confirmed (as wives and as workers) by their fulfilment of wifely duties: keeping the carpet hoovered, the furniture polished and, in particular, the windows shining. For men it meant disciplining oneself to regular employment, as described in the last chapter. In many respects men's consumption patterns can be understood as expressing their employee role, particularly in the case of drinking, as will be elucidated in Chapter Six. The moral credit earned by being a good worker, and the measure of a man's worth by his wage, were extended to his spending capacity. In establishing his son's credentials a man said in the same breath, "he's a *worker* . . . a big earner, can't stand idle," and the boast of being one of "the big earners" also meant being one of "the big money men . . . askin' what ye're drinkin''. Conversely lack of interest in consumer goods was interpreted, and criticised, as an implicit preference for idleness.

Physical objects had become visible symbols of inner worth, but the connection with hard work had become less essential, and big spenders had prestige almost in their own right. Whatever the origin of the employment ethic, Weber was right in his observation that whereas riches might have once been prestigious as a sign of the owner's devoted work and (by implication) his or her position as one of the elect, today they have become prestigious in themselves: ' the care for external goods . . . [has] become an iron cage.' (Weber 1930: 181). Here Baudrillard is in agreement:

> It is important to read social obligation, the ethos of 'conspicuous' consumption everywhere . . . a morality which is still imperative.
>
> So, under this paradoxical determination, objects are not the locus of the satisfaction of needs, but of a symbolic labor, of a 'production' in both senses of the term: *pro-ducers* – they are fabricated, but they are also produced as a *proof.* They are the locus of consecration

of an effort, of an uninterrupted performance ... the
heir of the principles that were the foundation of the
Protestant ethic and which, according to Weber, motivated the capitalist spirit of production. The morality
of consumption relays that of production, or is en-
tangled with it in the same logic of salvation.

(Baudrillard 1981: 33)

Stage of life course

Another dimension of the cognitive order that the material lifestyle of Cauldmoss reinforced was the differentiation of people
by age or stage in the life course. Here I will simply note two
interrelated ways in which age affected consumption patterns.
First, different kinds of commodities, whether clothes, furniture,
food or whatever, were considered appropriate to different age
groups and thus they signified one's stage in life, or that to which
one aspired. The most obvious examples were those goods that
confer adult status, such as cigarettes, alcohol, and motorbikes or
cars.

Second, consumption reflected age through an overall pattern
of spending, namely "having an independence". This phrase was
frequently used to describe one's economic circumstances in
relation to general financial worries, creditors, or one's parents.
It meant exercising personal choice in spending free from perceived constraint (the *cultural* constraints on spending were largely
invisible). The hallmark of having "an independence" for teenagers was paying "dig money" to their mothers. This was highly
important to the young person in establishing his/her status as
an adult through wage-earning, while for the parents, who often
payed much of the £10 or so back again as it was needed through
the week, it clearly established the contribution an ordinary
parent expected and the extent to which they were spoiling their
child by waiving or repaying the dig money (see Barker 1972). Men
over 30 recalled how they had longed to leave school for even the
most poorly paid, arduous employment, in order to make this
transition to adulthood. In 1984 teenagers were less ready to take
any job simply to have their own income (they could get £16.50 a
week on Supplementary Benefit – to be discussed in Chapter
Eight), but the wage was still the passport to the adult world in
which one exercised one's choice in the market (Willis 1984).

Gender: masculinity

The importance of gender in Cauldmoss was clear from the divisions of labour and recreation between the sexes, as we saw in Chapter Two. Gender categories were probably those most clearly expressed and reproduced by means of consumption; whether through the commodities used (e.g. clothing), who used them (e.g. cars), or the division of consumer tasks (e.g. purchasing or processing). Here I will restrict myself to highlighting the most important ways in which spending established masculine identity and the man's role in the family.

The connection between strenuous, disciplined employment and masculinity has been discussed in the last chapter. Since one's wage was a measure of one's worth and masculinity – the hard worker was a "big earner" – a man's consumer power was directly related to his esteem as a male. This was epitomised in the use of alcohol, to be described in the next chapter, but it encouraged greater expenditure in many other areas, particularly with food (buying meat), cars and courting women. Since, in the world beyond Cauldmoss, a woman's social status was largely determined by her husband's occupation (Leonard 1980), clues about young men's earning potential were used to screen potential boyfriends.

Some commodities were intrinsically masculine according to the way this concept was constructed in Cauldmoss. Frequently such goods were also expensive, but this was a secondary and largely independent way in which they denoted masculinity. Meat was the food most clearly associated with masculinity (see also Charles and Kerr 1988), which seems common to most cultures. Indeed, a recent revolutionary thesis argues that men's exchange of meat for sex was central to the origin of culture (Knight 1991). In Cauldmoss to relish steak epitomised manliness and male vegetarians were sometimes accused of being "pooftas". Sahlins traces the gender connotations of meat: 'back to the Indo-European identification of cattle or increasable wealth with virility.' (Sahlins 1976: 171). Another food that could enhance a man's masculinity in Cauldmoss was hot curry, sometimes eaten after an evening's drinking.

Large aggressive dogs or fighting breeds, such as Boston pit bull terriers (which were just arriving in central Scotland in the early 1980s), confirmed their owner's masculinity as if, being subject to his will, they were an extension of his strength and pugnacity: "I like taking him for walks, he's a powerful dog. Bull mastiff. You get attention . . . I love it." Some men took pride in the ferocity of their dog, such as the man who told two women a lengthy tale of how he had had to break a 2" by 2" piece of timber over his new Doberman's head in order to subdue it, as if it were an epic of man's mastery over brute nature. About half Cauldmoss households had a dog, the most common breed probably being the Alsatian. It was primarily the man's responsibility to feed and walk it, unless it was a woman's breed, like Scottish terriers or poodles, but many dogs were allowed to roam the streets free. Some women used large dogs as guardians when living alone or walking on their own at night, almost as surrogate males. Others asserted that Alsatians and similar breeds need a man's voice to control them, otherwise they are unreliable.

Control over powerful machinery also had masculine meaning, the hackneyed example being cars. In the early 1980s in Cauldmoss most women could not drive, even in car-owning households, and if they could they would rarely do so when travelling with their husbands, unless he was drunk. It was a strange sight in the village to see a woman at the wheel with a man next to her. However little money they had, men would try to buy cars with powerful engines; Morris Minors, Minis or Citroen Dyanes were rarely seen, and those that were belonged to women. The power of one's car was displayed through fast driving, and the extra brake lights young men were fond of installing in their rear windows emphasised their speed as they 'drove on their brakes'. Two mechanics relished telling Anne Marie Bostyn how they wrote-off two or three cars a month because they 'drive them so hard' : even powerful engines could not extend their physical capabilities far enough. This is a well known theme in the literature on cars (e.g. Bayley 1986: 7–8). Young men were socialised into the masculine use of cars through playing around on old motorbikes as teenagers, those that shied away from this minor initiation into adulthood being scorned.

Other machinery also boosted the user's confidence in his virility: chainsaws were far more suited to grown men than bowsaws; hand-drills or hand-shears smacked of elderly ineffec-tiveness. It was not only the power but also the danger involved in fast driving or chainsaws that made them manly.

These examples illustrate how the gendered meaning of

commodities need have no other logic than conventional association. Thus driving a fast car was more manly than riding a bicycle, even though the latter involved far more physical strength which in other contexts was associated with masculinity. Similarly the fashion for young men's clothes in the early 1980s (described above) and their highlighted or permed hair would have seemed positively effeminate a decade before.

The man's main role in the family was to provide his wife and children with the means to consume, and their standard of living (particularly evident in their clothes) was the principal way in which his responsibility to them was judged. The moral esteem of being a hard worker was above all the virtue of disciplining oneself to employment for the sake of one's family, as expounded in the last chapter. If challenged about their paternal roles men frequently referred to their material provision for the family.

Mothers faced most of the daily pressures from their children to conform to their friends' level of consumption in sweets, toys and clothing, and the children's style of living demonstrated both the mother's competence in managing the household budget and the father's ability to provide it. "Caring" parents sent their children to school in smart clothes, bought them proper school bags and ensured they had adequate spending money when going out. Mothers and fathers sometimes stated with pride that they never denied their children anything they might want, whether it was sweets, a bike, a stereo or, more recently, a home computer. This 'spoiling' was also intended, in the long run, to oblige the children to 'keep close' (Barker 1972).

A husband's ability to support his family was partly evaluated according to the frequency with which he took out his wife, and so it was very important that he should buy the drinks for them both (to be discussed further in the next chapter). Some men had their partners present themselves for inspection when they had finished dressing up to go out, which supported Veblen's theory (1899) that men exhibit their wealth or income through the fineries of their wives.

THE OBLIGATIONS OF RECIPROCITY

Introduction

The preceding section suggested that to be granted the esteem of working class respectability and village membership one had to

conform to a particular pattern of consumption, which constituted being "nice". Another force for conformity were the principles
of social exchange, which also acted as a catalyst to social involvement and consumption. These principles, in particular the norm
of reciprocity, shaped and often perpetuated personal relationships. In fact the relationships sometimes came to be defined by
the material reciprocated, for instance: "Old Jock: I take a drink
with him", or "Isabel always sends a Christmas card".

Social exchange has been the focus of sociological and social
anthropological theorising since at least the beginning of this
century (Ekeh 1974). Suffice to say the 'French' collectivist school
seems to be of greatest use in understanding social exchange in
Cauldmoss. Mauss states there is a fundamental 'obligation to
give' from which the other institutions of social exchange stem,
the obligations to receive and to repay.

> To refuse to give, or to fail to invite, is – like refusing to
> accept – the equivalent of a declaration of war; it is a
> refusal of friendship and intercourse. Again, one gives
> because one is forced to do so . . .

(Mauss 1954: 11)

The various theoretical classifications of exchange are numerous,
with infinite possible variations as to what can be identified as
part of the transactions (people, goods, services, opportunities,
etc.). However, to understand the significance of social exchange
in a particular culture this theorising is irrelevant unless it relates
to indigenous concepts. In Cauldmoss it would appear that three
different kinds of exchange were distinguished at various times,
though they had no indigenous names, they did not parallel
anthropologists' classifications and the distinctions between the
categories were not consistently maintained. The first kind of
exchange was noted in the last chapter: many villagers believed
that one should contribute to society in return for one's state
benefits (an example of Levi-Strauss's 'long term generalised
exchange'). I will not discuss this kind of exchange here, since it has
little connection with the value attached to specific commodities.

Short-term reciprocity
The second type of exchange recognised in Cauldmoss was that
form most clearly determined by the principle of reciprocity: that

a gift is never free and unless reciprocated it involves a loss of esteem (Gouldner 1973: 242). In men's everyday lives the main material things exchanged in this way were cigarettes and alcohol, while tea or coffee, biscuits and cigarettes were the main things exchanged in this form by women.

There appeared to be no recognition in Cauldmoss of anthropologists' distinction between 'immediate restricted exchange' and 'short-term generalised exchange'. Both were common to the use of alcohol, cigarettes and, for a few, cannabis. Alcohol was widely drunk by the whole adult population, though particularly by men, and is the subject of the next chapter. In the early 1980s smoking cannabis was restricted to a small section of mainly young men, while cigarettes were smoked by perhaps half the adult population, more amongst older than younger people, and amongst the young, probably more amongst women than men. Manufactured cigarettes were the norm, usually middle- or low-tar brands like Regal, Silk Cut or Benson and Hedges, but some rolled their own using Old Holborn or Golden Virginia tobacco. This was generally considered a means of economising and in company those with "tailor-made" cigarettes often proffered them to anyone rolling tobacco as if the latter would much prefer the prefabricated version. It was considered highly peculiar for a woman to roll her own cigarettes.

Housewives felt obliged to offer visitors a drink and snack at any time of the day. As one would expect, the hospitality was more elaborate and formal the less familiar the visitor was, but even close friends were usually given tea or coffee, and this was generally accompanied by chocolate biscuits (rarely plain ones), a slice of cake or fancy confectionery. In the evening, particularly after drinking (at home or in the pub) some "supper" was offered: a hot snack such as scrambled eggs on toast or cheese toasties. There was no suggestion that this hospitality was prompted by the presumed hunger of the guest, but the woman knew that she or her family had had, or would get, the same reception when they dropped in on their visitor.

Short-term reciprocity tends to act as an impetus for greater consumption as well as leading to more homogeneity in spending patterns. Once something has been given a chain of events is started which can only be avoided with social embarrassment, and the relationship which results from these events will in turn prompt the exchange of further goods. It should be possible for a group to conform to a low level of consumption as much as a high one, but a ratchet effect leads everyone to consume at the rate of the fastest, since one can always precipitate the next round but not (within the conventions) delay it. This largely explains why people feel obliged to 'keep up with the Joneses' in their household furnishings: not to do so would mean being excluded from the potential exchange of hospitality (Douglas and Isherwood 1979: 126).

When in a group people always offered their cigarettes around to the other smokers whenever they took one for themselves. However, if a few people who had previously been exchanging cigarettes were joined by others they might continue sharing their cigarettes amongst themselves. As with drinking, this reciprocity constrained people to conform to a common rate of consumption, which was usually that of the heaviest smoker since everyone received a cigarette when she had one. If someone had not finished her previous cigarette another one was laid beside her for the future. Consequently it was socially impossible to smoke a moderate amount (say ten a day); one either smoked as much as everyone else – perhaps twenty or thirty a day – or none at all. Frequently a person would empty half a packet of twenty in smoking two cigarettes, but in the long run she would receive ten back from other people. Clearly a smoker who expected to spend some time with other smokers felt she had to have a fairly full packet of cigarettes with her.

Giving Christmas cards or, less commonly in Cauldmoss, Christmas presents, were examples of immediate restricted exchange. When someone received an unsolicited Christmas card s/he was generally very anxious to return one as soon as possible, while often resenting that the sender should presume (and by doing so actually realise) such a relationship.

Long-term reciprocity

The third group of exchanges recognised in Cauldmoss were those in which things were given with little expectation that they would be returned, in an act described as "generosity", yet ultimately the giver expected the recipient to be indebted to her. Though he coined new terms, Sahlins pinpointed an important difference between 'immediate' and 'delayed' restricted exchange which was acknowledged in Cauldmoss (though rarely expressed):

It is notable of the main run of [delayed restricted
exchanges] that the material flow is sustained by pre-
vailing social relations; whereas, for the main run of
[immediate restricted exchanges], social relations
hinge on the material flow.

(Sahlins 1974: 195)

The most obvious example of delayed restricted exchange (where
the repayment does not have to be immediate or exact) was the
nurturing of children by their parents, where the expectation of
reciprocity was latent and not stipulated by time, quantity or
quality. Cross-culturally, this kind of exchange is most common
between close kin, but the immobility of the Cauldmoss population meant that a gift from a neighbour or credit from the shop
could be returned over a long period in almost the way that
kinship links endure. A nice example that shows how the relationship expressed through friends' gifts could parallel kinship
ties was the giving of money to babies and infants (usually put
into the cot or pressed into the parent's hand). This was commonly a token piece of 'silver', and the inevitable escalation of
standards meant no one would invite dishonour by giving less
than the largest silver coin, which was fifty pence. However, it
was not always a token gift and parents could be urged to accept
£5 notes for each of their young children. This helps perpetuate
relationships between families over generations since 'the relationship is in the feeling of indebtedness not in the gift.' (Leach
1982: 154)

Having one's close relatives for a main meal was usually
perceived as long-term reciprocity, but inviting friends, one of
the principal forms of restricted exchange in middle-class culture, was extremely rare in Cauldmoss. The second survey found
that council households were less likely than private households
to report having visitors for meals, and only a tenth of the council
visitors were friends as opposed to relatives, compared with a
third of the visitors to private households.

Helping friends, and more particularly kin, to find jobs was
probably the most important economic form of long-term reciprocity. The significance of personal kinship networks in job
recruitment has previously been discussed (Chapters Two and
Four). Long-term reciprocity was also important in relation to

consumption, though it did not, in general, act as a catalyst for greater consumption in the way that balanced reciprocity did, since the relationship associated with the exchange already existed. Examples of close kin engaging in this kind of exchange included parents' material provision for their children and bingo players sharing their winnings with their siblings. The principle of long-term reciprocity was neatly encapsulated in the saying heard in Cauldmoss that "a gift to a friend is no loss."

Gift giving was a central part of weddings, and the bride could be preoccupied with preventing guests duplicating presents, and establishing what gifts must have cost, right up until the "show of presents". This and the hen night were the main events for women prior to the marriage. The presents were put on display, generally in the bride's parents' house, and all the female wedding guests were invited to view them, the occasion usually being accompanied by tea, sandwiches, cakes and alcohol. One of the main topics of interest was the price of each gift, and discrete comments were made in praise of the expensive ones and belittling those that were clearly cheaper than one's own. This interest in the size of presents was partly a recognition that they were statements of the guest's perceived relationship to the bride. There was clearly scope for ambiguity in this, so a guest might try and establish a closer relationship than was previously recognised or might distance herself with a modest present. Expensive gifts can also be a straightforward assertion of affluence, and some were criticised for being "too showy".

The items given were almost exclusively household utensils and furnishings, such as towels, kitchen equipment (from simple tools to microwaves), furniture, silver decorations, clocks, bedding and so on. This was the traditional way in which one's friends and relatives, particularly of an older generation, helped with one of the major financial burdens of one's life: establishing a home.

Social exclusion through reciprocity

Although the principle of reciprocity often stimulated consumption and made it more homogeneous, the obligation to reciprocate gifts could also discourage people from social involvement. Since certain forms of social exchange implied particular relationships between those involved, people who did not want to establish such a relationship tried to avoid accepting the initial gift. In Cauldmoss exchanging meals in each other's houses was restricted almost entirely to close kin or affines, Sunday 'dinner' being the principal occasion. This seemed to be treated as a form of long-term reciprocity. Clearly people were well aware of the special relationship they had with those who came to eat in their house, and they were extremely cautious in entering this form of exchange with people outside their family. Such familiarity might have brought with it other obligations and demands.

Short-term reciprocity established a degree of equality between the participants which meant disliked acquaintances were sometimes excluded, such as a woman whose husband's relatives had never stepped into her house since the day after he died: "But I don't owe them nothing and they don't owe me nothing, so that's ixie pixie." It could also exclude those who considered themselves of a higher status than others (cf. Frankenberg 1966: 160). On the other hand those who knew they could not afford the level of consumption of their fellow villagers also avoided reciprocal relationships, for very different reasons. This led to people spending their leisure time with others of similar economic means, and could fragment consumption patterns rather than make them more homogeneous, a topic I will return to in Chapter Eight.

CONCLUSION

The main theme running through this description of the material lifestyle of Cauldmoss has been the struggle to maintain respectable standards and reproduce the social relationships which distinguished "nice" folk from "the wasters". A subsidiary theme has been the pressure to conform to customary behaviour and thus reproduce other cognitive categories that constituted the culture of the village. Another element of conventional consumption was the expression of belonging to the village; this will be discussed in Chapter Seven in relation to a contradictory pattern of more privatised spending. Before turning to these issues of social change, however, the analysis of consumption will be illustrated by focusing on the use of one particular commodity: alcohol. This description of drinking will be related to both the themes in village consumption identified in this chapter and those to be considered in Chapter Seven.

6

Drinking

THE IMPORTANCE OF DRINKING FOR CAULDMOSS MEN

This chapter concentrates on one particular commodity that has a central place in the culture of Cauldmoss: alcohol. In the last chapter material lifestyle was analysed in terms of various underlying patterns, the commodities themselves only being described in relation to the various themes discussed. Here I will look at the matrix of factors affecting consumption from a different angle, by focusing on one good in particular.

In a study of masculine consumption drinking is especially suitable for a case study since it was one of the few areas where men were in control of expenditure (once their spending money had been allocated: discussed in the previous chapter). The importance of drinking for Cauldmoss men was evident from both their conversation and behaviour. They discussed it as if it was intrinsic to social life and one of the main reasons to increase their earnings. Apart from church activities and the Masons there were few social occasions without alcohol, and all the major ritual events marking the passage of time in the year and in people's lives were celebrated with drinking.

Men who did not drink at all were exceptional, and their abstinence was frequently commented on by other villagers and themselves: "never stepped inside a pub all my days!". They generally asserted a moral superiority in this eccentricity, and others, particularly women, often respected it.

The literature on alcohol is enormous (Crawford 1986), but there have been few general studies of drinking culture in Britain. Two important social histories are Brian Harrison's account of Victorian drinking habits (1971), and Mass Observation's sociological investigation into the pubs of Bolton in the late 1930s, edited by Tom Harrison (1943). Both of these have been damningly criticised by Hey for concealing the power relations which exclude women from 'public' houses. Her book *Patriarchy and Pub Culture* (1986) provides an excellent analysis of the intensely chauvinistic male culture of pubs which is usually shared by those who write about them. However, the study relies almost entirely on secondary sources, and detailed ethnographies of British pub life seem to be limited to Whitehead's feminist study of a Herefordshire pub (1976), Smith's short participant observation study of social space and the publican's role in one pub (1981), Gofton's analysis of changes in traditional working class drinking habits in north east England (1984) and Hunt and Satterlee's study of pub life in a Cambridgeshire village (1983).

As with most recreational drugs, the use of alcohol is enmeshed in social constraints and obligations. This chapter addresses different constituents of the social value of drinking, in an attempt to describe and understand the use of alcohol. The ethnography will concentrate on public drinking behaviour in the pubs and clubs of Cauldmoss, partly because this was easier to observe than domestic drinking but, more importantly, because in 1984 it still represented the norm for alcohol consumption amongst most people (particularly men) in the village.

There were several reasons why some men did not frequent the pubs or clubs at all, apart from the obvious one that they might not drink alcohol. A few who were rarely seen drinking in fact remained dry for a couple of months and then went on a binge or a "bender" lasting a weekend or a week, only stopping when they collapsed or the money ran out. Others had been banned from pubs or clubs, usually for a limited period, for deeds such as fighting, being abusive, "mooching" (cadging drinks and cigarettes), exposing themselves in front of the barmaid, and so on. These people drank at home with a "carry out". The bingers and those banned from the pubs might fit Douglas's hypothesis that the more drinking follows a generally inclusive pattern in a society the more a person suffering social rejection is likely to 'turn to compensatory drinking, to possess at least the symbol of what he does not have' (Douglas 1987: 9).

At the weekend pub and club goers often returned in a group to someone's house after closing time, bringing back "carry outs" to prolong the night's revelry, but the main people who drank at home were women. Another group were those (usually from privately owned houses) who did not want to associate with the pub clientele and who tended not to share the status values expressed in the traditional patterns of public drinking. They will be considered in the final section of the chapter, along with the young who drank in the local town.

BELONGING TO THE VILLAGE

Locations of drinking

Most drinking was done in the three pubs and three clubs of the village. Besides liquid refreshments they all provided pool tables, darts and colour televisions, of which pool tables were by far the most popular. Each pub had its own distinct character which was partly the legacy of previous managements, despite the efforts of new landlords to override this, and partly a result of the social distinctions perpetuated by the clienteles. This was a feature of the social stratification in Cauldmoss described in Chapter Three.

The old hotel, which stood at the village crossroads, was still renowned in the early 1980s for the heavy drinking, violence and soliciting by local prostitutes that had supposedly been common-place a decade before. Although for several years fighting had been unusual and the only "prostitute" was an old woman, the pub remained stigmatised and "nice", respectable folk did not want to be associated with it. In an attempt to attract couples rather than male heavy drinkers, in 1983 a new landlord entirely redecorated the pub, installed plush seats in the lounge bar, bought an extra large television screen, and organised weekly entertainments such as singers. This had little effect, at least in the first year, and, in keeping with its lawless image, young people still regarded the old hotel as the best pub in which to smoke cannabis.

Opposite the old hotel was a pub known as Billie's, after the landlord, which attracted predominantly older men, and which was favoured by members of the Orange Lodge. Women were even more scarce here than in the old hotel, and the atmosphere was closer to that of the traditional hard-seated, linoleum floored Scottish working man's bar. Men using the betting office next door often popped in and out between it and one of the pubs, placing a bet and then watching the race on the pub television over a drink.

The third pub, called Nancy's (it had a landlady), lay three-quarters of a mile outside the village. It was described by locals as "nicer" or "quieter" than the other pubs, but this quiet made it difficult to run profitably and throughout the early 1980s the owner was trying to sell it, only continuing the business with reduced opening hours. Couples were more likely to visit this pub than the others, and on Saturday nights live entertainment lured in extra customers.

The bars in the three clubs were used by many men inter-changeably with the pubs. The main social club had been built on the site of the old Miners' Welfare by the Masonic Lodge, which had felt that social events held in the Masonic Hall itself were hindering Masonic business. It was still run by the Masonic Lodge social committee which charged £1 to men and 50p to women for annual membership of the club, the subscriptions being used largely to subsidise drinks. The most popular use of the social club was bingo, almost exclusively patronised by women, but the games bar was frequented by men who were often joined by the women after the bingo sessions. Women going drinking by themselves in a group were more likely to come to this club than either of the others or to the pubs. Because the social club stayed open a few hours longer than the pubs at the week-ends it normally filled up with a lively crowd around midnight.

In contrast to the social club few people went to the Masonic club simply to use its bar but, rather, to attend weekly concerts, quizzes or bingos. The Saturday night concerts drew the largest numbers, in which members of the audience were expected to sing individually to the accompaniment of an accordionist (to be described in the following chapter). As might be expected very few Catholics ever used the Masonic club; the Saturday night concerts usually culminated in Protestant hymns and always ended at midnight with the National Anthem.

The Bowling Club was the only institution amongst the pubs and clubs that was regarded as "snobbish" or "clannish" by those who did not use it. Membership fees per annum of £10 for men and £8.50 for women were claimed by some villagers to have been specifically designed to exclude the less affluent. However, since many men paid this amount for drinks in one night, it would seem that the fees were interpreted according to a prior evaluation of the club's clientele. The "respectable" section of Cauldmoss were more likely to drink here than elsewhere in the village. However, there were fairly lax rules for signing in non-members and some men frequented the Bowling Club as well as the pubs who were by no standards "respectable", being unemployed, often shabbily dressed and heavy drinkers. The Club was open throughout the year, and even in the summer during the bowling season many members came to drink rather than play bowls. Players were predominantly over 40 years old. As with the other clubs, there was a pool table and colour television. Thursday was a "ladies' night" which did not exclude men but meant they stayed in the background behind the predominantly female clientele (see the discussion of women's leisure: Chapter Two).

At talent contests, discos, Gala Day sports quizzes or 'Mr and Mrs' contests, a bar was set up by one of the pubs or clubs wherever the event was held, such as the community centre, the upper floor of the Masonic Hall, or the school hall. The organisers of the Gala Day were careful to ensure that each landlord or lady had an equal chance to provide the bar at the different functions. As in the pubs and clubs, women never bought the drinks unless they were in a group on their own.

Wedding receptions were often held in the community centre or one of the clubs. At least one round of alcohol was usually provided by the bride's family, either as the guests' first drink from the bar or in the form of filled glasses distributed by the caterers. The most elaborate weddings had champagne, but it was acceptable to offer a choice of whisky or sherry, with which the newly wedded couple were toasted. After the initial drinks guests usually bought from the bar in the normal fashion for the rest of the evening. A similar arrangement was typical of other social events initiated by (or focused on) particular individuals, such as a hen night, stag party, or celebration for someone retiring from work.

Integration in, and belonging to, the community

For men, visiting the pubs and clubs was their most important form of integration into the community on a weekly basis. In Chapter Seven we will see how such involvement in the recreational life of the village was considered by many to be an indispensable part of their lives. It was very difficult to gauge the typical amounts of alcohol drunk. A formal survey falls foul of the under-emphasis or exaggeration that dogs most enquiries (see Ashley 1983: 58), and the limitations of our own tactful questioning have already been mentioned. However, an impression from the second survey was that most employed men in council houses went for a drink two or three times a week, while a minority never went for a drink and another minority went out practically every night. In marked contrast the majority of employed male private householders only very rarely visited the pubs or clubs. For men in council houses one of the main attractions of drinking, judging from the way they talked about pubs, was participation in the main male social nexus of the village.

A great advantage of the pubs and clubs was their neutrality in terms of hospitality. To a large extent men could determine the extent to which they interacted with each other, ignoring people, exchanging a brief greeting, or having a prolonged conversation and swapping drinks. By meeting in the public house the level of furnishing was of little interest, the privacy of someone's living room was not infringed and conversely no one felt obliged to accept a similar imposition in return.

Although about a third of each pub's customers were regular clientele who rarely visited any of the other bars, many men moved between the pubs and clubs during an evening. When drinking without their wives they generally acted in a fairly independent and spontaneous way. They would turn up individually at one bar, meet friends by chance and perhaps later move on to another pub and different company, and it was unusual to prearrange meetings in a pub, or to gather with other men in order to go to a bar. Since the bars were nearly all fairly close it was not unusual for men to drop in at several to find a particular person. When going out with his wife, however, a man normally decided with her beforehand where they were going and they spent the whole evening there.

Since much of men's recreational life went on in the pubs or clubs they were important for establishing economic contacts. The informal way in which many jobs were found has already been emphasised (Chapters Two and Four) and pubs were one of the principal places to hear of vacancies or, for local small employers, recruit workers. Furthermore pubs, and the old hotel in particular, were the main places for selling goods that had been acquired informally.

Drinking in the pubs and clubs was not only a way to partici-pate in village life but also an assertion of one's membership of the community. Nancy's, outside the village and "nicer" than the other pubs, and the Bowling Club, which often had visiting teams and was more "snobbish", were the least parochial drinking places in Cauldmoss. Conversely Billie's and the old hotel were felt by their patrons to be at the heart of village life, a sentiment that was expressed by their coolness, and sometimes hostility, towards outsiders who entered. Strangers passing through Cauldmoss were prompted to use the lounges rather than the public bars, and sometimes the landlords actually encouraged them to drink elsewhere outwith the village, particularly if they seemed "respectable". Some of the incomers to Cauldmoss who had been identified as undesirable were conscious enough of their unpopularity not to drink in the bars, while the few that did were ostracised from conversation and risked being provoked into a fight. Of course strangers who were introduced by a local, and sometimes even those who introduced themselves, could be given a warm welcome in the old hotel or Billie's, but it was clearly understood that the clientele were extending the hospital-ity of *their* community to a guest. The central place of pubs in Cauldmoss social life, as well as the lack of alternative venues, was illustrated by young men who still frequented them despite using alternative drugs to alcohol. One group used to sit together in a corner of the old hotel, stoned on local "magic mushrooms" or smoking cannabis and hardly touching the beer in front of them, unconcerned that most people in the pub had condemned them for being "on the dope".

Drinking was the principal feature of a spending ethic which encouraged gregarious leisure within the village and inhibited upward social mobility (to be discussed in the next chapter). Using up 'surplus' income on drink, which was generally re-garded by men as legitimate, prevented workers acquiring goods that would assert a higher social status. There were, however, non-egalitarian aspects of this institution, such as heavy drinkers earning the prestige accorded to "hard workers" and, more im-portant, the rules of reciprocity leading to drinking circles differentiated by spending capacity. This seems to run counter to Douglas and Isherwood's thesis (1979) (see Chapter Seven).

Despite this divisiveness, however, they remained divisions *within* the working class, rather than divisions between different classes which could arise if some workers accumulated capital.

Hogmanay

Membership of the village was also expressed in a ritualised way at Hogmanay, in which alcohol played an integral part. From midnight on 31 December for three or four days hospitality was provided to all visitors, and villagers welcomed the chance to show they had forgotten old grudges by having people in their houses whom they had previously condemned as wasters, bad mothers, thieves, or whatever. The media for expressing this hospitality were always the kiss or (between men) the handshake and the exchange of spirits. It was notable that, apart from kissing and handshaking, of all the traditions of Hogmanay, such as dark men bringing coal and silver into the house, the offering of salmon sandwiches or eating black buns, it was only the exchange of alcohol which remained almost ubiquitous in Cauldmoss. (I will return to the analysis of New Year ritual later.)

By cutting across the personal antagonisms and status boundaries of everyday social life Hogmanay reunited the community. Like the Whalsay spree in the Shetlands, New Year restated 'the principle of access to all local households' (Cohen 1985: 95). The spirit of fellowship went beyond Cauldmoss itself, and people felt particular honour in giving hospitality to a complete stranger, but in practice the festivities were experienced as an expression of village solidarity. It was as members of their household but also as members of the community that people gave hospitality to strangers.

MALE SOLIDARITY

Spatial segregation of the sexes

Drinking in the pubs and clubs of Cauldmoss was an assertion of belonging to the village, but it probably had greater value for men as a confirmation of masculinity and male unity. In Chapter Two we saw how domestic work, employment and leisure were all structured according to gender. Part of the spatial dimension of this fundamental social boundary was that the pubs were at the centre of the men's domain, in contrast to the home which was the women's sphere. The way men learnt to retreat from this area of female authority has already been mentioned.

For many women much of their social life took place in the home, particularly if they still had children to care for. This provided an alternative venue to the clubs and pubs if they wanted to spend an evening drinking and chatting, and women sometimes gathered at the house of a mutual friend to do this. Many households kept a supply of alcohol to offer visitors: a bottle or two of spirits (nearly always vodka, and maybe whisky), lemonade or Iron Bru to mix with it, and a few cans of beer. Sometimes a bottle of spirits or liqueur was bought that evening specifically to drink at someone's house, for instance after a bingo session. Most women would far more readily drop round to a friend's house in the evening, where they could relax in the private, domestic, female sphere of a living room, than go to the pub.

There were various degrees to which women were excluded from the drinking establishments. Apart from the Bowling Club there were usually few women in any of the clubs or pubs – perhaps about one woman to ten men – and they were nearly always accompanied by either a man or a few other women. However, the social club was sometimes filled with women after a bingo session, Nancy's had a less exclusively male atmosphere than the other pubs, and in all pubs the lounges were less dominated by men than the public bars. On Saturday nights, and when there was a special fund-raising function, the clienteles of the clubs and pubs often consisted predominantly of couples. When women accompanied "their men" they generally acted in a support role, rarely taking a leading part in the conversation and never buying drinks. The passive role of women was illustrated when a couple told me who the ten people were that they had "sat in company" with the previous Saturday night: they simply listed the five husbands, their wives being taken for granted. The obligation for women to dress up and act as a decorative accompaniment for men has already been mentioned (Chapter Five).

The presence of women in bars was treated in various ways. When accompanying their partners at the weekend in the respectable manner described above, women were accorded the respect due to them as guardians of their families' "niceness" (see Chapter Two). As others have noted (Martin 1981), one of the everyday ritualisations of age group and gender boundaries is swearing, the practice of which amongst men generally confirms equality and companionship while its absence marks the presence of children or respected women. Men normally made an effort to avoid swearing in female company, which usually did not last long but was then accompanied by frequent apologies. This is an example of the apparently superior status of women which Barrett explains as 'compensation' (1980: 109). Middle-aged women who visited a pub once a week with female friends were generally regarded as fairly respectable, but some "nicer folk" criticised them. They were usually widowed or separated which made them vulnerable to sexual "patter", and few men adjusted their language because of their presence. Less respectable, in the eyes of other villagers, were women who frequently drank in the pubs (either with a male partner or, worse, alone); they were likely to be seen as of "the bad element". Sometimes aggressive swearing was consciously used to embarrass and exclude such women from the pubs. Another feature of this masculine exclusiveness, in particular in the old hotel and Billie's, was the speculation that any young women who drank on their own were "loose" or "on the game", simply because of their location (see Hey 1986).

Drinking also expressed a man's role in employment, and in particular his earning capacity, to be discussed in the next section. The man's role as provider for his wife, and thus her dependence on him, was exemplified in men "treating" women to drinks. This practice also manifested the woman's position as a visitor in the man's domain, and so it was doubly powerful as a symbol of the social relationships between the sexes. To reverse it would have challenged the fundamentals of gender difference, and men virtually never allowed women to buy them drinks, especially if they were middle-aged or older. Similarly few women in Cauldmoss considered violating this convention: "If we're going out, *he* pays. I dinnae pay. I dinnae believe in that!" Even though the husband might have begged £10 off his wife before they left the house, and even when women were contributing equally to a kitty, it was always the men that went up to purchase the drinks.

Pints to sustain masculinity

The boundary between the sexes was expressed in the use of alcohol not only spatially and temporally, but also by the quantity and type of alcohol drunk. In discussing gender the association of masculinity with hard physical work was noted as a feature of patriarchal relations (Chapter Two). Hey has shown how this male strength is thought to 'need' replenishing:

Beer in quantities tops up the manly body: 'refreshes the parts other beers cannot reach', an advertising jingle which captures precisely the physical *and* sexual undertones. Women on the other hand don't need to 'restore' their 'strength', being weak creatures by nature: what they never have they never miss.

(Hey 1986: 52)

In Cauldmoss men were as constrained to drink beer from pint glasses as women were constrained not to, if their gender identities were not to be threatened. (Some female friends who were drinking pints in a neighbouring town were accused of being "dykes" [lesbians] by a male customer.) If men got a half pint to succeed a full one they would almost invariably pour it into the larger glass, and the only time they drank from half pint glasses was when they had a "half and half", that is, a half pint of beer with a whisky (originally half a gill). Most men expected to drink at least three pints in an evening at a pub, and on the weekend probably at least five. Twice this amount, or the equivalent in spirits, was not considered excessive, so long as the man could hold his drink, and eight or ten pints might have been typical for a heavy drinker on his main night out at the weekend.

A man's masculinity was not only sustained with a large amount of beer, but also with suitably strong ale, which was associated with physical strength (cf. Gofton 1984: 13). To drink Guinness in Cauldmoss could be seen as pretentious unless one's masculine prowess was already established; drinking "heavy" or "special' was standard male sustenance, while drinking lager had only lost its feminine connotations in the late 1970s. None of the bars sold real ale in 1984, but had they done it would almost certainly have been evaluated according to its alcohol content (as well, perhaps, as its middle-class image). Towards the end of the evening some men indulged in a "wee half", referring to a quarter gill (in fact a fifth) of some spirit, usually whisky, vodka or rum. It was almost exclusively older men who drank whisky with half pint chasers throughout the evening, and a few men just drank spirits mixed with water (whisky), Coca Cola (rum) or orange juice (vodka) but without any beer. Being able to "take" a lot of alcohol, whether in the form of spirits or strong beer, earned masculine esteem, and the number of pints certain men were reputed to be able to consume (between fifteen and twenty) was mentioned with respect by lesser drinkers. However, there was rarely competitive drinking to demonstrate one's greater capacity (cf. Mars and Altman (1987) on the exhibition of manliness in Georgia), since this would have undermined the solidarity of male drinking.

Although the legitimate amount for women to drink was far less than that for men, drinks clearly designated as female included several strong beverages: cider, sherry, and vodka with lemonade. Apart from bottled sweet stout which was occasionally drunk by older women, lager was the only beer women drank, and it was usually with lime which made it an exclusively female drink. Sherry was offered as an alternative to whisky for women at weddings, but many of them preferred to drink the latter, usually mixed with lemonade or Iron Bru. This was despite the fact that whisky was associated with heavy or harmful drinking (cf. Plant 1979; Blaxter, Mullen and Dyer 1982) and was thought by some in Cauldmoss to provoke fights, being described as "Scotsman's poison".

Solidarity amongst men

The pub was the central place for men to acknowledge and renew their membership of male society, women's limited participation being strictly demarcated in terms of space, behaviour and the type and quantity of alcohol drunk. In Hey's terms it was 'a paradigm of male domination made possible by female exclusion, control, and oppression' (1986: 14). This was where patriarchal ideas were most powerfully transmitted: in jokes stereotyping women as fools or sex objects (cf. Whitehead 1976); in the support given to men with "women troubles"; in the moderately competitive virility and, more fundamentally, in the association of "having a good time" with almost exclusively male company. Consequently to drink in the pubs was to establish one's solidarity with one's fellow men. This sense of fellowship was perhaps most evident in the most exclusively male preserve of all, the men's toilets, where, whether or not they were total strangers and however drunk they might be, men invariably greeted each other with "Right!" or "All right pal?".

Licensed intimacy

To establish the relative importance of cultural factors and physical (pharmacological) effects in drinking behaviour is a complex subject. Much research has been done in this area and it appears that expectations about the effects of alcohol, developed from personal experience and folklore, have considerable influence on behaviour (Crawford 1986). Many authors agree that intoxication and drunken demeanour are separate phenomena, the latter being a form of learnt behaviour that is appropriate to the culture in question. Here I wish to describe some of the familiar behaviour associated with drinking in Cauldmoss, and show how people interpreted it.

One of the striking aspects of men's demeanour when they had been drinking was their physical contact with each other, which would have been ridiculed as effeminate or homosexual if they were sober. In earnest conversation drunken men grasped each other's hands to emphasise a point, in greeting they were likely to squeeze hands affectionately, and when joking they might tickle each other or even hug, kiss, or stroke each other's heads. In conversation they were also likely to be far more emotional than when not drinking, and prone to personal confessions, such as their unrequited love. They were also more extrovert in performing before an audience, in particular being ready to sing when they might never have considered it sober. All these actions could be purely learnt behaviour for drinking occasions, but they were perceived as resulting from alcohol's suppression of inhibitions and were legitimised as such. Similarly, Anne Marie Bostyn observed that women drinking amongst themselves might talk almost exclusively about sex with a preoccupation that would have appeared excessive if they were sober.

Sometimes drinking and its physical after effects were used as an excuse to avoid some approved activity. This was particularly interesting when the activity avoided had masculine connotations. At the summer sports competition (on a Saturday) one of the "hardest" men in Cauldmoss was encouraged to race in front of a large gathering: he shouted back that they should have seen him at two o'clock that morning, then they would not ask him to run. This quip was quickly followed with an overt reference to his manhood: when the organiser called out "Married women!" for the next race he shouted "Yes please!". The masculinity attributed to heavy drinking was also sometimes used ironically to validate a man's inability to get an erection because of "brewer's droop".

In the same vein alcohol was used both to excuse fighting and, in its absence, justify one's lack of aggression. Men frequently explained away their violence by saying how drunk they were, and even when (as with a man who bit off somebody's finger) they acknowledged "it was an ignorant thing ta da", they still considered their inebriation should mitigate the crime. To some extent women condoned this attitude, as I found when I tried to placate a mother who had heard that her son had been involved in a fight the previous night. On learning that I had seen the initial argument she quizzed me about her son's state: was he drunk? I assured her he had not been, thinking this would vindicate his conduct, but on the contrary his mother was even more annoyed and despaired of her son's pugnacity. On other occasions men said they resisted being provoked into a fight because they were sober, an explanation which credited them with the urge to fight but just enough self-control (when sober) to prevent it. Most people in Cauldmoss thought that drinking (in particular whisky) made one physiologically more prone to violence, and a few men abstained completely because, they said, any amount of alcohol drove them to fight.

It seems that the supposed pharmacological effects of alcohol frequently allowed men to abnegate responsibility for their actions, while the masculinity attributed to heavy drinking legitimised behaviour that would normally be regarded as decidedly unmanly.

Ritual reversal: the hen night

Social anthropologists have long recognised that crucial cultural categories are sometimes marked by rituals in which there is a reversal of established roles. By acting out the opposite roles in a very specific, framed event, normal relationships are reaffirmed through the contrast. The "hen night" in Cauldmoss was an excellent example of such a ritual reversal. It highlighted the customary behaviour appropriate to each sex by formally disrupting and inverting it on an occasion to celebrate the end of a woman's unmarried state.

One particular hen party in Cauldmoss began with ten female friends meeting the bride-to-be, Sadie, in the social club, where she had previously paid the barman £10 to cover a first drink for everyone who might turn up. One of her pals arrived with a paper jacket and tall pointed hat with streamers which the bride-to-be put on, and a noisy procession set off with Sadie carrying a decorated potty full of salt. The women rang a bell, beat a tin tray and sang "Way hey, kick the can, Sadie Wilson's got a man!"

as they walked from one bar to another. In each the predominantly male clientele were approached for cash which they put
into the potty. This was placed on the floor and the bride-to-be
had to jump over it three times, "for fertility", it was said. (The
salt was kept to sprinkle on the doorstep of the new house after
the wedding.) In the road between the pubs and clubs the women
stopped cars and demanded money from the male drivers, who
got a kiss from the future bride in return. Going back to the social
club where they had begun, the women made yet more noise with
their tray, bell and singing, and one remarked that "Ah didnae
ken lassies could be so noisy!". Now serious drinking began, the
women putting £1 into a kitty several times, and by the end of the
evening they had had at least eight drinks each, mainly vodka,
whisky or rum. One of the women was missing when the party
disbanded at about midnight, and she was discovered very in-
toxicated sitting in the toilets. After this Sadie behaved even more
drunkenly than she had previously done as the group stumbled
homewards. She finally got her pal's father to drive her the last
200 yards back through the scheme, having first fallen asleep in
his cupboard under the stairs.

The hen night was a reversal of normal gender roles in several
ways. For women to make a great deal of noise, accost men
directly and proceed around the village with the main actor in
ridiculous clothes sharply contrasted with their typically passive,
quiet, deferential role in public. To accost men in the pubs (and
also in their cars) violated the masculinity of these central male
spheres, and by getting thoroughly drunk the women indulged
in behaviour that was usually only licensed for men.

To return to the physical effects of alcohol: its use on these
occasions was socially constructed and being inebriated was
intrinsic to the ritual, as with Hogmanay. Before the event the
participants eagerly anticipated an orgy and afterwards the highlights of drunken behaviour were reviewed repeatedly, such as
one woman going to bed with her fur jacket on, or another
smashing someone's garden gate as she failed to clamber over it
when taking a short cut home. It was as though to validate the
occasion and make it truly memorable it had to come high up in
a notional Bacchanalian league table of previous celebrations. For
men a stag night was a less memorable event, since male drunkeness was more commonplace and consequently less valuable for
marking change in a significant way (cf. Leonard 1980: 152).

EMPLOYMENT

A man's role as a wage earner was a third aspect of male identity expressed through public drinking in Cauldmoss. Although there was a general idea that alcohol revived one's energy when doing "thirsty" strenuous physical work (cf. Harrison 1971: 39), such a direct physical link was not important in Cauldmoss. Men were rarely employed in circumstances where they could drink on the job and when there was the opportunity they rarely took it: drinking alcohol was valued primarily as a socially regulated activity in very specifically defined contexts, not as a suitable refreshment when thirsty. (There might possibly have been a legacy of the strict prohibition on miners having anything to drink prior to, or during, a shift.) The connection that did exist between alcohol and employment was more to do with earning capacity and the temporal structure of the week.

Many people perceived the frequency of men's "nights out", and particularly their nights out "with the wife", as a clear expression of their earning capacity. Drinking money was the surplus left once the immediate obligations of household spending have been met. A man bemoaning how much "the coin" had been taken off "the working man" in the previous ten years illustrated the point by saying that, whereas working men used to go out four nights a week "bevvying", now they could only go out for two. Men who went to the pub frequently were assumed to be "doing all right".

The link between levels of earnings and drinking meant that big drinkers and spenders could claim the moral worth of "hard workers" (see Chapter Four). One of the few remaining miners in Cauldmoss told me proudly: "I'm the top machine worker in Scotland, put that on your form . . . aye . . . you know . . . status, status quo as they call it . . .". He claimed to have been earning twice that of any man in Cauldmoss at his peak, and he greatly relished the esteem granted: "you know, when you stand at the bar and say 'I'll buy yous a round'." Furthermore, as we saw earlier, working hard and disciplining oneself to the arduous routine of employment was considered manly, which reinforced the association between drinking and masculinity. The interconnections between the different factors can be put diagramatically (Figure 6.1).

Moral attitudes towards alcohol reflected the assumption that

FIGURE 6.1   The interconnections between drinking, masculinity, work and earnings.

drinking money should be the surplus after supporting one's family. Thus young men without children and older men whose children had left home could drink much more before arousing disapproval than a young father. Two unemployed men who regularly went on "benders" together were judged differently, not only because one was an incomer, but more importantly because he was the father of five young children. His drink-induced poverty aroused moral outrage, whereas the regular scrounging of his unmarried pal was generally tolerated. Apart from family responsibilities there was a further consideration amongst some that a person should have *earned* their drinking money, or maybe have won it in the bookies, but not have received it in a giro. These values lay behind the resentment that was sometimes directed at unemployed men drinking, to be considered in Chapter Eight.

The link between pub drinking and earning capacity was particularly strong because the usual practice was to have several pints in one visit. As mentioned above, most men expected to have about three pints or more, and to enter a pub with money for only one was definitely "ignorant", despite the frequent euphemism "I'm going for a pint". Men's ideal drinking pattern was to have a "session", meaning a long spell of drinking over four or five hours. Most drinkers probably only had a proper "bevvy session" once or twice a week, on Friday or Saturday after pay day, but it was generally regarded as the model to which other pub visits approximated.

Friday and Saturday nights were certainly the most popular times to visit the pubs or clubs in Cauldmoss. About half the employed men in the village went out drinking on a Saturday night, most of them with their wives. Rather fewer men went out on a Friday and this was less predominantly a couples' evening.

The majority of these men did not go out to a pub more than once during the weekdays, and, more commonly, not at all. There were clear practical reasons for drinking at the weekend – having more cash available, and having the Saturday or Sunday to lie-in – but it also structured one's week and so gave more meaning to one's time away from employment. Men's unproductive recreation in the pubs and clubs was a reversal of their working role during the week, further exemplified when couples went out together and the men provided the sustenance for their wives (by fetching and paying for the drinks). The week's work was marked out, and was differentiated from the weekend (or Sunday) of leisure that followed. This interpretation suggests another reason why the employed resented seeing those out of work celebrating on a Saturday night.

ADULTHOOD

In Chapter Five age was shown to affect the way material lifestyle was evaluated in various interrelated ways. There was a shared perception that certain commodities were appropriate to particular age groups. In relation to alcohol the most obvious examples were lager and vodka, which were preferred far more by younger drinkers (of both sexes), and "halfs and halfs" which were usually drunk by men over about 55. For a young man to have ordered a whisky and chaser would have invited ridicule; this was seen as an intense form of drinking learnt through many years' experience.

Certain kinds of spending demonstrated one's adult "independence", one of which was participation in conventional pub drinking. Growing up was directly associated with manhood, employment and becoming economically independent through one's earnings: drinking in the pubs or clubs was an expression of all three (cf. O'Connor 1978). The prohibition of public drinking to under 18s made it one of the transitions towards maturity, either as a pretence or a confirmation of adulthood. Since drinking was also a step towards manhood, mothers were often fairly tolerant of under-age male drinking, perhaps not wanting to inhibit their sons from learning their gender roles (Martin 1984: 34), while men frequently indulged it.

The young were less keen to drink in "sessions" in the village pubs and were more attracted than their elders to the bars, discos and nightclubs of the local town. To them these provided a more exciting prospect, particularly for those who hoped to meet someone of the opposite sex, or who were already courting. Transport was problematic since the last bus left the town at 11 o'clock, so the lucky ones were given lifts by car-owning friends while the others resorted to sharing taxis or, occasionally, persuading an indulgent parent to collect them. It was not possible to study the drinking patterns of the Cauldmoss young in the local town in any detail. Although the more upmarket venues there were a great attraction, the majority of youngsters probably still learnt the main part of their drinking behaviour from their own village. Long before they could legally drink they were familiar with the local clubs and pubs that their parents and elder siblings used, both by hearsay and by entering them on the occasional errand or for a surreptitious drink. When they did go drinking in the town it was normally with a group of fellow Cauldmoss youngsters, so they took with them the norms of their community. We will return to the different drinking patterns of the old and young in the final section of this chapter.

RECIPROCITY

Public drinking was valued by men as a means of affirming various aspects of their identities: as members of Cauldmoss, as males, as workers and as adults. Drinks had a further value if they were exchanged: along with cigarettes they were the most convenient and generally acceptable articles with which to symbolise an egalitarian relationship, which was done by means of a reciprocal transaction. In the last chapter three kinds of exchange were identified which, in various contexts, villagers recognised. The exchange of alcohol, like that of other social drugs in Cauldmoss, cigarettes and cannabis, could be described as short-term reciprocity: either immediate one-for-one reciprocity between two people, or short-term 'generalised' reciprocity between each person in a group and its other members.

The esteem earned by buying other people drinks has been touched on above in relation to earning capacity. Between men there was not normally the expansive statement "I'll buy yous a round" and the consequent conspicuous generosity that the mining machine worker was proud of, and which is often assumed to typify drinking patterns in pubs. In fact men tended to meet up accidentally in pubs or clubs, as has already been described, and it was quite common for them to buy drinks on their own even though conversing with several others. Often only a pair exchanged drinks, and when drinking groups did emerge it was usually informally, with three or four people being typical. In large gatherings of, say, half a dozen couples at a Saturday night concert, the normal practice was to make a kitty to which all the husbands contributed the same amount. Though this still necessitated a drinking group with the same spending capacity, it avoided the conspicuous generosity of round buying; as one man said, "it's no shame on you or me, like, if you're only there with a couple o' quid". (He then went on to say that they usually started the kitty by all putting in £5.)

When a man was about to buy a round, rather than overtly stating this he usually discreetly asked the others individually "Pint o' heavy?" or whatever, or if it was obvious what they were drinking would simply go and buy them drinks along with his own. As soon as one person had done this, acknowledged by a nod or "Cheers", the drinking group was formed and its members would reciprocate in turn. If women were present they would be bought drinks by the men. Buying drinks in such a group established the male members as equals – as men, as workers and as earners – but since the exchange was completed almost immediately the relationship was not maintained by long-lasting obligations.

The most formal exchange of alcohol was in the rituals of Hogmanay. Most people in Cauldmoss bought a bottle of spirits (in the past almost inevitably whisky, but by the early 1980s often vodka) which they did not open until midnight of 31 December, and then did not consume themselves but poured out into others' glasses. Throughout the night, whether receiving visitors in one's own home or going "first footing" to others', each person kept his bottle to himself and offered some to everyone he met for the first time that year, never drinking any himself. The festivities lasted several days and even on 3 or 4 January someone entering a living room full of people was likely to go round offering a drink to everyone present. This is a classic example of generalised exchange.

Ambiguities in the gift

There were occasions when men stood drinks without expecting them to be reciprocated. This was not done frequently and was not normally ostentatious. Most men did not grandly announce their intention to buy others drinks because it would have been seen as too boastful, while the recipients did not eagerly and gratefully accept because it would have been too demeaning. Instead there was an almost silent recognition of status difference which often left great ambiguities in the gift-giving. Sometimes the difference in social position was quite evident and unproblematic: the youth, student or pensioner felt no loss of honour in accepting drinks from a big earner, and as has already been noted, men practically always bought women drinks. On the other hand the buyer might dismiss offers to reciprocate at the time as if content with the esteem of being the harder worker and greater provider, but in fact note and resent the recipient's lack of insistence and his implicit acceptance of a status differential. The recipient was often put in a situation where he had to assert considerable will in order to repay drinks, or had to consciously make a way to do so in the future. Beynon clearly experienced this problem when studying Halewood car workers. He remembered one man who would:

> go out with you for a night, buy lots of beer, give you fags, beat you at darts and tell you stories about his family. When you met him the next day he'd say 'Here he comes, the man with no hands. You want to watch out for him. Don't go out with him for a night unless you've a spare fiver and a pocket full of ciggies.'

(Beynon 1973: 112)

Many men were glad to be accorded the esteem of buying rounds so long as they did not find themselves penniless through supporting a scrounger. The dividing line between the two could sometimes be very thin.

At times there was a complete misinterpretation of the obligation to reciprocate, when the conventions were not mutually understood. A miner who got his student nephew a job in the pit during the holidays was greatly affronted when the young man offered to buy *him* a pint the following Saturday night. The high-earning miner felt it was his role to provide for the impoverished student, while the student was obviously unaware of this expression of status and simply wanted to show his gratitude for having been found the job.

NON-TRADITIONAL DRINKING PATTERNS: STATUS AND GENERATION

It is clear that traditional patterns of public drinking developed in connection with the social relationships resulting from employment. Confining their drinking to the village, the original occupational community, and spending 'surplus' earnings on "sessions" and round buying made men's pub drinking a central institution in perpetuating the traditional, restricted status of working-class men distinct from "snobs". However, changes in the economy and employment which led to the breakdown of old status group structures, considered in Chapter Three, had, it would seem, simultaneously disrupted the social relations underlying traditional drinking patterns. In Cauldmoss the most important consequences of these changes, as they affected drinking, were the diversification of male employment with the disappearance of the occupational community and the greater involvement of the population in the status values of mass consumption. However, as I have explained earlier, my findings do not allow an historical analysis. We can simply note the co-existence of other patterns of alcohol use in Cauldmoss in the early 1980s which did not perpetuate traditional status values in the way that pub drinking did. These alternative patterns of drinking were distinct in terms of location and the type of drinks consumed.

Although the most common form of entertainment when going out was to visit the pubs or clubs (over half of those who had gone out in the previous week had gone to such places, according to the second survey), a minority of Cauldmoss villagers preferred to meet their friends in their homes and share drinks with them there. The advantages of this way of meeting for women have already been mentioned, but some men also preferred it. In keeping with national trends (Allan 1979; Charles and Kerr 1988) it was predominantly the more middle-class, private householders who had this pattern of entertainment. The second survey found that, of those who had been out in the previous week, two-thirds of the council tenants had visited pubs or clubs and only a twentieth had gone out to visit friends or relatives, while a quarter of the private householders had visited pubs and clubs and nearly half had visited friends and relatives.

To continue with this simple dichotomy, older men in council houses generally only drank at home on special occasions, such as gatherings for a marriage, death or Hogmanay. Younger council tenants were rather more likely than older ones to have non-relatives round for a meal. When they did so the "tea" was eaten fairly quickly with little conversation and no beverage to accompany it; the sociable part of the evening was sitting around the fire drinking cups of tea before and immediately after the meal, and later in the evening drinking cans of beer and spirits. This was akin to the pattern of pub drinking with a specific period devoted to talking and consuming alcohol. At the end of the evening "supper" was usually provided.

How far this generational shift reflected middle-class influence or was a distinct development is uncertain. In households with middle-class lifestyles the meal was far more prolonged, the most sociable part of the evening being focused around the table rather than the fire. Alcohol rather than tea was drunk beforehand, and wine often accompanied the food, which was followed by coffee and perhaps more alcohol. Sometimes wine was only drunk with the meal, and before or after it beer and spirits were consumed; this represented an intermediate stage in moving away from the conventional pattern of drinking in Cauldmoss.

The preference young people had to drink in the bars and discos of the local town has already been mentioned. In part this was simply a reflection of young people's wish to escape the constraints of their village, and in particular engage in entertainment that included both sexes at an age when they were courting. As such it was not very different from the preference that older generations had to travel beyond Cauldmoss when they were young. However, it also represented a wider historical change in patterns of drinking: weaker conventions about the location and the types of alcohol drunk, less emphasis on exclusively masculine drinking and less concern with drinking circles and session drinking. As Gofton and Douglas found in north east England, a 'culture' of drinking regulated according to 'community and work roles' was no longer being clearly transmitted between the generations (Gofton and Douglas 1985: 503). Cauldmoss teenagers experimented with cider, Carlsberg Special Brew, cheap wine and other unconventional drinks, none of which could be consumed steadily in an evening's session without excessive inebriation. Furthermore, they were not inhibited in mixing these drinks. Older men considered this an abuse of alcohol and condemned the young who did it as "plonkies". This weakening of traditional restrictions opened alcohol use to the creation of new cultural values by the manufacturers: the success of drink advertisements both reflected and encouraged this dissolution of drinking norms. Thus vodka had come to replace whisky as the principal spirit drunk in Cauldmoss, lager had become an accepted drink for young men, and new brands of lager were adopted as readily as new pop groups.

> Fashion, rather than tradition, shapes their patterns of consumption in drink as in other aspects of their lifestyle, such as clothes, food, music, sexuality. The criteria which are used to grade individuals and groups derive from the industries which cater for consumption, rather than from groups formed in the workplace or the neighbourhood.
>
> (Gofton 1984: 17)

Gofton's analysis did not fully apply to young men in Cauldmoss in the early 1980s, for the new values were still modified by the traditional conventions of the village, as described above. In particular, the male bonding and masculinity that characterised Cauldmoss drinking were hardly reduced when visiting the local town.

The transience intrinsic to fashion not only affected the types of drink consumed but also the bars in which they were drunk. Many in the local town were regularly revamped in different styles, becoming 'fashion items' themselves (Gofton and Douglas 1985). Aware of this competition for the custom of the Cauldmoss youth, the landlord of the old hotel refurbished his pub and installed a massive video screen. Another change undermining the traditional notion of concentrated drinking was the provision of bar snacks at Nancy's. This was introduced to revive her flagging trade, and was generally regarded by villagers as a confirmation that Nancy's was a "nicer" pub than the other two.

CONCLUSION

Drinking has been analysed as one of the few areas of consumption in which men were in direct control of expenditure. The central place of public drinking in the male culture of the village can be understood by the way it established and strengthened men's identities as members of Cauldmoss, as masculine, as "hard workers" and as adults. Furthermore, alcohol provided a useful symbol by which to express equality through a reciprocal exchange. The traditional pattern of drinking with its gregarious ready spending constrained upward social mobility, but alternative contexts for drinking, at home and in the local town, and alternative types of drinks, suggested the decline of these conventions. This change was undoubtedly related to changes in employment patterns and opened this sphere of consumption to manufacturers to create new cultural values for their products. The new patterns of drinking were only one example of a dynamic in consumption which contradicted traditional norms of spending. This dynamic, and the way it conflicted with the expression of community belonging through consumption, is the subject of the next chapter.

7

Contradictory Patterns of Consumption

This ethnography of material lifestyle in Cauldmoss has so far focused on how consumption reproduces cultural categories and social relationships, and has described the symbolic value commodities had in expressing cultural distinctions. This may have suggested that the material lifestyle of Cauldmoss was unchanging, which was not the case. From the inhabitants' accounts of their and their parents' consumption in the past, it was clear that Cauldmoss had not been insulated from the changes in material lifestyles affecting the rest of Britain, though the specific content of these changes probably varied considerably by area. Campbell has described this dynamism – the 'apparently endless pursuit of wants' – as 'the very essence of modern consumption' (Campbell 1987: 37). By drawing on three of the four interpretations of consumption outlined at the start of Chapter Five ('cultural', 'productionist' and 'hedonist') it is possible to explain the insatiability of consumer desires for some villagers.

This impetus to develop new patterns of consumption contradicted a different theme in Cauldmoss spending: that one's material lifestyle expressed one's solidarity with the community. This could be characterised as a more traditional ethic of consumption, but it would be wrong to assume that it necessarily predated less restricted consumer aspirations. The tension between the two patterns of consumption might have existed a century ago, though it seems likely that it had become far more accentuated since the Second World War. The first part of this chapter will describe how material lifestyles were changing in Cauldmoss and the second part how this conflicted with the reproduction of community relationships through social integration.

THE DYNAMIC OF CONSUMPTION

Social and economic historians have traced the existence of mass consumption and the dynamism of fashion at least as far back as the sixteenth century (Mukerji 1983). However, a prerequisite for fundamental changes in consumer demand was the breakup of the *ancien regime*, which transformed the nature of objects in society (McKendrick 1983: 20). Once the rigid social order had broken down the process of signification between material object and social status became dynamic, with emulation an increasingly important factor in consumption patterns (Miller 1987). Industrialisation greatly increased the capacity of manufacturers to produce means of social discrimination, so that the whole population could be incorporated into the system. But at the same time the industrial revolution created a risk of enormous over-production, and thus ever increasing mass consumption became a necessity for the capitalist economy (Williams 1965: 323). This was aided by a reorientation of working-class culture from the workplace to the home in the second half of the nineteenth century (Daunton 1983).

Goldthorpe has argued that social developments this century have facilitated further growth in the consumer expectations of the working class. As a result of the decay of old status group structures:

> normative restraints on what are seen as 'appropriate' rewards, entitlements and opportunities are weakened. Moreover, this process can only be encouraged as the ethos of consumerism and continuing material advancement secures wider acceptance, and as the limitations on wants and lifestyles imposed by traditional communities and subcultures, especially those of the working class, are undermined.

> (Goldthorpe 1985: 129)

Although the withering of normative constraints and aspirations for upward social mobility were necessary for the growth in consumption this century, they seem unlikely to have been sufficient. That would have meant there was an enormous pre-existing demand for goods; it is more likely that desire was stimulated by the social processes of differentiation and imitation (Simmel 1957), by the interests of producers (Baudrillard 1981) and by illusionary hedonism (Campbell 1987).

Historical legacy

For some commodities there was an important historical dimension to their meaning, which limits synchronic semiological analyses of consumption. These goods were of great importance to their owners principally because they had been unobtainable in that person's past. The value of white bread as opposed to brown, meat with every meal rather than as a luxury, "butcher meat" rather than rabbits, wall to wall carpets rather than lino or wood, could be largely explained in terms of the legacy of previous poverty. Conversely, the central place of an open coal fire in the living room had been inherited from an era when coal was relatively cheap and such energy inefficiency could be afforded.

The production of numerous new commodities, lack of which allowed the younger generation in the early 1980s to distinguish the impoverished, seemed to have had little devaluing effect on the status symbols an older generation had retained from the past. Many parents consciously aimed at providing their children with goods that they themselves had been deprived of when young, such as a bicycle, new clothes rather than secondhand ones, and so on. Of course they rarely acknowledged that the relational significance of these goods had changed, and that the bicycle which had been beyond their parents' means might be the equivalent of the home computer that they could not afford for their child in 1984. Instead the increased productivity of manufacturing, and the fall in the real price of commodities, was experienced by many as progress, confirming a deeply held assumption that in the long term things would probably get better. One consequence of this general faith in progress was that one had to improve one's position continuously (in subjective terms), since staying still would in fact mean a regression in relation to society as a whole.

The legacy of historical conditions was not, however, the most important determinant of the significance of goods: rather it was an aberration from the general arbitrary and relational meaning of commodities (most clearly epitomised in fashion). The impetus for continual change in material lifestyles, beyond the symbolic importance of cleanliness and renewal, will be understood in terms of three theoretically distinct, but empirically interrelated, factors. They are: manufacturers' constant redefinition of the commodities that represent particular standards, modern imaginative hedonism and the desire of some consumers for upward social mobility.

Manufacturers' redefinition of meaning

The dynamism of consumption is often considered to be the outcome of capitalist interests. According to this Marxist perspective desires and needs are created in order to maintain the social relations of production. So as to keep workers dependent on selling their labour their wants are constantly renewed which keeps demand ahead of improved productivity (Preteceille and Terrail 1985). This approach has been developed furthest by writers in the Frankfurt School, who accord advertising a key role. Exchange value is thought increasingly to dominate modern culture with traditional forms of association being replaced by 'an atomised, manipulated mass who participate in an *ersatz* mass-produced commodity culture targeted at the lowest common denominator.' (Featherstone 1991: 14).

Marxist critiques of the commodity have been extended by the application of semiology, one of the most important authors in this field being Baudrillard (1981). Following Saussure his structuralist analysis of goods emphasises the arbitrariness of both the sign and the concept signified, which helps us understand the perpetual inflation of material living standards.

In respect to Cauldmoss, it seems that manufacturers by and large built on existing cultural values and had limited ability to create desire for new commodities *de novo*. Commodities were purchased and used because they had cultural value, only one component of which was functional value (see Wight 1987). Since the link between sign (the consumer good) and signified (culturally ascribed value) is for the most part arbitrary, there is infinite scope for manufacturers to give new meanings to signs (commodities) simply by manufacturing more of them.

There are basically two ways by which manufacturers are able to constantly stimulate further aspiration for new products. First, the production of a greater quantity of the same signs, such as chocolate biscuits, meat, armchairs, televisions or cars, makes them cheaper and more commonplace, thus making them less meaningful than they previously were, whether they symbolised affluence and respectability, conscientious parenting or whatever.

The second way in which new meanings are manufactured is when the production of a greater variety of each commodity creates more gradations of value. So whereas at first simply owning a good, like a bicycle or car, had considerable social significance, later on it is the type of commodity that is significant, whether a BMX bike or a powerful model of car. At one time in Cauldmoss ownership of a large screen black and white television was very prestigious in comparison with owning a mere radio. But by 1984 the black and white television was no longer opposed to the radio but to a colour set; the size of the screen had little significance anymore but instead the presence of a remote control or a video recorder was important. Since then satellite dishes have introduced a new distinction between villagers. In an almost inevitable inflation of material standards simple ownership of a good becomes less meaningful in itself, and instead it is the particular version and style of the good that has social value (see Sahlins 1976: 215).

Manufacturers clearly have a vested interest in changing the material criteria by which fundamental social roles are assessed (for instance which toys constitute a sufficiently generous present from a loving parent), just as their interests are furthered by the accelerated obsolescence that is intrinsic to fashion in general. Advertisements work on the basis of providing new materials for expressing elements of status and identity that were of pre-existing concern. They hope to define new standards for assessing traditional roles. For instance television advertisements showing men giving enormous boxes of chocolates to their lovers on Valentine's Day suggested that those who did not express their emotions with this level of spending were either lacking in love or were mean.

Modern hedonism

Campbell (1987) has developed a hedonistic model of human action which distinguishes between 'traditional' and 'modern' hedonism. The traditional hedonist is preoccupied with sensory experiences that satisfy him/her, and tries to maximise the

number of life's pleasures s/he enjoys, such as eating, drinking,
having sex and playing games. However, a fundamental problem
for traditional hedonists is that the more satisfied they are by their
sensory experiences the less pleasurable the experiences become,
so that they are easily satiated.

Modern hedonism is concerned not with satisfaction but with
gaining as much pleasure as possible from life, pleasure being
envisaged as a potential quality of all experience.

> In order to extract [pleasure] from life, however, the
> individual has to substitute illusory for real stimuli,
> and by creating and manipulating illusions and hence
> the emotive dimension of consciousness, construct his
> own pleasurable environment. This modern, autono-
> mous, and illusory form of hedonism . . . explains how the
> individual's interest is primarily focused on the mean-
> ings and images which can be imputed to a product .

(Campbell: 203)

Campbell's theory accounts for the insatiability of modern consumer wants in three ways: first, 'modern hedonism' replaces
'traditional hedonism' whose sensory potential is finite; second,
the imaginative nature of modern hedonism means 'the joys of
longing' become greater than the pleasure obtained from the
'real' consumption of the commodities, leading to repeated dis-
satisfaction on acquiring and using goods; and third, imaginative
hedonism creates a demand for novel products because the supposed newness allows the consumer to project idealised pleasure
on to them, which s/he could not do with familiar goods. This
thesis explains 'that most central of all institutions of modern
consumerism – the phenomenon of fashion' (ibid.: 93).

A basic problem with this theory is the relationship between
the 'voluntaristic, self-directed' character of consumption and the
'cultural ideals [that] are necessarily implicated' (ibid.: 203).
Campbell stresses the individualistic nature of modern consumption, but presumably the daydreams that give individuals
pleasure are largely shaped by their culture. Thus the enjoyment
someone in Cauldmoss got from choosing, ordering and looking
forward to the delivery of her three piece suite was a personal
experience, but it originated in part from subcultural values
which made the newness of one's suite a source of esteem.

It also seems obvious that the imaginative pleasures that cultural products can prompt can be enjoyed communally (a contradiction of Campbell: 92). For instance, the illusions and daydreams that might arise from a television series, such as *Boys from the Black Stuff* or *Dukes of Hazzard*, can be shared, developed and modified through conversation or expression in graffiti, as was the case in Cauldmoss in the early 1980s. Presumably when people exchanged fantasies based on images drawn from their television viewing, advertisement viewing, or perhaps their exaggerated recollections of drunken experiences, they were engaging in imaginative hedonism, even though it was clearly not autonomous.

Much of the material lifestyle of Cauldmoss would be termed 'traditional hedonism' by Campbell, but there were examples of the illusionary pleasures that constitute modern hedonism. Although advertising was a means for manufacturers to stimulate demand, it also provided illusionary pleasure in itself. Within Cauldmoss the main sources of adverts were magazines, newspapers and the television. For a village of approximately 600 households in 1984 the local newsagents sold about 550 daily newspapers, 750 Sunday papers, 110 women's magazines and numerous other specialist magazines. Most of the products represented in these magazines were beyond the price range of the readership in Cauldmoss, yet they enjoyed imagining the pleasure to be gained from them: 'the line between representation in the interests of a particular manufacturer and distributor (i.e. advertising), and images produced primarily for entertainment is barely distinguishable' (Campbell 1987: 92).

The same applies to television advertising. The pattern of television viewing has already been described; though for much of the day it was usually only the children that watched with any concentration, the adverts often diverted adults' attention away from whatever else they were doing. Their efficacy is clearly a moot point; what is certain is that they were widely known in the village and provided a source of images and metaphors: several people were known by nicknames which came from television commercials.

An example of how material lifestyle could be used to facilitate daydreams were the elaborate fireplaces already mentioned. For instance, stone-facing of roughly finished sandstone blocks with a large mantel of knotted pine was intended to give a ranch-like feel to the room, another expression of the Country and Western ethos widely subscribed to in Cauldmoss. Such a fireplace could cost between £20 (when a friend did the bricklaying for free) to around £150.

Changes made to kitchens in Cauldmoss might also have illustrated how commodities could provide props for fantasies of a different way of life. Although the original replacement of council-installed kitchen cupboards and shelves usually had considerable functional value, subsequent refitting of kitchen units demonstrated the extension of fashion and its intensification in this area. Manufacturers' brochures clearly intended to attach an air of Scandinavian elegance to pale wood units, in contrast to older painted ones, and to give oak units with diamond-paned glass the affluence and authenticity of old English country houses. The furthest kitchen modification had developed by 1984 was one with a breakfast bar: this divided what had previously been a largely private room into the female space (around the cooker and sink) and a public space where even male acquaintances were invited.

For many women and the young of both sexes going shopping was one of their favourite leisure activities. Usually this meant a half or full day in the local town, but a day out to the shopping centres in Dundee, Edinburgh, Stirling or Glasgow was far more exciting. While the ostensible purpose of these trips was usually some specific purchase, such as a new carpet or a present, as much pleasure seemed to derive from window-shopping as from the satisfaction of buying the intended article. In fact a day looking in the shops, interspersed with refreshments in the cafés, was enjoyed without any other purchase at all. Campbell argues that this pleasure comes not only from the aesthetic appreciation of goods and their display, but also from the imaginative use of the objects seen; that is, from mentally 'trying on' the clothes examined, or 'seeing' the furniture arranged within one's room' (Campbell 1987: 92).

A similar imaginative use of goods was men's admiration of expensive and powerful cars that occasionally passed through the village, often watched longingly until they passed out of sight. If they were in company comments to their mates usually indicated they had been picturing themselves at the wheel, such daydreams presumably facilitated by television adverts.

Aspiration to upward social mobility

The erosion of traditional restraints described above led to the widening of villagers' reference groups and the legitimation of aspirations to upward social mobility, processes greatly facilitated by the mass media. Young people were far more affected by these developments than the older generation, for reasons mentioned above.

Baudrillard argues that aspiration to social mobility, and a certain threshold of disposable money, is a prerequisite for fashion (Baudrillard 1981: 49). At a macro level the illusion of change and personal social advancement that comes from following fashion in fact disguises 'a profound social inertia' (ibid.: 50). This can be represented by the metaphor of a downwardly moving escalator. People are spread out up the escalator, all trying to climb higher but remaining stationary as the stairs (analogous to the succession of fashions) move beneath their feet. At the top are the elite, and everyone beneath them is destined to follow in their footsteps in a vain attempt to improve their position; the polka dots Princess Diana wore one month were sold in the High Street stores the following month. Neo-Marxists might extend the metaphor to argue that manufacturers control the speed of the escalator.

Modifications to the interior design of houses sometimes illustrated the tenant's aspiration to higher social status. The most expensive fireplaces were those that involved lowering the base of the hearth to floor level, or the elaborate construction of receding brickwork from the fire right up to the ceiling in the form of a false chimney, as if imitating the fireplace of a traditional French farmhouse. Other households had a whole room put aside as a 'dinette', furnished to be expressly used as a dining room, while the latest lowered ceilings or louvre doors were installed in others.

For some of the younger generation in Cauldmoss holidays had come to indicate the kind of social status to which they aspired. Simply having the luxury of not being compelled to work was not in itself honourable in Cauldmoss (in contrast to Veblen's thesis: 1899). What was regarded as prestigious was the form of holiday that one had. Distance travelled, type of accommodation, length of stay and climate (most of which were reflected in suntan) were all taken as indicative of cost, which was the overriding criterion by which esteem was granted.

Cars were probably the goods chosen, bought and owned most self-consciously for their social value as distinct from their instrumental use. In several respects cars seem to come close to Baudrillard's idea of the commodity as essentially 'sign' value: the creation of images by automobile designers and the confirmation of these images by the rich exemplifies how the code is controlled by the elite, while the ubiquitous currency of this system of values, even amongst those (as in Cauldmoss) who could never afford the more prestigious signs, demonstrates how people are destined to follow a code over which they have no control. Furthermore this system of signs is subject to fashion, which, in being of value only in relation to what is not in fashion, has the essential arbitrariness of sign value.

Although masculine esteem was gained through the sexual imagery of powerful cars, whether customised old Escorts bought for £50 or new Capris, the more general significance of cars was their image of worldly success, expressed simply through expense. Other dimensions of social value, such as 'prestige of intellect' for Volvos (Bayley 1986), were unimportant in Cauldmoss. Ironically the symbolic value of expense was confirmed by the many men who modestly asserted a purely functional purpose for their car: "just to get from A to B". They were acknowledging that others imputed credit-worthiness, wealth, or diligence at one's job from the probable cost of one's car.

One model to which some granted particular prestige irrespective of its cost (that is whether or not it was so old it was beyond passing a legitimate MOT test) was the Jaguar. Presumably this was related to the conventional hierarchy of company cars in many British firms, which had a Jaguar at the top for the chairman (Bayley 1986). The only Jaguars in Cauldmoss were well over five years old, but they greatly enhanced the self-esteem of their owners.

Whereas the shame of impoverishment may be seen as an important part of traditional respectable values, and ready spending could enhance masculine esteem, the fetishisation of money that was sometimes voiced in Cauldmoss seemed to be an extreme expression of unrestricted aspiration for social mobility. Money was what was supposed to both enable upward mobility and prove it. Younger villagers frequently stated their view that money dominated everything: "It's always money, wherever you go . . ." or, "They say money's no' everythin', but it is. Ninety-nine percent!". This orientation was reinforced by the tabloid papers, which comprised the main part of men's reading material, with their constant theme of venerating wealth (Seabrook 1986 and 1987b).

A pub conversation illustrated the value some villagers attached to money. A young barman in the old hotel boasted to his clientele that he had an Isle of Man bank account and that he planned to have enough money to stop working in twenty years' time. Someone asked him what his trade was, which he would not answer. Another man, Billy, told him to reply: "M-O-N-E-Y – that's your trade: money. That's the name o' the game: money." I suggested that money would not necessarily bring happiness. The barman replied, "It gets you ninety-nine percent", and Billy added: "a rich cripple gets a fuckin' better life than a poor cripple".

In marked contrast to traditional values younger people sometimes said, with a note of pride rather than inadequacy, that they "couldnae afford to live on less" than their current wage, or that they would need *at least* x amount to live on. When such statements came from single people without family commitments they emphasised the importance of money in their evaluation of their own worth.

BELONGING TO THE COMMUNITY AND
NOT BEING A SNOB

The accelerated changes in consumption patterns described above undermined one of the key features of the conventional material lifestyle of Cauldmoss. This was the Durkheimian idea that the continual reproduction of the village as a community necessitated a degree of social integration to confirm shared conceptual categories. In general the use of goods was very much taken for granted, an unthinking replication of the 'normal way of life'. It was only when someone acted differently from the convention, so identifying her/himself as somewhat apart from the community, that the everyday conformity to the standard patterns of consumption could be seen to be an expression of belonging to Cauldmoss.

Identity with the village was intertwined with one's social identity within the status hierarchy. In Chapter Three it was noted that there was a boundary above the category of 'respectable working class', even if it was more vague and far less

ritualised than that between the respectable working class and
the "bad lot". Identification with one's fellow villagers created
powerful constraints on social aspirations: a great sense of equality was felt amongst the bulk of the population and for anyone to
leave this tightly defined group of their own will undermined the
status of the rest. Since one's status was demonstrated largely
through lifestyle, the homogeneity of the tight group was principally expressed through consumption. It is clear, therefore, that
the kinds of spending stimulated through manufacturers' manipulation of demand and modern imaginative hedonism, both of
which were facilitated by the greater legitimation of upward
social mobility, conflicted with conventional consumption patterns.

Most inhabitants made a direct connection between upward
social mobility and abandoning one's membership of the community. When asked what people most condemned in Cauldmoss a
young woman replied:

> People will condemn ya if you try ta act a class above
> the rest, if you try ta act like a snob. I think that's about
> the worst you can get. Just about everybody will con-
> demn you for that.

Her boyfriend agreed: "People get classified as that [a snob] even
if they're no. . . .maybe get a motor on the road, guid claes an'
things like that. . ."

When asked what they would do if they won the pools (Second
survey), a fifth of our sample said that having a lot of money
"wouldnae change me, I can tell you that the noo. Money
wouldnae change me!". They were predominantly older people
in council houses, and this assertion was most frequently heard
from villagers over 40. It seemed to be a statement of solidarity
with the rest of the village, a denial of having any serious wish to
"better oneself". We have seen how the longer one had lived in
the village the more one had invested in one's personal reputation and the more importance one attached to the opinions of
other inhabitants. Conversely younger villagers felt less constrained to adhere to the conventional material lifestyle in the
village than their parents' generation, at least until they saw their
future as being there.

Although occupation was of minor importance to villagers in
identifying each other (Chapter Three), particularly in contrast to
public patterns of consumption, occupational mobility was also

a clear sign of leaving the main core of the community. This could be problematic for those with more traditional values, in particular parents whose children followed managerial careers, a point I will return to.

Organised collective leisure

An essential part of the conventional lifestyle that expressed one's belonging to Cauldmoss was participation in collective leisure activities in the village. Many people felt that such involvement was an indispensable aspect of their leisure, and sometimes even of their whole lives. A pensioner reflected on how her life passes "You've just got to take it as it comes, ken, . . . 'cos you never know the minute. . . When I'm no longer fit to go to the bingo, that's it . . ." – she will just waste away, just as her husband did as soon as he no longer had the strength to visit the pub. He would sit at home drinking canned beer from a glass, but he would swear "ye cannae get a guid pint unless you got your feet in the sawdust." For men the pubs and clubs were clearly the principal loci of shared leisure, as described in the last chapter. Here I will restrict myself to a description of organised collective leisure in the village.

The community centre was the principal venue for organised recreation, funded by the regional council and staffed by a community worker, who was an outsider, and two local people, a secretary and a caretaker. Some events were organised by the community worker, some instigated by her and run with the help of volunteers, and others were independent of her.

The great majority of regular centre activities were pursued exclusively by people under about 25, despite the community worker's attempts to broaden participation to other age groups. There were youth clubs for three age groups from 4 to 18 years old, several different football clubs, the Unemployment Club, and a number of short-lived clubs like judo and disco dancing. Since nearly all children in Cauldmoss (apart, significantly, from some of the incomers) progressed through the youth clubs these were important institutions initiating them to village life. Consequently many older people viewed the centre as primarily a facility for the young, which was self-fulfilling since it discouraged the involvement of older people.

There were a few activities specifically organised for older people, the main ones being the "old folks' " lunches twice a week provided by the local authority and the weekly Over 50s Club bingo.

Apart from a flourishing badminton club, 25 to 50 year olds only participated in community centre activities for occasional functions like prize bingos, "Mr and Mrs contests", sports quizzes for fund-raising and dances or discos that might be arranged privately or for an organisation. People nearly always attended the dances and discos in couples, and on most of these occasions a licensed bar was installed.

The primary purpose of the voluntary organisations in the village, the most important of which was probably the Womens' Rural Institute, seemed to be to provide leisure activities for like-minded villagers, although they usually had some extrinsic rationale. Prize bingos, whist drives or domino sessions were organised to raise money while concerts, "Scots' nights", dances and discos were arranged purely for entertainment.

There were several venues that could be hired for these functions: the centre, the school, the Masonic Club, the church hall or the social club. The "concerts" were organised most frequently by the Masonic Club (every Saturday). Usually one of the half dozen local musicians was booked (who most commonly played the accordion, sometimes the piano or guitar), and singers always came from the audience. The latter usually had a repertoire of a few set pieces each, mainly 'easy listening classics' (e.g. 'Paper Roses') and Country and Western songs, but also Scottish folk songs or hymns (particularly Protestant ones like 'The Old Rugged Cross'). It was generally known what others could sing and only the strongest willed could resist collective requests for particular songs. In 1984 this tradition of producing one's own music was still strong in Cauldmoss amongst those over about 30, and a wide range of women and men were prepared to sing, not only at Saturday night concerts but also at weddings and Hogmanay parties. Most would never have considered performing in front of a strange audience, which illustrates the close-knit, communal atmosphere at these occasions.

Dances had much the same form as discos except that a band took the place of the disc jockey with his hi-fi equipment. On special occasions the dancing was accompanied by a buffet, prepared beforehand by several women and served up halfway through the evening. People expected, and nearly always got, a set assortment of food which would include ham, lettuce, French bread, white rolls, sausages, a dish with eggs, cheese and crisps. These events cost between £1 and £2 to enter, and unless it was a church social there was either a bar or people brought their own "carry-outs" of alcohol.

A ready spending ethic

The obligation to be involved in village life and the constraints on upward social mobility were both contained in a ready spending ethic. This characterises the consumption patterns of 'traditional proletarian' communities according to Lockwood (1966: 251), who based his analysis on *Coal Is Our Life*. Dennis explained in two main ways why the miners of Ashton used up their surplus income (after 'necessities') in drinking and gambling: to enjoy life while they could because an accident or unemployment might end their pleasure tomorrow, and to maintain a lifestyle that was developed when young on low wages, which they would probably be forced to return to again and which was the norm for the whole town (Dennis *et al.* 1956: 138–40). Lockwood stressed the Durkheimian integration involved in such gregarious leisure, when intense social networks lead to an obligation to join in 'public and present-orientated conviviality' (Lockwood 1966: 251). This kind of expenditure is associated with an allocation of the wage in which the wife receives a set amount of 'housekeeping money' each week, as discussed at the start of this chapter.

From a functionalist perspective the ready spending ethic prevents anyone from converting a temporary wage differential into permanent capital ownership, thus causing damaging social divisions (Douglas and Isherwood 1979: 168). Evidence to support this argument might be drawn from the 1984–5 miners' strike, in which disunity could have been exacerbated by the concern of some miners' to pay their house mortgages, recently acquired under Thatcher's government (Coulter *et al.* 1984: 178). However, the thesis shares the problem of much functionalism: how to relate the 'needs' of the social structure to individual behaviour. It would seem that subjective intention is principally negative: people are constrained from spending money on a house or car for fear of ostracism as a snob (cf. Dennis *et al.* 1956: 146), and this then leaves them with little option but to spend on immediate consumption.

Whichever interpretation one emphasises (and they are not incompatible), a high regard for expansive spending on entertainment was frequently expressed in Cauldmoss. For instance a man who went to the club every night of the week (except Sunday) told me:

> I'm lucky in that my wife is really tight – if it was up to me I'd no' have a penny. . . I'd spend it as I got it, you never know what will happen the next day – Maggie might have a war to get you in to.

An example of such spending came from a young man in a summer job as a cement finisher in Aberdeen. He worked over fourteen hours a day and cleared £180 a week, yet he returned to Cauldmoss without any savings. Instead he boasted of his beer paunch and tales of women and all night discos.

Gambling

The drinking patterns described in the preceding chapter provide the most obvious example of the ready spending ethic; another example is gambling. This took three main forms in Cauldmoss: placing bets at the bookmaker in the centre of the village, an exclusively male pursuit; filling in the pools or the newspaper bingo at home, engaged in by both sexes, and going to bingo sessions, which was almost entirely a female activity. The exceptions were a few elderly men who sometimes attended local bingo sessions and some middle-aged men who accompanied women to "big-money" games in clubs in nearby towns. In 1984 probably the majority of households did the pools or one of the recently started newspaper bingos, at least a third of the women went to bingo sessions but a much smaller proportion of men went to the bookies. Those who put lines on the horses could be divided between moderate spenders who put from 50 pence to a few pounds on bets, and a few very serious gamblers who frequently placed bets of several hundred pounds and sometimes won over £1,000. This latter group were greatly admired by the small-time gamblers at the bookies, but criticised as too excessive by most other people, although gambling in general was only condemned on moral grounds by about a tenth of the population (First survey).

It was only with the pools, and more recently with the newspaper bingos, that the principal motive for gambling could be regarded as the wish to escape from one's working class conditions. Many people felt that their weekly payment (often about

£1) provided their only chance of significantly changing their situation, and when asked what they would do if they won (Second survey) a quarter said they would buy a house, some would also leave Cauldmoss, some would stop working and others would start "a wee business" or invest it because "it'd be the one chance you had".

However, the intentions of others were more in keeping with the 'vigorous and frivolous' leisure of Ashton (Dennis *et al.* 1956: 130), even in relation to sizeable winnings. They would spend the money going out, drinking, on clothes or on a great holiday, and one woman said she would blow it all: "It's fun money, ye can spend it all: no' as if you earned it. . ." (cf. Hoggart 1957: 137). Most of the pensioners asked said the winnings would go to their children, and as mentioned previously, a fifth of our respondents stated that winning the pools "wouldnae change me". For men who used the bookies in Cauldmoss the excitement of winning seemed to be more important than the consumption afterwards, unless it was to celebrate the win, reaffirming it. In fact a lot of winnings were spent either on celebratory drinks, thus broadening the social dimension of gambling, or on further bets.

The motive of having a bit of fun while you can and, above all, doing it with a lot of other people, was even more clear with bingo. This could be played almost every night in Cauldmoss, at either the social club, the Masonic Club, or at the centre, but most players only went once a week on a regular night. Neither the money spent (about £2 for an evening) nor that won at bingo (typically £5–£10, exceptionally £40, in Cauldmoss) was very significant in terms of the overall household budget (see Dixie with Talbot 1982: 9). Even when a really large sum was won, such as £200, the winner was likely to distribute the money amongst her relatives and friends and keep only a small fraction for herself. Thus, as with the conventions for drinking, spare cash tended not to be accumulated. As elsewhere (Dixie with Talbot 1982), in Cauldmoss bingo was primarily a social activity: "I do it for to socialise with other women, because they *are* mainly women." (Note the immediate legitimation of a woman's leisure by affirming it is almost exclusively female.) One of the callers in the village said that bingo was all women have got in Cauldmoss:

> There are only pubs and clubs, and most women dinnae want to just go drinking. A wee game of bingo

is their night out. So long as it's no' at the cost of the
weans' food I dinnae grudge a woman a wee night out
at bingo.

Some women travelled to neighbouring towns to play bingo for
much higher winnings than those in Cauldmoss, but the books
were correspondingly more expensive. In contrast "prize bingos", which were fund-raising exercises, were not played for cash
but for donated prizes (which ranged from ordinary household
items, like tights and tinned food, to hampers of food or a huge
teddy). They were seen as rather more respectable, being for a
worthy cause and less obviously gambling, and were attended
by churchgoing women who were proud not to play bingo for
money. The communal nature of prize bingos was sometimes
highlighted by winners giving away large prizes, for instance a
young woman announcing that she would donate the sack of coal
she had just won to the oldest person in the room.

Were it unmodified by conflicting values, this traditional ethic
of expansive spending would provide an example of how economic circumstances and cultural values can reinforce and
reproduce each other. A norm of ready spending inhibits substantial change in life chances since, even when it is possible,
people are discouraged from accumulating even a little capital.
The histories of some Asian families provide interesting cross-
cultural comparisons of work and spending ethics and the
possible economic consequences of these values (e.g. Maan 1992).

THE BALANCE BETWEEN RESTRICTED AND UNRESTRICTED
EXPENDITURE

For the sake of this discussion it is useful to characterise the
contradictory patterns of consumption described in this chapter
as two ideal types (Weber 1949: 90). The first pattern might be
labelled 'unrestricted' and the second 'restricted'. Although the
different values underlying them were typical of different generations (young and old respectively), individuals rarely subscribed to one norm to the exclusion of the other, and in their daily
practices they often had to negotiate between the two. If pressed
everyone would have recognised the need for some balance
between more gregarious, restricted expenditure and more individual, unrestricted expenditure, but they differed over what the
balance should be.

The largest employer in Cauldmoss characterised two groups in the village. Some of his lorry drivers spent £30 a week in the club drinking and bragged about it, while others saved that amount and might buy new cars with the money. The latter were resented as "miserable so-and-sos", but once they had bought their cars the others were jealous. Both types of consumers worked as hard as each other.

> I suppose this is where the snobbish bit comes in . . .
> The dividing line is near enough between the people
> who make use of the money they earn and then those
> who are proud of spending big money.

Practically all employed heads of households in Cauldmoss made a regular payment to some form of long-term saving scheme (while half of those unemployed and retired did so: Second survey). Nevertheless, spending for immediate pleasure was considered by many (particularly men) to epitomise traditional values and distinguish ordinary people from "stuck-up folk". The latter were often condemned for being so reluctant to use their money: "That cunt I'm working for – he'll no' spend anything . . .".

A few men, including one in his 30s, earned enough to run a car but chose not to do so. They embodied the more extreme of traditional restricted values, in being focused inwards on the community with little desire to widen their range of social contacts, and in not granting esteem to car ownership.

It was older people, however, who generally accorded more value to membership of the community, along with being "nice", commitment to work and conforming to gender roles. Because of these concerns they were far less subject to the dynamism of consumption and more content with their existing belongings. For instance, many old people were satisfied with furniture in a style dating from their youth, such as solid, dark stained wood. Its biographical significance, as the furniture with which a couple started their married life together, or perhaps furniture chosen with a now deceased spouse, was of far greater importance than its worn and (to the young) unfashionable appearance. Any extra money the old might have had was more likely to be spent on their children or grandchildren than on their own furnishings (Second survey).

Generational differences in villagers' opinions about the upgrading of their council houses were illustrated when the council renovated the "steel houses" on the scheme. In doing so they had to rip out the lowered ceilings and refitted kitchen a tenant had installed a year previously. Most people in Cauldmoss had great sympathy for the family and condemned the council, but some older villagers argued that compensation was not deserved since permission for the alterations had not been sought, and some went on to criticise such home improvements in general.

Improving one's council house seemed to have particular resonance in the balance between gregarious leisure and domestic consumption. On one occasion excessive spending on decorating was described as "terrible. . .it's like a disease", and this kind of scorn was nearly always directed by men against women, an example of the informal sanctions shaping women's spending of the wage. Similar normative limits to home furnishing and concern not to let it become anti-social have been documented for the working class of Bergen in Norway (Gullestad 1984).

Amongst the various features of material lifestyle that were sometimes regarded as snobbish – unusual food, unconventional clothes, elaborate furnishing, expensive cars – home ownership was the only one that dramatically transformed one's life chances, as well as indicating one's aspirations to transcend the stricter bounds of respectable working class status. It was therefore remarkable that, hypothetically, such a move was not widely condemned, which suggests considerable change in attitudes in the previous few decades.

After the Second World War people were resented for thinking they were superior simply because they had moved from a "but-and-ben" to a council house with a modern toilet: their pretensions were ridiculed by reference to the rings of the pail that were still imprinted in their buttocks. In the early 1980s, however, only a few villagers claimed they had no wish to buy a house at all. These were mainly older villagers (over 50) who said they preferred to enjoy their social life and have holidays abroad rather than be "scraping to own their own house". One young man, renowned for his unconventional views, berated his fellow villagers for being too "materialistic" which led them to want to buy their houses rather than spend on drinking and eating. He ridiculed those who gave up decent food and their social lives to pay a mortgage, "when they could be in a council house". This expression of the ready spending ethic echoed those who scorned new private housing schemes as "spam valley", referring to the diet first-home owners were reduced to in order to afford their mortgages, but it was not usual amongst younger people in Cauldmoss.

The vast majority of villagers would have loved to have bought their own homes, but they knew that the stigma attached to the village would make it very difficult to sell them in the future, and so financially reckless to buy in the first place. Consequently by 1984 of the three-quarters of the Cauldmoss population who lived in council houses only two tenants had bought their houses, enabled under the Conservative government of 1979–83. A second reason against buying was the design: "Wouldn't dream of buying *this* house. Not unless it was – like in two together. . . but no' this four in a block. And if it was in a nice bit . . ." A prerequisite for home ownership was the privacy of a detached house, or at least one that was semi-detached. It is unsurprising that the few people that did buy their council houses in the villages around Cauldmoss changed the doors, replaced the windows or put stone–cladding over the harling. This clearly demarcated their own property, providing visible material testimonies to enhance their sense of personal ownership.

Discounting the problems of location and design, the long term ambition of many people in Cauldmoss was to own their own home. In describing the advantages of home ownership most people emphasised the value of being able to make major improvements on the house without "doing it for the council", such as fitting radiators to the back boiler, and everyone agreed that houses would be looked after much better if privately owned. Several people mentioned the value of home ownership as an inheritance for their children.

For many aspiration to owning their own home was also related to the importance of keeping one's house looking respectable, in terms of being clean, tidy and in good repair. However much effort they might put into keeping their house "fit for visitors" as tenants, their work could be undermined by paint peeling off their front door or a damp patch coming through the living room wall. These were the kind of frustrations that led some to long to be fully in control of their homes.

No one mentioned ideological objections to buying council houses. "I believe there's quite a few who'd like to buy their houses," one man commented. "That's against Labour policy – and I don't know why." Whatever villagers' attitudes to specific issues like home ownership, nearly all found themselves, in particular contexts, caught between the contradictory values of restricted and unrestricted social aspirations and their associated patterns of consumption. There were numerous examples of people accompanying apparent evidence of superior status with apologies or disavowals. Thus a man told me how he took his family out to a restaurant in a nearby village every Saturday night, and when I expressed mild surprise he immediately added that it is not really "special" anymore since everyone can afford to go out for a meal now.

Hospitality to unfamiliar visitors could cause great anxiety, a balance having to be found between honouring the special guest but not suggesting any pretensions of status. In the course of impressing on me his working-class origins, the minister told me how deferential villagers were when he visited them, always bringing out their best china although he was happiest drinking from a mug. "I've no' left my class," he asserted. A few weeks later when Anne Marie Bostyn and I visited him he served us coffee in mugs but with saucers beneath them. This expression of broader themes in 'apparently insignificant things' is elegantly summarised by Williams, writing about older Aberdonians:

> while hospitality demanded honouring the guest with [cups and saucers], egalitarianism required at the same time their disavowal, with the result that numerous conversations reaffirmed, at the appropriate moment, the solidarity of plain mugs.
>
> (Williams 1990: 261)

A similar example was the common practice in Cauldmoss of making a joke when one's host put a milk bottle or carton on the table. Quipping "We've got a milk jug just like that!" simultaneously notes one's host's inability to meet the finer requirements of respectability and legitimates it by including oneself in this failure.

For the minority of parents whose children had risen substantially in the occupational hierarchy, or were at university, their pride in their child's achievements had to be tempered, in wider company, by asserting s/he "hasnae forgotten her roots". Ironically this was easier to maintain because nearly all such upwardly mobile children lived in the Scottish cities. A woman who proudly described the lavish lifestyle of her eldest daughter who had moved to Dundee as a consequence of her husband's career as a Woolworth's manager, was also pleased to think that "she doesn't forget when she had nothin' – started out in a council house".

CONCLUSION

In Chapter Five the compulsory nature of consumption was described. Those villagers who wished to live within the moral community of Cauldmoss had to meet certain standards of repectability and reproduce the principal cognitive categories of the culture by conforming to customary consumption. In this chapter I have argued that this static conformity only partially describes consumption in Cauldmoss. Contradictory material lifestyles have developed in response to several interrelated external influences: the weakening of normative restraints on upward social mobility, the manipulation of the meaning of commodities by manufacturers and the move towards modern imaginative hedonism. Many villagers experienced a tension between these unrestricted patterns of consumption and a spending ethic that expressed belonging to the village.

8

Unemployment

We have seen that categories of respectability are central to the culture of Cauldmoss and to villagers' identity. One's reputation as a worker, and for men, specifically as an employee, is one of the key criteria by which respectability is judged. While most of the fundamental cultural categories in Cauldmoss have some kind of material expression, few are denoted so clearly by commodities as that of being "nice". A particular material lifestyle is the backbone of this conventional respectability, and this lifestyle is doubly important as a demonstration of one's commitment to disciplined employment: evidence that one is a "hard worker".

It has been emphasised, however, that consumption and employment were evaluated differently according to age, gender, residence (whether private or council housing), orientation towards the village and aspiration to social mobility. In general older people retained an extremely strong employment ethic in the early 1980s which was not shared by the young, while the latter aspired to a much higher material living standard than the old. The older one was and the longer one had lived in the village the more one's social status was founded on one's reputation for morally correct behaviour over a lifetime, rather than material aspects of respectability.

What becomes of this system of meaning, in which employment and consumption are crucial, when nearly forty per cent of the male workforce is unemployed? Do those without jobs for a long period develop new values that give rise to a subculture of unemployment, or do they strive to approximate the conventional behaviour of the employed and subscribe to the values underlying their consumption? In previous chapters a state of 'full' employment was assumed as a useful heuristic device that allowed the predominant norms of the 1950s to 1970s to be described. In fact from the late 1970s unemployment in Cauldmoss became increasingly widespread: this chapter will explore how men struggled to retain their self-esteem in the face of mass unemployment.

THE RISE OF UNEMPLOYMENT

In the 1971 Census 6.4 per cent of the economically active population of Cauldmoss were registered as seeking work, when the unemployment figure for the whole of Scotland in April 1971 was 5.7 per cent, and for the local group of employment exchanges 5.5 per cent. The aggravated unemployment in Cauldmoss was probably largely due to its isolation; the cost of bus fares considerably reduced the incentive to take low paid jobs in the conurbation, and employers would choose people living nearby in preference to those in outlying villages (see Chapter Four). From July 1979 unemployment in the area started to rise steeply as successive foundries and other industries closed. In the 1981 Census the economically active seeking work in Cauldmoss were recorded as 15.4 per cent, while the figure for the local 'travel to work area' was 12.6 per cent and for the whole of Scotland 12.8 per cent. In 1983 a major mill in a nearby town was "streamlined" and 700 jobs were lost, pushing the unemployment rate for the local travel to work area up to 19.6 per cent.

Our own questionnaire surveys which covered 10 per cent of Cauldmoss households indicated the level of unemployment in the village in the summer of 1982 and again in December 1985. These figures were presented in Table 4.1.

Since Invalidity Benefit (combined with Invalidity Allowance) was considerably higher than Supplementary or Unemployment Benefit (see Table 8.1 below) there was a great incentive to claim it as long as possible if one had no hope of finding a job, or to register as an invalid when already unemployed. Our impression in Cauldmoss was that nearly all of those on Invalidity Benefit would take a job offered to them if it paid more than their benefits, and therefore this group has been included in calculating the unemployment rate.

Note that although male unemployment fell from 37 per cent to 31 per cent between 1982 and 1985, its distribution changed. More private house residents became unemployed in this period, and whereas in 1982 male council tenants suffered unemployment remarkably evenly between age groups, by 1985 young men had a far higher rate of unemployment (53 per cent) than older men (22 per cent). The proportion of women in employment fell amongst both council and private house residents between 1982 and 1985, the reduction being in full time rather than part-time jobs.

The survey findings suggested that about a third of those who were unemployed at any one time during this period were likely to remain so for only a short period.

It is important to acknowledge that the economic circumstances of those registered as unemployed varied considerably, a point noted elsewhere (e.g. Ashley 1983: 15; Sinfield 1981: 92). For instance in the second survey sample the fourteen households with unemployed men included: two where the wives had full time employment; two where the fathers had recently taken early retirement from the pits and therefore had substantial redundancy pay; three privately owned houses; one where the husband had regular work on the side, and another where a widow lived with her oldest son who was in a well paid job and her youngest son who had occasional undeclared earnings. At the other end of the scale were two council houses each occupied by a single man. One was aged 61 with no chance of work again, had been unemployed for over ten years and had used up all his savings, and the other was a younger man in serious debt, whose wife had recently left him taking practically all the household furnishings. Clearly, aggregating the findings from these respondents obscures the circumstances of those in greatest financial hardship, and reduces the contrasts between them and those in employment. Nevertheless it is necessary if one wants to compare different groups rather than individual case studies.

A further factor which blurred the distinction between the material living standards of those out of work and those in work was the poverty trap (to be described below), which could mean that people in employment had the same net income as those on the dole.

References to the 'unemployed households' in the second survey sample will include three other households which depend on welfare benefits apart from the fourteen mentioned above. In one a woman whose husband had left her was bringing up three young children, and in the other two the interviewees were on Invalidity Benefit. The homogeneity that will be suggested in describing the unemployed is, therefore, something of an abstraction, but having emphasised this point it is useful to concentrate on what can be regarded as typical behaviour of the unemployed without having constantly to mention the exceptions.

In contrast to Jahoda's focus on the *latent* benefits of employment (Jahoda 1982), the following section will concentrate on its most overt benefit – earning money – and look at what the lack of money means to those without jobs.

Before continuing one general feature of unemployment in Cauldmoss must be stressed: the monotony. Boredom was perhaps the predominant experience of many on the dole (cf. Coffield *et al.* 1986: 68), due to lack of money, the inability to plan ahead, and the constraint felt particularly by older men to keep out of public social life. When discussing their daily lives this was a feature the unemployed repeatedly emphasised: "so much time on my hands," "Cauldmoss is *absolute* boredom when you're on the bru", or: "There never used to be enough hours in the day for me when I was working. . . now, I know what like an hour is . . . it just drags round."

THE ATTEMPT TO MAINTAIN A CUSTOMARY LIFESTYLE

The domestic division of labour

Contrary to the optimistic assumptions of several sociologists in the early 1980s, there seems little evidence from that period that working-class unemployment either transformed the gendered structure of domestic life or modified the meanings underlying conventional consumption.

In Cauldmoss the customary allocation of tasks in an employed household was based on the interrelated factors of a gendered division of labour and the man's principal role as wage earner. The justification for a husband's non-participation in domestic work, apart from its essential femininity, was that he had already sacrificed himself for the family through employment, which might suggest that male unemployment would prompt significant changes.

Several studies have addressed this subject and nearly all confirm what was found in Cauldmoss: that domestic gender roles are remarkably entrenched (e.g. Marsden and Duff 1975; Morris 1985; McKee and Bell 1986). Losing their principal masculine role within the household, that of the breadwinner, made men defensive of gender boundaries rather than open to change, as Morris found in her study of redundant Welsh steelworkers (Morris 1985: 414). Furthermore, from the women's viewpoint increased domestic work by their husbands would have been problematic: it could disrupt their routine, infringe on their space and threaten their recreational life (Roberts *et al.* (eds) 1985: 366). The gender order was regarded as natural to the extent that women were concerned that their husbands should not be "womanish" (cf. Hoggart 1957: 55). On a material level, very few women whose husbands were out of work were in formal employment themselves (to be discussed below), and so the conditions for role reversal rarely existed.

There were some unemployed men who breached the taken for granted gender roles: usually young husbands without long term experience of employment, or "incomers" who had married Cauldmoss women (see Chapter Two). Interior decorating, domestic cleaning, such as scrubbing the steps, and cooking children's meals when the wife was out were sometimes done by unemployed husbands, while one or two young fathers (from outside the village) actually shared responsibility for feeding their babies and changing nappies. Yet these examples only blurred the divisions of labour and did not represent a fundamental change in conventions.

There appeared to be a slight increase in women's financial control in unemployed households. The results of our second survey suggest that couples were more likely to share financial decisions if the husband was unemployed (Wight 1987). In most families the wife cashed the giro at the post office, and where she was managing the finances she usually gave her husband money only as he needed it, in contrast with employed households where only a quarter of wives did this. On the other hand, casual wages the husband might have earned on the side could usually be disclosed at his discretion.

Spending

One of the most striking aspects of the unemployed's spending patterns was their conservatism. In general they spent their limited income with the same objectives as their counterparts in employed households; new means of economising developed, but not alternative patterns of consumption. The levels of state benefits (Table 8.1) give some idea of the challenge women faced in managing the household income when their husbands were out of work:

TABLE 8.1 Levels of state benefits per week from November 1983 to November 1984.

Supplementary benefit		Short term	Long term (unemployed NOT eligible)
Single householder		£26.80	£34.10
Married householder		£43.50	£54.55
If living in another's house	adult	£21.45	£27.25
	16–17	£16.50	£20.90
	11–15	£13.70	
	under11	£ 9.15	

	Standard	Increase for dependent adult	Increase for dependent child
Unemployment Benefit	£27.05	£16.70	£0.15
Invalidity Benefit	£32.60 *	£19.55	£7.60

* plus Invalidity Allowance paid according to age when injury occurred: £7.15 if aged below 40, £4.60 if below 50, £2.30 if below 60.

Source: Department of Health and Social Security.

Although the figures from the household money budgets are unreliable (see Chapter One), they nevertheless indicate how the unemployed reallocated their resources. From Table 8.3 below it can be seen that unemployed households' overall spending *per capita* was about 56 per cent of that of employed households. The main difference in how this constricted income was spent was that proportionately more went to fuel, food and alcohol, which was balanced by disproportionately large savings in clothing, 'services and entertainment' and cars. The highest priorities were heating and eating.

Poverty as the inability to participate: not fulfilling traditional values of "working men"

The tenacity of values associated with full employment can be attributed to several factors, to be discussed in the concluding chapter. An important consequence of this conservatism was the degree to which the unemployed experienced poverty. From the earlier analysis of consumption in terms of social obligation

TABLE 8.2 Average percentages of reported expenditure on different household items by employment status.
(Total stated expenditure excludes housing costs and tax payments
in order to make figures comparable.)

	No. of households in sample	Heating & light	Food	Alcohol & drink	Tobacco	Clothing & shoes	Large household goods	Other goods	Car	Bus	Services & entertainment	Miscellaneous	Total
Employed	9	13	33	3	6	8	2	5	13	2	5	8	98
Unemployed	9	25	42	5	4+	2	2	6	6	2	2	5	101

Source: Household budget survey.

TABLE 8.3 Per capita averages of absolute weekly expenditure on different
household items by employment status.
(Children under sixteen counting as half).

In £s

	No. of households in sample	Heating & light	Food	Alcohol & drink	Tobacco	Clothing & shoes	Large household goods	Other goods	Car	Bus	Services & entertainment	Miscellaneous	Total
Employed	25.5	5.8	15.0	1.6	3	4.0	0.8	2.4	5.8	0.8	2.4	3.4	45.0
Unemployed	22.5	6.4	10.3	1.2	1	0.4	0.6	1.4	2.2	0.4	0.2	1.2	25.3
Unemployed's spending as percent of the employed's expenditure		110	69	75	33	10	75	58	38	50	8	35	56

Source: Household budget survey.

(Chapter Five) it follows that poverty should be seen as relative to 'the conditions of life which ordinarily define membership of society' (Townsend 1979: 915), as Adam Smith observed two centuries ago (Smith 1892: 691). Since the unemployed shared this definition with the employed – in particular in defining what constitutes a respectable standard of consumption (as adults, women or men, parents, etc.) – their deprivation was unmitigated by subscribing to alternative cultural values.

The experience of poverty was exacerbated by the strongly held view that if one could not conform to the conventional style of living one had to withdraw from social activities. According to the second survey unemployed men only "went out" in the evening half as frequently as those in employment (on average 0.7 rather than 1.5 nights a week), and were more likely to go to the relatively cheap bingo than to pubs, clubs or dances. They were loath to go drinking unless they could participate in the conventional pattern. This involved having a substantial amount of money (at least £5), and in practice meant going out one night a week or a fortnight, according to the frequency with which they received their giros, which allowed them to spend on a par with villagers in work. Usually they went out on the weekend following their giro payment, but some (particularly teenagers) had their evening out on the Thursday it arrived. Very similar findings come from a study of young unemployed people in north-east England:

> This was one of the many tactics the young adults used to maintain their self-respect; they felt the need to participate in the customary activities of the community for two or three days a fortnight, and for this it was worth being broke for the other ten days.

> (Coffield et al. 1986: 62)

Having money in one's pocket to buy cigarettes and a drink was essential for a man's self-esteem, thus few of the unemployed were prepared to exhibit their poverty by entering a pub with only money for one pint – in fact to do so was described as "ignorant". When a social occasion was unavoidable yet there was no spare cash, money would often be borrowed to avoid having to spend frugally at the event.

The need to meet the conventional level of consumption in

order to participate in the public sphere was illustrated by the necessity of suitable clothing, whether to drink in pubs, go to discos or play football. A graphic example was the effort that a long-term unemployed man put into getting respectable clothes for the Orange March. He was set on joining "the walk" and for four months he and his partner saved in order to buy a smart jacket and shoes. Even though this ceremonial occasion was not commercialised, for the unemployed to participate involved a minimum level of expenditure. Some coping strategies achieved a compromise between conventional consumption and withdrawal. For example, standing around outside the pub, sometimes described as 'loafing' in the literature (Bakke 1933; Morgan 1992), maintained contact with one's mates without involving the indignity of sitting inside not buying.

A further reason why several unemployed men spent the middle of the day standing at the central crossroads outside the pubs was that they wanted to keep out of their homes which they regarded as feminine spheres. Others took up several hours in long walks, while very few men on the dole passed the time together in each other's living rooms, though they did occasionally have lengthy conversations in the garden or in garden sheds, again illustrating the segregation between the sexes. Teenage young women were far more likely to spend time together in one of their homes, as their mothers did in between their various domestic and parental duties. In this respect women were better placed to maintain their social involvement on a meagre budget.

For middle-aged and older unemployed men whose self-esteem was largely founded on the respectability of being a "hard worker", the shame of idleness was doubly experienced. Not only were they workless, but they were unable to achieve the respectable level of consumption that expressed one's commitment to employment. Traditional patterns of drinking provided one of the most important ways of demonstrating one's status as a "working man", as well as giving men access to the main male social nexus in Cauldmoss. It is unsurprising, therefore, that the inability to visit the pubs frequently was considered to be one of unemployed men's greatest social deprivations.

The notion that drinking several pints (or at least not ekeing out one pint all evening) is the reward for disciplined employment and enhances one's esteem as a "hard worker" was illustrated by the resentment sometimes directed towards unemployed men drinking. This undermined the connection made between work and rightful access to alcohol. For instance a working man made his brother feel he "was no' entitled to a pint of beer" when they met in the pub. However, the overt expression of such attitudes was becoming less common as the unemployed increasingly came to be seen as the victims of the economy, rather than as individual deviants. Nevertheless, older unemployed men with a strong employment ethic tended to exclude themselves, feeling they should not enjoy themselves, or at least should display a frugal lifestyle (see Fryer and Payne 1986: 239).

In 1983 an ITV *'World in Action'* programme particularly caught the imagination of people in Cauldmoss. The Conservative MP Matthew Paris attempted to live for a week on Unemployment Benefit, having claimed that it would not be difficult, and the television cameras recorded his failure. What most struck people in Cauldmoss was the way he ended up penniless in a working man's club "mooching a drink". They considered this thoroughly demeaning: instead of remaining at home discreetly, the obvious strategy to retain one's dignity, he seemed to flaunt his poverty by passing his time in the club unable to buy a drink.

The strongest pressure to conform to conventional consumption patterns came from the obligation to engage in social exchange in Cauldmoss. It might be thought as easy to comply with a low level of consumption as a high one, as Piachaud argued (Piachaud 1981: 420). However, the ratchet mechanism described previously led everyone to keep up with the most generous host, or consume at the rate of the fastest drinker or smoker, since one could always precipitate extra consumption but not decline from reciprocating it.

The divisive effect of conventions of reciprocity led to drinking circles separated according to the men or couples' means (cf. Dennis *et al.* 1956: 154), and recognising this unemployed men frequently excused themselves from getting caught up in round buying (see Coffield *et al.* 1986). Men made redundant frequently remarked how they could not afford to go out with their old friends who were in work:

> Ye couldnae afford to run about wi' them; like if they're goin' off to a dance . . . you cannae afford it. You meet

the *real* bru people. [Your employed friends] will no'
come down and say "I'll take you oot the night."

This man concluded from his experience on the dole that:

It's obviously a true saying, if you've got a few bob in
your pocket you've plenty of friends, if you've no
money you've no friends.

A woman whose husband was unemployed made the same
observation when describing how their friends reacted to her
husband being laid off:

Quite astonished they were: we've not got any friends
any more . . . .We used to mix with a lot of friends but
we don't see them anymore. We just can't keep up, with
the way we live an' the way they live . . .

Certain spending acquired particular significance as a hallmark of solvency for the unemployed, such as the ability to eat
butcher meat regularly or feed one's pets adequately. In the
second survey several older people established that they would
not economise on meat: "We wouldnae do wi' out our meat,
anyway! There's a lot o' things we could do without as long as
we got our meat! No extravagances – plain meals." Several times
unemployed men mentioned to me how much they fed their dogs
(up to two and a half tins a day for an Alsatian) as if this were a
guarantee that they were not yet destitute. The worst stigma was
to beg, as the incredulous comments about the Conservative MP
"mooching a drink" illustrated. Even though hitch-hiking, a
formalised kind of begging, had become generally acceptable
amongst many young people in the rest of Britain, the unemployed in Cauldmoss were, like their fellow villagers, loath to
pursue this means of travel openly.

To expand on Townsend's description, it could be said that
poverty is not only the inability to fulfil one's normal roles in
society, but also the inability to take part in the social differentiation signalled by purchased commodities without being
demeaned. This had particular resonance for those whose aspirations were unrestricted and reference groups were far-flung,
both of which were more likely if one was young. Hence the
humiliation for the young unemployed, least committed to village life and probably most influenced by the mass media, to

dress in unfashionable clothes. Similarly cars were important to self-esteem: when made redundant men were usually loath to sell their cars, and some kept them on the road even though, as one man said, he was never able to fill more than the reserve tank. The unemployed were very conscious of the public display of impoverishment when they were forced to sell or replace their cars: "you've reduced your style. . . you're going down." Whether or not they owned cars themselves, the unemployed respected others with costly models, pointing admiringly at Jaguars or excitedly recounting how they had got a lift in an acquaintance's new Capri.

The hierarchical ranking of goods had most importance if they were conspicuous, like clothing and cars. Children's Christmas presents were discussed so widely, mainly by the children themselves, that they were effectively public as well. Although the children's expectations were inflated by months of keenly watched television adverts, this stimulation of demand was taken for granted as an inevitable part of modern life. In describing her worries about Christmas presents a mother on benefits never bemoaned the expense of her children's wishes, nor did she criticise the advertising that had prompted them. Indeed, she objected to the idea of banning such advertisements until children had gone to bed, saying that they allowed parents to learn what their children wanted for Christmas.

Though it is widely agreed that poverty should not be defined in absolute terms, the wider implications of *relative* deprivation are not always fully appreciated. To show that the unemployed in Cauldmoss were not in threat of losing their subsistence – except, perhaps, in their own cultural interpretations of what constitute biological "necessities" – is not to belittle their experience of poverty. On the contrary, a relative concept of poverty emphasises how the unemployed's sense of impoverishment permeates practically all areas of their lives as a consequence of the social differentiation of goods. "You're not *living*, just surviving: you just about exist".

Parenthood

The heavy moral responsibility to bring up one's children correctly, borne primarily by mothers, has already been described (Chapter Two). Again, one of the key objectives parents had was to maintain a conventional standard of consumption for their children.

This was crucial for the "young uns" to retain their self-esteem, which in turn reflected on their parents' respectability (Chapter Five). The colour television was frequently retained specifically for the children, and, in fewer families, so too was the video (three-quarters of the unemployed with videos had young families: Second survey. One of the commoner reasons for getting into debt was: "For the likes of clothes for the kids. You *had* to take them on credit," and the unemployed prioritised the provision of meat in their children's diets (see Kerr and Charles 1986: 147). The treatment of children's needs as paramount is a common finding of most studies of poverty throughout Britain (Marsden 1970: 211; Marsden and Duff 1975; Clarke 1978; Burghes 1980 and Ashley 1983: 56).

Children's demands were, of course, largely determined by the expectations of their peer groups. Every evening the ice cream van drove around the scheme with its siren tunes and few parents could withstand the whining of their children for money when their playmates had just rushed off for sweets or crisps. Ashley (1983: 56) suggests that the prioritising of children might stem from their strong comparative reference groups, whereas their parents on low incomes were often isolated. In Cauldmoss, on the contrary, the intense social networks ensured that most parents felt pressure from other adults to bring up their children in a suitable way, in part defined materially, and this exacerbated the stimulus from their children's own peer groups.

The clearest example of this double pressure came with Christmas, children's presents being the subject of much discussion, particularly amongst the beneficiaries themselves. It was mothers who experienced this pressure most: a sixth of women said they would like more money for Christmas (Second survey) whereas no men mentioned this. The amounts parents reported that other parents had spent on *each* of their children were as high as £200. Even if they thought these figures were exaggerated they made Christmas a trying season for households out of work: "There'll be an awfae lot in Cauldmoss sore-hearted because they've nothing for their weans at Christmas."

The sort of pressure parents were under, mainly as a result of advertising, and the inability or disinclination of those on benefits to withstand this pressure, was graphically illustrated by Ann, a mother of three recently deserted by her unemployed husband. She told me how throughout November she had been fretting about Christmas because her two daughters (aged 8 and 6) both wanted new bikes which would cost about £100. She definitely could not buy a bike for only *one* of them. One evening she was worrying about it again when she suddenly resolved: "Fuck it, Ann. If they weans are wantin' to get a fuckin' bike, you'll just have to fuckin' get it." The following day she went to a chain store in the local town which was encouraging customers to join their Christmas club and bought two bikes which together cost £134. She arranged to pay this off at £20 a week, out of her Supplementary Benefit, Child Benefits and limited support from her husband who had recently found a job. At the same time she bought her 3 year old son a £67 go-cart which she was paying off at £15 a week. She went on to mention that she had already got some other Christmas presents for her daughters, the main ones being a portable television costing £54 for their bedroom and an electrically operated horse that cost £18.99.

Young men's unemployment

We saw earlier that by the mid-1980s unemployment disproportionately affected the young (Table 8.1). Those without children devoted more of their money to clothes, alcohol and entertainments than did those with young families, which corresponded to the spending patterns of their counterparts in work.

The second questionnaire survey found that dependence on cheap or outmoded clothes was the prime source of frustration for the young unemployed: "Ye cannie dress yourself on £25 a week. You've a *right* not to be scruffy", one lad asserted. Being unable to renew one's clothes for the community centre discos or for an occasional night out in the local town was particularly demeaning given the importance of fashion to the young's self-esteem. The community worker described how teenagers from unemployed households might alternate two sets of clothes between discos, while others were like Willy with "one good set of clothes that he sometimes wears: trousers, white shirt and his woollen tank-top." Very few young people had Brian's attitude:

> He doesn't bother – which is good, I mean, but I mean some will see that as 'he can't afford it', and others will say 'that's just Brian, it doesn't matter'. But there's not a great many people like that.

Clothing illustrates the way in which the spending of the unemployed, though clearly reduced overall, was shaped more by cultural factors than economic logic. The widespread adoption of punk fashion in Britain at the end of the 1970s can be seen as a response to mass youth unemployment and/or a reaction to the norm of smart, expensive clothes. The normal hierarchy of commodities was reversed and used as a means of distancing one's group from established society, as with hippies, Rastafarians, American blacks (with soul food: Sahlins 1976: 176) or Newfoundland Pentecostalists, all of whom 'created a new system of symbolic status. . . which denied the validity and legitimacy of the symbolic arenas from which they regarded themselves as excluded.' (Cohen 1985: 62). In Cauldmoss, however, the unemployed did not adopt punk fashion as a way of coping with restricted income. On the contrary, they wanted to wear the same kind of clothes as those in work, and the only punks in the village were all incomers who adopted this style as an overt expression of not "belonging" (described earlier: Chapter Five).

Young unemployed men felt their poverty particularly keenly in respect to courting. They were excluded from the main places for meeting young women, and the expectation that to "get off with lassies" one needed money, particularly for drinks, gave them an enormous handicap. When I suggested to three unemployed lads that a girl who is on the dole herself might understand that they have no money and be attracted without it, they laughed: "So she'll no' want you. She'll be looking for someone with money." The problem of chatting up girls was often mentioned: They say "What do you do?", and you say "Fuck all – that's it!". One lad described how at a disco "they soon suss you out if you've got a car and what job you're doing", and "when you go back to their place their parents suss you out even deeper." Without a car or a good job "it doesnae matter if you look like Robert Redford."

Some parents reflected that their unemployed children were growing up more slowly without the transition conferred by earning a wage. They lacked the self-confidence of financial autonomy as they supplemented their "bru money" with free food, cigarettes and "subs" from their families (see Willis 1984: 476). Teenagers who paid £10 dig money out of their £16.50 Supplementary Benefit and had to scrounge off their parents to buy clothes or go out at the weekend had only a limited experience of one of the most important elements of adulthood, the ability to make consumer choices and feel they were determining their own lives. Teenagers' practice of spending much of their dole on one or two evening's drinking related to the way pub drinking signified spending capacity and maturity. Most pupils preferred to leave school at 16 in order to receive Supplementary Benefit in their own right, rather than rely on their mothers' continued receipt of Child Benefit.

It is ironic that although the young unemployed were financially more dependent on their parents, in Cauldmoss, where council housing was readily available, being jobless gave one an opportunity to get one's own house long before it could be afforded if one were employed. Since rent and rate rebates made accommodation effectively free for the unemployed, and Single Payments were available (until April 1988) to pay for most of the necessary furnishings and appliances, teenagers on benefits could set up their own homes with little delay. This was a dramatic departure from the established tradition of saving for several years in order to buy enough furniture to make a home, before which many couples would not marry. The ease with which the young unemployed acquired their own houses without working annoyed many middle-aged and older people in the village. They used to be particularly incensed by the size of Single Payments for furnishings (the most notorious reports being around £600 or £800), but these were phased out following the 1986 Social Security Act. To older people it seemed fundamentally wrong that the unemployed should get so easily what they had worked for over many years.

Though young people did not seriously countenance a future for themselves without jobs, their attitude towards regular employment was rather different from that of their parents' generation. Paid work was regarded more simply as a means to an end – money – and the moral value of disciplined work was far less important to them. An indication of this different orientation was their participation in the Unemployment Club in contrast with older unemployed men.

The Unemployment Club at the community centre was intended to provide recreational facilities and social contact at a nominal cost (10p weekly subscription) for the unemployed. It met two afternoons a week and the principal activities were the same as those practised by males in the Senior Youth Club:

football, pool, space invaders, sitting around talking and drinking fizzy sweet drinks, tea or coffee. In fact of the two dozen or
so who went to the Unemployment Club the majority were
members or ex-members of the Youth Club, and most of them
were male, reflecting how young women tended not to see themselves as unemployed. No adults above 30 joined in, which the
community workers acknowledged was disappointing. In part
this was due to the general association of the centre with youth
activities which discouraged adults from participating in anything. However, it also related to the older unemployed's
withdrawal from social activities, their unwillingness to present
themselves publicly as workless, and their reluctance to engage
in institutionalised recreation, as if fearing this would signify
their permanent exclusion from "proper jobs". Although the
young unemployed did not want to be denied jobs forever, their
main concern was poverty and boredom. Had the Unemployment Club offered them the kind of leisure facilities that their
age-mates in work were able to afford, they would probably have
been fairly happy to pass away their time there in between
sporadic jobs.

ORIENTATION TO EMPLOYMENT

The restrictions on people's material lifestyle were one of the
most serious consequences of unemployment in Cauldmoss, exacerbated by the tenacity of material standards of respectability
and the esteem granted to "big spenders". We have seen how the
unemployed struggled to conform to the conventional patterns
of consumption of the village, and when this was untenable they
tended to withdraw from social involvement. Given this experience of unemployment, what strategies did people adopt or
develop to try and improve their circumstances?

Seeking employment

Virtually no one coped with unemployment by changing their
orientation towards paid work. Employment was so central to
the culture of Cauldmoss that few men over about 25 abandoned
it as a goal in life, although the unemployment trap (to be discussed below) set limits to people's willingness to work. When,
occasionally, someone said s/he no longer wanted to find a job
it was usually interpreted as temporary resentment at unsuccessful searching: "deep down in their hearts they dinnae mean it".

The few people who, at some stage, told us that they no longer intended to work again all sought employment keenly at some subsequent date.

The initial reaction of older men to redundancy was to maintain their familiar routine, simply replacing their job with the search for employment. They tended to get up at their routine time and then visit the Job Centre, scour the newspapers or try to pick up some details of vacancies informally. The unemployed were well aware that personal contacts provided their best hope of finding a job, but the tendency for segregation by income in leisure activities perpetuated the position of the workless, since they had less social contact with those knowledgeable about jobs (as Sinfield also found in North Shields (1970: 230)). The pubs and clubs were particularly important places for gathering information about vacancies, but, as we have seen, traditional drinking culture excluded the unemployed even more than their lack of money. As Sinfield noted two decades ago, 'because of the large element of chance and the role of family and friends, finding work was no indication of the intensity of the search. . .' (Sinfield 1970: 224).

From October 1982 it was no longer necessary to register at the Job Centre in order to claim benefits, but many in Cauldmoss still did and nearly all the unemployed visited it at intervals. Older people initially did this every fortnight or so, but since it confirmed what slight prospects they had – unless they possessed particular skills – visits generally became intermittent. The jobs that were available have been described in Chapter Four, but these were usually taken by those already employed. According to officials in the Job Centre employers generally preferred to take on those currently in work rather than the unemployed, and the longer one had been out of work the less chance one had of being recruited.

The unemployed also sought work through adverts in the newspapers – mainly the weekly local paper – and some had depressing tales of the number of letters they had written and the small proportion of firms that had even replied, let alone given them any hope of an interview. Married men were much less willing than single males to take work which involved living away from home, but when lack of local jobs became apparent most considered working anywhere in Scotland.

Some Cauldmoss school leavers attended the Careers Office

every week, as they were advised to, but after ten weeks or so of paying £1.50 bus fares without any sign of finding work they generally gave up. For many of the young unemployed phases of a few weeks' keen job hunting gave way to disillusionment and much longer spells where their main concern was simply to avoid boredom. Sometimes something would prompt them to search for work again – a plan to buy a stereo, the intention to get married, or a friend's luck in finding a job – and then the pattern of job hunting and disillusionment began again. An example of this sporadic effort to find work was the way people applied for the government TOPS courses but on learning there was a five month waiting list abandoned the idea. Five months later they would return to the Job Centre hoping to begin the course, although they had not registered on the waiting list.

Men made redundant initially sought work of the kind they had just done, largely because experience was their greatest strength in the labour market. In Chapter Four it was noted that, in contrast to the predominant values, some skilled workers identified with their occupations, and when unemployed this self-identity was often maintained. Such identification with a trade meant these men were unwilling to take on work which they considered to be less prestigious or to retrain. When an unemployed time-served electrician eventually took a job as a postman many thought this was demeaning, and from his abject appearance as he went about his work it seemed that he shared or had internalised this opinion.

In describing the values associated with employment I argued that paid work was, in part, a means of establishing one's worth, calculated in monetary terms. This makes it understandable why the unemployed were loath to take a job paying significantly less than they had previously earned, and it was usually only after several months of fruitless job hunting that they would consider such a move. (This contrasts markedly with McLaughlin's findings in Northern Ireland that the main determinant of wage levels sought was the estimated household need (McLaughlin 1991)).

> Many see it as a defeat ... Taking lower pay often means accepting a poorer job with less status and requiring less of their skill – it means a lowering of standards that may be never regained.
>
> (Sinfield 1981: 43)

Adult men were unlikely to take work paying them net less than £10 to £20 more than they received on benefits, and if working on the side (while claiming benefits) they usually demanded about £10 a shift.

Another aspect of this persisting equation of wages with worth was the reluctance of men in the Unemployment Club to do anything productive unless they were paid for it. "If there's no money behind it they're not interested," the community worker commented. The director of a local Action Resource Centre characterised the minority of unemployed men who were willing to do voluntary work as being in two groups. They had either previously done voluntary work in uniformed organisations (a very few), or were middle-aged ex-skilled workers who had taken voluntary redundancy, maybe had a wife working, could manage adequately (through large redundancy payments or savings) and, most important, saw themselves as retired.

Alternative forms of employment

Several alternative forms of employment were developed by government agencies as a limited response to the reduction of jobs in manufacturing industry. The most important in Cauldmoss, and probably throughout Britain, were those aimed at school leavers: the Youth Opportunities Programme (YOP) and the Youth Training Scheme (YTS) which succeeded it.

During 1981–2 there was a Youth Opportunities Programme in the community centre, organised by the community worker, and many teenagers in the village participated. However, the appeal of this scheme was not so much employment experience nor the wage (generally regarded as pitiful), but the opportunity to be doing something with one's mates in the village. When it ended few school leavers were prepared to travel to similar schemes in the local conurbation because of the extra cost in time and money.

Young people's response to the YTS highlighted the generational differences in orientation to employment. The concept of what one's time and labour was worth (Chapter Four) was not only shaped by training and previous earnings. Some of the young unemployed in Cauldmoss, who had never worked since leaving school, were not prepared to attend a YTS regularly for £21.25 a week (their take-home pay after paying half their bus fares out of a wage of £25). Although some called them lazy, the young people themselves said they would be "suckers" to work for such a miserable wage. In this they had the tacit support of the adult community, who described YTS as "slave labour" and saw such programmes as exploiting youth unemployment. For most of those who refused YTS places £10 a day was the minimum wage they considered adequate, and some were not prepared to accept low pay while training for marketable qualifications like computer operating. There is considerable evidence to suggest that Cauldmoss youth were not exceptional in their disdain for low pay. In October 1983 nearly half the 300 places on a year's Manpower Services Commission course in technical subjects, from engineering to computer studies, could not be filled at the local technical college. At a national level, in January 1984 the government ordered two investigations into unemployed youngsters' refusal to accept low-paid jobs or join government training schemes (*The Guardian* 1 February 1984).

In our first survey the one example of paid employment which was not described by the majority as "work" was taking part in a YOP. The responses suggested it is not regarded as *real* work because of its temporary nature and minimal pay.

A few men in Cauldmoss used their redundancy pay to establish their own businesses, as advocated by employment agencies. One man set up as a self-employed roofer when a local builder paid him off, another started a mobile shop, and another waited over a year until one of the village grocery shops came on the market and bought that. However, most of the unemployed in Cauldmoss were deterred from self-employment by their almost total lack of business experience and the difficulty of finding a potentially profitable enterprise in a severe recession (despite the Enterprise Allowance Scheme). No Community Programmes were set up in Cauldmoss during the first half of the 1980s.

THE UNEMPLOYMENT TRAP

There were some in Cauldmoss who could only command a net wage roughly equal to, or lower than, the welfare benefits to which they and their families were entitled. This has been termed the 'unemployment trap'. It was due to a combination of low wages, high levels of direct taxation with low thresholds, the sudden cut-off point in eligibility to means tested benefits, and the costs incurred through going to work (travel costs, work clothes etc.). One contemporary study estimated that 20 per cent of the workforce were in this position (Parker 1982: 37; see also Ashley 1983: 30–2). Although in the early 1980s benefits bore the same relation to average gross earnings as they did in 1948 (Parker 1982), right-wing analysts attributed the unemployment trap to high levels of benefits rather than low wages and high marginal taxes. Consequently acknowledging the very existence of this disincentive to formal employment was politically charged. Some authors argued, from survey data, that there was no unemployment trap (Atkinson and Micklewright 1985), but whatever the political convenience of this position it denied the world experienced by the unemployed of Cauldmoss.

Those on the dole who had the exceptional luck of being offered a job, but who would have only earned about the same or less than their current benefits, had to decide whether employment or consumption was more important to them. This clarified fundamental priorities which had previously been obscured by the compatibility of the two goals. Unless a job was likely to provide the opportunity for a future, better paid career, in general the young in Cauldmoss thought the disadvantages of low paid work greater than the frustrations of unemployment, when one's consumer power was roughly the same in each case. A woman on the dole calculated that:

> I would really need to be gettin' an awfie good wage before I'm goin' to leave Cauldmoss to work ... Ah would need to be makin' £60 for me to be making £20 [on top of] what I'm gettin' the noo ... I think that's mostly everybody's attitude in Cauldmoss.

Others in Cauldmoss said they would only work for a net gain of £10. For those with young children their role as parents led them to maximise the net income of the household, whatever their attitude to employment might be. Both single men and fathers did not want to "make a mug" of themselves by working without any net gain (as in Belfast (Howe 1986: 14)). Furthermore, opting to remain unemployed left open the possibility of temporary undeclared jobs which could significantly augment one's income.

Another dimension of the unemployment trap was the disincentive for women whose husbands were "on the bru" to seek formal employment unless very well paid, which was extremely unlikely around Cauldmoss. Their earnings were deducted pound for pound from the couple's benefits (cf. Morris 1987). Thus in our second survey we found that while slightly over half of the wives of employed men had full or part-time jobs, only a fifth of those women whose husbands were on the dole had any employment. The benefit system exacerbated income differentials between what Pahl calls the 'middle mass' and a deprived underclass of claimants (Pahl 1984: 320).

Some people did take jobs that did not increase their net income, and others remained in formal employment even though they were aware they could receive the same income in benefits out of work. In some cases there was the expectation that temporary low pay would be improved, but for others remuneration was not the overriding motivation to work. For these employees the non-material benefits of their jobs were more important, such as time structure, changed environment, masculine identity, and, above all, the virtue of disciplined employment which remained even though the necessity did not currently exist. The few people we knew with such a commitment to employment were all in their late 50s or over, while many pensioners suggested that they worked, or would have worked, for no net increase in income. A woman tried to explain why her 60 year old husband continued working although he could get as much money on the dole: "Older folk *will* work hard, no' like the young ones. I don't know, it's something *in* the older people. You won't get the younger people doin' it . . ."

It is important to note that research in Northern Ireland has found it is usual for unemployed people to be ready to work for less than the wage levels they had previously said they 'needed' to return to work (McLaughlin 1991: 494), rather than exceptional as I have suggested in Cauldmoss. Since there were very few formal jobs available during the main period of fieldwork I was unable to explore this in Cauldmoss, but my findings seem at variance with those from McLaughlin's research five years later.

Thus the unemployment trap highlights the distinct values that different age-cohorts held towards employment and consumption already discussed in earlier chapters. Unemployment did not give rise to a new orientation to employment, but rather accentuated previously existing variations between age groups. Skilled workers were reluctant to change their occupation in response to unemployment; there was a persisting equation of wages with personal worth; there was very little response to government incentives for self-employment, and the sexual division of labour in the home usually remained as it had been when it was premised on the man's wage earning role. Practically everyone still sought employment and no one seriously countenanced a future without jobs. However, the young regarded employment more simply as a means to an end – money – rather than a central part of their moral identity. In this their experience of the shrunken labour market was probably an important influence, but there appeared to be little variation in outlook between the young who were in work and those on "the bru".

WORKING ON THE SIDE

One of the most important strategies by which the unemployed in Cauldmoss could fulfil their traditional role as "workers", albeit in a restricted way, and avoid the unemployment trap was to "work on the side". This means taking temporary and often part-time work without the employer or worker paying National Insurance or tax, and without the earnings being declared to the Unemployment Benefit Office.

Harding and Jenkins (1989) have argued that 'informal' and 'formal' economic activity should be regarded as representing poles of a continuum, and the notion that a 'hidden' or 'black' economy exists as a distinct economic sphere is a myth. Several features of work on the side in Cauldmoss seemed to support this analysis. The (apparent) availability of informal jobs appeared to be influenced by the overall level of economic activity in the region and by the sub-contracting policies of large employers, and these "side jobs" were found through the same social networks as those operating for formal employment. Furthermore, working on the side was not an innovative strategy in response to unemployment but had long been practised by people with full-time formal jobs, in which case it was usually known as "moonlighting".

Most informal work available to the unemployed in Cauldmoss was in the building industry, both as sub-contracted labour on large sites and as self-employed roofers, bricklayers, and so on. Jobs were also found in small drilling firms, haulage, cleaning, farming and milk rounds, and for young women, as babysitters and dog walkers. Informal self-employment included haircutting, gardening and occasional taxiing. In general very low wages were paid: adult men were unlikely to work for less than £10 a shift, but teenagers would accept £1 an hour.

Obviously it was very difficult to assess the extent of work on the side in Cauldmoss, and there is no reason to suppose that the particular conditions of the local labour market that provided such opportunities in the early 1980s were typical of the economy as a whole (see O'Higgins 1980; Leach and Wagstaff 1986: 119; Harding and Jenkins 1989). Those who did semi-regular "side-work" gave the impression that half the unemployed were "at it", while those who had rarely been offered informal work suggested it was virtually unobtainable. This illustrates the extent to which such jobs were the patronage of particular social (largely kinship) "cliques". Since work on the side was gained almost entirely through personal contacts kinship links played an even greater role in recruitment than they did for formal employment. Others have shown that informal economic activity tends to exacerbate the polarisation between the employed and unemployed because it is those in jobs who get the opportunities for undeclared work (Pahl 1984; Morris 1987b). In Cauldmoss work on the side polarised the unemployed themselves, since it not only enhanced the income of those involved but greatly improved their chances of being offered formal jobs "on the books".

Some people reflected that there were far fewer "side jobs" around in the early 1980s than had previously been the case, suggesting that opportunities declined with the wider recession, as Pahl argues (1984: 93–8). However, Howe documents many ways in which the unemployed can engage in informal employment even when very poor and living in an area of high unemployment (Howe 1986: 25), which fits with our observations in Cauldmoss.

Of fifty-nine unemployed men that I knew in Cauldmoss I had no information about the employment activities of twenty. Of the remaining thirty-nine, thirty-six had worked on the side irregularly while three had never done so. Nearly all the local employers, in building, haulage, farming, drilling and coal distribution, employed people who they knew were signing on, though some only did so temporarily on this basis. The advantages to employers of an informal labour market could be considerable, which will be touched on later in the Conclusion, as will the wider political consequences of widescale working on the side. The length of informal jobs varied enormously, a few lasting for a year or more but most being sporadic and very short-term. Some jobs entailed a few weeks' work in a row, but more frequently someone might be asked to do two shifts in a week and then nothing for a month. This irregularity was one of the many reasons why informal employment was generally regarded as unsatisfactory. It rarely offered any financial security and did little to provide a temporal structure to a man's life.

Working on the side provided most of the immediate things sought from employment – money, a different environment and different company – as well as satisfying the moral imperative to be employed (see Marsden 1982: 198). Men commented that it made them feel equal again to those employed legally: as Jock put it, "When I'm working on the side I don't count myself as *any* cunt, I'm *graftin'* for it." Even a temporary job could be sufficient for a man to reassert his esteem as a "working man" which was so central to traditional values (cf. Howe 1986: 20 for similar findings in Belfast and Wadel 1973: 31 for Newfoundland).

The financial incentive for the unemployed not to declare their occasional earnings was enormous, and came about principally because of the abrupt cut in benefits when one began to earn. In the early 1980s a quarter of the unemployed in Britain only received Unemployment Benefit. For each day they earned more than £2, benefit was withheld for that day (about £5 per day for a single adult). For the three fifths (approximately) of the unemployed who received either Supplementary Benefit or Supplementary Benefit *and* Unemployment Benefit, their benefit payments were reduced pound for pound as soon as they earned over £4 *in a week*. This lack of tapering in the reduction of benefits, combined with the withdrawal of rent and rate rebates and the payment of income tax and National Insurance, meant an effective marginal tax rate on each extra pound of income of between 60 and 70 per cent for the unemployed until they earnt over £105 a week (Parker 1982: 32).

When each £1 earned was reduced to 40p if declared, it is obvious that many men who were already on very low incomes chose to break the law, particularly since their personal identities were largely based on their family roles as "breadwinners". A further important disincentive to declaring one's employment if it lasted more than a fortnight was the cumbersome bureaucratic procedure of signing off and signing on again, which involved several journeys to the benefit offices in the local town and delayed giro payments. The anomalies and unfairness of the tax/benefit system which encouraged people to work informally were frequently commented on in Cauldmoss. As one unemployed man told me: "They're creatin' the situation for you to diddle them out of tax and benefit. . . but if I had the choice I'd rather do it legal. . ." (see Harding and Jenkins 1989: 42).

Most of the unemployed were eager to take work on the side, so long as they could conceal it. In the first survey jobs on the side were described in a similar way to legal employment, most people calling them "work", and only a small minority described them as a "sideline" or something similar. The lack of any specific term to describe the unemployed's undeclared jobs suggests that they were not regarded as very different from ordinary employment. Occasional "fly jobs" were generally condoned and considered morally distinct from other illegal economic activity. However, those working on the side were sometimes condemned by vindictive villagers who disliked them on other grounds, or were jealous of their employment opportunities. Some of those 'working on the books' resented *their* taxes going to pay the benefits of those in informal jobs, and if their earnings were little more than their possible income from benefits they particularly condemned men with regular work on the side. Full-time undeclared jobs were widely condemned. However, even amongst those formally employed, it was usually recognised that the secretiveness, irregularity and lack of protection made "side jobs" far less desirable than legal work. "Good luck to them!" was the general consensus.

Undeclared earnings amongst those formally employed were considered more legitimate than the unemployed's work on the side (cf. Ashley 1983: 45), though there were few opportunities to "moonlight" in the early 1980s, in comparison with the previous decade. The virtue of employment, and fact that a man can rarely do too much, was nicely illustrated in the Glaswegian Matt McGinn's popular folk song *Three Nights and a Sunday*:

> I work aw day and I work aw night,
> Tae hell wi' you Jack, I'm all right;
> Three nights and a Sunday double time.

                                        (Buchan and Hall 1973: 12)

Although the employment ethic legitimised work on the side, the unemployed still feared "grassers" and had to be discreet, so that a casual job only earned a man the respectability of a worker amongst his family and immediate friends. Phone calls or letters to the Department of Health and Social Security could lead to "snoopers" being sent round in cars to watch houses, or pressure being put on individuals to sign off. Those caught claiming the "bru" fraudulently had to repay their benefits, but only one or two people in Cauldmoss were caught out each year, which suggests rather less officiousness by the fraud squad than was often assumed by the unemployed. The motive nearly always attributed to people "grassing" was jealousy. An unemployed man summed it up:

> It's funny in Cauldmoss: everyone's in the same boat being unemployed, but there's always two or three men who'll ring up the bru. There's an awful lot o' spite in a wee village – someone'll think, 'I've no' got a job and he's workin'!'

An official at the local Department of Employment confirmed this, saying that the vast majority of the numerous letters they received informing on fellow villagers seemed to be motivated by personal animosity. Those working on the side had to be discreet in their consumption as well as their employment, particularly in re-establishing their esteem as workers in the pub, for changed patterns of spending quickly aroused curiosity. The increased social isolation of those unemployed with informal jobs might have political implications, which will be mentioned later.

Researchers interested in the characteristics and development of illegal economic activity during the recession of the early 1980s have been criticised for fuelling periodic 'moral panics' about so-called 'welfare scroungers' (e.g. Harding and Jenkins 1989). Ten years later the government has responded to an enormous budget deficit by promising to attack those who have already suffered most from its economic policies: there are to be further 'crack downs' on benefit fraud (1992 Conservative Party Conference), despite evidence that tackling tax evasion is more cost effective (Smith 1986). In this political climate the discussion of illegal means of coping by the unemployed warrants justification. There are several reasons why I did not omit this subject from the ethnography out of political expediency.

Most important, it must be recognised how the benefit/tax system operated (and still operates (e.g. McLaughlin 1991)) to discourage the unemployed from 'active problem-solving behaviour normally rewarded and encouraged in the employed population' (Fryer and Payne 1986). Very few of those on the dole wanted to be pushed into undeclared employment and denied the dignity of presenting themselves publicly as "workers", but not acknowledging their financial circumstances makes a radical overhaul of the tax/benefit system (e.g. Leach and Wagstaff 1986) all the less likely.

If it is accepted that the 'informal economy' is part of, and dependent on, the larger economy (Harding and Jenkins 1989), it makes it all the more necessary to consider how the most disadvantaged fraction of the working class are pressured into conditions of employment that allow maximum exploitation by employers. The availability of cheap, unprotected labour is one of several reasons why a cynical right-wing government might welcome widespread working on the side. Another is that illegal coping strategies provide some financial cushioning for the most enterprising of the unemployed, as well as compromising them, thus inhibiting political action.

AUGMENTING WELFARE BENEFITS

The increasing importance of material lifestyle rather than moral repute in villagers' self-esteem, particularly amongst the young, put most claimants at the bottom of the social hierarchy. Given the differentiation of commodities, even a minor increase in income was therefore an improvement in social status. This constituted a considerable incentive to adopt any means to augment one's benefits. To borrow money, be supported by one's kin, to "fiddle" or to steal were all ways of responding to unemployment which ameliorated one's low esteem as determined by consumption, in the way that working on the side restored one's social standing in terms of the employment ethic.

Kinship support for the unemployed

When discussing welfare benefit levels several of the young unemployed emphasised that their parents were subsidising them, providing what both generations regarded as an essential supplement to "bru money". The costs of unemployment were spread to close relatives, but this informal redistribution of resources was limited by the conventions of reciprocity. The young unemployed who still lived with their parents had never achieved economic independence from them, and so a continuation of financial support was not a great indignity, although it perpetuated their pre-adult status (as discussed above). Teenagers with employed parents frequently received "subs" for cigarettes and clothes, were often given a regular amount at the weekend to go out for a night, and usually ate more than their nominal £10 "dig money" covered.

The unemployed who had their own homes, and particularly those who had previously been employed, were far more resistant to debt relationships with their parents or other close relatives, and strove to reciprocate any help they got. Nevertheless, parents and employed siblings were still important to them at financially difficult times (when several bills arrived at once, or new clothes were needed), or in allowing an occasional treat (such as borrowing money to go to a rock concert or a special dance).

Kinship support in kind was usually less demeaning than in cash, since the monetary value was vague. Having unemployed relatives round for Sunday or Christmas dinners was a common way of helping them, as was the loan of resources such as a car (filled with petrol) or a caravan for a weekend trip. While most unemployed adults were reluctant to receive gifts from their relatives they often felt they should not preserve their own dignity at the cost of their children's wellbeing. Consequently much kinship support for the unemployed skipped a generation as grandparents gave generous presents to their grandchildren, thus reducing the expense of clothing and toys. Even this kind of help could be resented if there was any hint that it implied a failure in the parents' role, and, as with all aid between relatives, feelings were most tense between affines.

Credit

The unemployed were wary of falling into debt, and many had cautionary tales of relatives or friends who took on too much credit and ended up with their furniture under threat of confiscation. Yet they also regarded borrowing money as unavoidable "if you're in our position": "If your man's no' working ye've got to"; or, "Folk cannae really live noo without it. Nobody *wants* it, but ye've *got* to." It was particularly useful for intermittent large expenditures like clothes or Christmas presents. Several of those on the dole had been committed to paying off large loans at the time they were made redundant, which was one of the employed's great fears: "if you take out a loan and are knocked out of work you're in a pickle of bother then!". The same proportion, four-fifths, of employed and unemployed council tenants reported using credit (Second survey), while slightly under half of the unemployed had a "club" in comparison with two-thirds of those in employment (Second survey), presumably because of restrictions on membership.

Several of the employed thought that those out of work borrowed simply to maintain their previous standard of living. The local "Provi cheque" agent said that when they lose their jobs people "want to keep up" in the eyes of others. "Obviously, even passing outside your house, people see your standards. People keep up the flan for a year maybe, but they cannae keep up the image. . ." Yet he did not issue a cheque unless he felt confident that the recipient would be able to repay it.

Anne Marie Bostyn and myself only knew of three households in Cauldmoss where unemployed people failed to meet their repayments on furniture or clothing and were either taken to court, had them repossessed, or found some illicit way of getting the necessary money. Since failure to meet one's debts was a great indignity these individuals were extremely discreet about their financial problems and it was likely that several other unemployed families had the same difficulties.

Fiddling and theft

There was a general consensus in Cauldmoss on the relative immorality of various different illegal means of supplementing one's benefits. In approximate order of increasing illegitimacy they would have been ranked: working on the side, poaching, collecting fuel, buying stolen goods, defrauding the authorities, stealing from large institutions and, most condemned, stealing from "your ain folk". Different people, however, drew the boundary of acceptable behaviour at different points on this continuum. The main differences of opinion were between the older and younger generations, between those employed and those "on the bru", and (to a lesser extent) between women and men.

The extent to which these moral evaluations shaped the unemployed's behaviour was complicated by how public the activities were. Some of the least immoral acts (such as collecting coal) were the most public and therefore inevitably damaged one's personal reputation. Conversely, the most intensely condemned acts (such as theft) could maintain one's respectable working-class status by providing the means to continue one's material lifestyle. But this was a high risk strategy since if caught one not only ended up with a reduced income (due to the fine) but, unless very lucky, was also exposed as a criminal. Many people in Cauldmoss eagerly turned to the court pages of the local paper before reading any other news.

Those over about 60 claimed that "in our day" the miners did not even steal off their employers. They condemned outright most small thefts and fiddles and despaired that for many young ones, "if it's no' too hot, it's no' too heavy". For older people moral integrity and reputation as "a good worker" were more important to one's self-esteem than one's pattern of consumption. According to these traditional values working on the side restored one's dignity as a worker and breadwinner, and its illegality was usually overlooked. After all, the activity was not in itself illegal, it was made illegal by government regulations.

Rather less respectable was the collection of fuel. Unemployed men dug out carrier bags or (if lucky) hundredweight sacks of low-grade coal from abandoned open-cast sites or exposed seams, and wood was collected from nearby copses. These were rapidly being depleted since live trees were cut as well as dead ones. Another source of "free" fuel was peat; some people who had access to a car or van helped themselves at night to stacked peat that had been cut commercially. Collecting one's own fuel was one of the few areas of the domestic economy that had developed in response to unemployment (see Gershuny and Pahl 1980).

The majority of those "on the bru" did not collect their own fuel, and those that did were mainly long-term unemployed. It was a fairly public strategy that displayed not only that one was unemployed but also so impoverished one had to adopt unconventional means to survive. Consequently if one was trying to maintain one's respectable status one would put off "coal howking" expeditions as long as possible, especially if the fuel had to be barrowed or wheeled on bicycles because a car was unavailable. Most "nice folk" in employment regarded it as an honourable way for those on the dole to cope, being a return to a practice well known in the area's history, particularly during the 1930s, and being seen as close to "real work". However, they also saw it as rather demeaning, though it was more a sign of fallen status than the cause of it.

A few men poached salmon or deer, though this was not restricted to the unemployed and, indeed, the need for a car to get to remote lochs and glens often impeded them. Poaching appealed to masculine qualities even more than digging coal, the skill, endurance, risk-taking, and cunning involved boosting masculine esteem. Though not a respectable activity the legitimacy of historical tradition, combined with a general sympathy for the landless against the landed, meant some "nice folk" condoned poaching and happily bought the produce.

Defrauding the authorities was morally more contentious, older people and those in employment usually condemning it. Fixing the electricity meter to provide virtually free energy was one of the commonest fiddles amongst the younger unemployed in Cauldmoss. Since they were at home for much of the day, a free substitute to coal made a substantial contribution to the household budget. Occasionally claimants managed to trick the DHSS into making unwarranted payments, lump-sum Single Payments for exceptional needs being the easiest to tap. One of the commonest frauds, both in village hearsay and as reported to us by the actors, was to appeal for a Single Payment to buy some household necessity which they already possessed. This would be taken round to a friendly neighbour before the officer arrived to discuss the claim. The payments could be three times the weekly giro (e.g. £70), but we never heard of anyone getting away with more than one such fraud.

The nature of the activities, the legal penalties and the disapproval by local people meant few knew who was fixing their meter or fiddling the DHSS, unless the perpetrator had confided in them, in which case s/he assumed it would be connived at. Many villagers believed that the incomers habitually defrauded the authorities although they had little evidence to substantiate it. The fact that more incomers confided in us various fiddles than did "local" people probably only reflected our own status as outsiders. Those "on the fiddle" implied that their actions were not morally problematic: "It's a load of hooey folk cannae live on the bru," one woman told me, "you just have to know the corners and dodges."

The thefts committed by people in Cauldmoss varied enormously in the way they were evaluated. Raiding fields for potatoes was almost validated by the hard work involved, while succumbing spontaneously to temptation, as much shoplifting was described, was generally considered less reprehensible than premeditated acts. However, thefts from the rich or large stores (e.g. stealing £20,000 worth of grandfather clocks or breaking into a large clothes shop in a nearby town) were thought far less culpable than thefts from small shopkeepers, the school or the church hall, although the former usually involved more planning. Burgling shops, particularly if large and outwith the village, was seen as virtually victimlesss crime in contrast with burgling private homes, the most vigorously condemned kind of theft.

Sahlins has noted how what he calls 'negative reciprocity' is usually transacted between those at greatest social distance (Sahlins 1974: 195); in Cauldmoss the Pakistani grocer suffered far more shoplifting than the other three run by local people, and burglary was usually committed by lads from the council scheme on incomers living in private houses. The worst kind of theft was an offence against one's "own kind" – either neighbours, kin or those equally impoverished – and this was nearly always condemned except where people suspended judgement through kin loyalty.

Judging by those who confided in us or were caught, it seemed that only a minority of the unemployed engaged in theft and nearly all of them were under 40. However, few would refuse to buy cheap goods that had been "acquired" and stolen goods were often distributed through the pubs. Some individuals were known to have the right contacts to "fence" articles, and an unemployed slaughterhouse man was ready to process stolen sheep or poached deer.

The social dimension of these acts suggested that it was not simply the poverty of unemployment which encouraged crime. In Cauldmoss there was an element of competition between criminals which was inseparable from the masculine qualities expressed through these activities. Even employed and older men were generally less moralistic about fiddles and thefts than were women. Another aspect of these activities was the thrill of taking a gamble to beat what was perceived as an unfair and impersonal system, in order, as Henry puts it, 'to gain control over personal action' (Henry 1978: 65). The masculine competitiveness and risk-taking were effective ways to relieve the normal monotony of life on the dole.

For some younger people the importance that spending capacity had for their self-identity, which was closely related to their extra-village reference groups (see Chapter Three), meant monetary gain was almost self-legitimating (cf. Henry 1978: 118). One of the "nice" lads in the youth club justified avoiding a £5 fare saying, "Money's money after all. You got to save it where you can." For those whose self-esteem was largely based on material lifestyle, this financial rationale justified the obvious way to cope with the indignity of poverty: supplementing one's giros illicitly. They felt "forced" into "making do" or "cheating". A woman whose husband was unemployed said, 'I wouldnae condemn a thief. If someone stole five pound from my purse I'd say, "Poor cunt, he must be that hard up to do that"'. She said you have to expect women "to stick a few things in their bag in the Pakis nowadays", for, as her husband added, "You've got to get everything you can, nowadays".

The worse one's deprivation was felt to be, the more legitimate was the action which one was constrained to follow. A man who had been unemployed for four years told me: "to be honest, I think it's a case of survival. You do anything you can to live at a level that's not starving."

CONCLUSION

Since consumption was as important as employment in constituting people's respectability, financial deprivation was as serious a consequence of unemployment in the social life of Cauldmoss as the loss of latent benefits of paid work. The main theme of this chapter has been the social experience of poverty and the ways in which the unemployed responded to it. The meanings that employment and consumption had for the employed were by and large shared by those on the dole. There was no subculture or counter culture of unemployment which had arisen in Cauldmoss in response to 30 per cent male unemployment. Consequently the experience of unemployment was all the more frustrating: inability to match conventional spending patterns meant one could no longer express one's status as a "hard worker", while for younger people with less restricted aspirations their lack of money put them at the bottom of the hierarchy of spenders. The unemployed still aspired to fulfil the same fundamental roles as those who were in work – as adults, as parents, and so on – but since they judged these roles by the same material standards they were inevitably demeaned.

The differences in norms that did exist were between different age-cohorts. Those who grew up before the Second World War had a strong employment ethic which was not shared by those under about thirty, while the latter had much higher material expectations than their parents. The generational differences were starkly revealed by the choices that had to be faced by those in the 'unemployment trap'. "Working on the side" was a strategy which ameliorated many of the problems of unemployment, particularly for those with a strong employment ethic, while other illicit means of augmenting one's benefits helped to restore the self-esteem of younger people whose identity was largely based on their material lifestyle.

9

Conclusion

The ethnography presented suggests that the behaviour and values of Cauldmoss inhabitants were largely shaped by parochial relationships. The social cohesion of the village can be understood in Durkheimian terms. It was founded on the common past inherited by all those "belonging" to Cauldmoss, and was reproduced through a common interpretation of the fundamental cognitive categories that made up their world. Idealised notions of community life – common interests and fellowship – had their most formal expression at Hogmanay and the annual Gala Day.

Much of the literature on unemployment emphasises the loneliness and poverty of being without work (e.g. Marsden and Duff 1975; Sinfield 1981: 54; Seabrook 1982), but within Cauldmoss local people had a dense network of relatives and friends with whom to retain contact, and no transport costs were involved in doing so. However, being unemployed within a community had contradictory effects on the experience of poverty. On the one hand there was frequently a redistribution of resources amongst kin, with those in work helping out the claimants, yet on the other hand the unemployed's social proximity to the lifestyles of wage earners meant a greater pressure to consume and thus a stronger sense of social and material deprivation.

Although Cauldmoss has been analysed as a community, the significance of external macro-sociological factors has been emphasised. The most important was the general stratification of British society: the Cauldmoss population was dependent on the labour market and subordinate to their employers. Most saw themselves as "working people" and destined to remain so as part of "the order of things". With the exception of skilled tradesmen, lack of control over their working conditions led to a thorough alienation from their jobs, but it also led men to esteem the small part of their working lives still within their influence: their masculine discipline to the job. The moral evaluation of men's work was interpreted as an *employment* ethic, which combined both men's alienated role in the work force and their masculine role in the family.

The three interrelated factors – gender roles in the family, alienation and the employment ethic – help explain the traditional concerns of the Labour Movement: trade unions' concentration on monetary demands and the 'family wage'; the low priority of greater control in the work place or a shorter working week, and the exclusion of women from many jobs and their low wages when they were employed.

A second important external factor was the way different styles of life and the prestige attached to them were created and promulgated on a nationwide basis in the interests of producers. The way people in Cauldmoss responded to this was largely determined by the degree to which they had 'restricted' or 'unrestricted' social aspirations.

Another macro-sociological factor directly relevant to this book was the state welfare system, and in particular the benefits paid to the unemployed. These were understood largely in relation to the employment ethic and people's interpretation of the obligations of reciprocity.

Within Cauldmoss the most important form of stratification was that of social status. There was a fundamental division between "the nice folk" (respectable) and "the wasters" (rough), although within each group there were further gradations of honour. "Being nice" not only incorporated crucial material factors, such as housing and occupation, but was constituted by a wide range of normative cultural practices as well, such as dress, furnishings, disciplining oneself to one's employment, leisure activities and sexual reputation (all, of course, with gender-specific standards). Consequently issues of social status had far more salience in people's daily lives than social class, and, I suggest, this would have been so even if the social class composition of Cauldmoss had been less homogenous. Class position was taken for granted by most villagers as the parameter of their experience, only to be transcended by a one-in-a-million win on the pools or, over time, through their children's upward social mobility, while respectability was a pervasive concern in their every day decisions. Villagers were constantly creating and recreating status distinctions.

In so far as one can generalise from the Cauldmoss findings presented here, it seems as if the social honour, rights of association and control over information that are the privilege of higher status groups might explain the motivation behind much consumption, since one's material lifestyle is one of the most important criteria of status. Since the level of consumer demand is crucial to the working of the national economy, and therefore the interests of capital, social status has more than parochial importance. There were other ways in which social status related to the class structure. Membership of the respectable working class created and reproduced different life chances from those available to "the wasters". The most important factor was access to employment, which was largely through personal contacts, but opportunities for marriage also had important material consequences, even within a fraction of the working class with little wealth.

Three different approaches were used to analyse consumption in Cauldmoss: 'consumerist', 'productionist' and 'hedonist'. In large part the use of commodities can be interpreted as the compulsory expression and reproduction of social relationships, in particular those of gender, work, social status and belonging to the community. However, different patterns of spending existed in the village which did not conform to, and sometimes contradicted, the cognitive order constructed through traditional consumption. This more individualistic spending, which was related to wider reference groups than the village and less restricted aspirations to upward social mobility, was interpreted in terms of the 'productionist' and 'hedonist' perspectives. According to the former approach it could largely be explained in terms of manufacturers' stimulation of demand. Certain features of this more privatised consumption could, however, also be interpreted in terms of the shift from traditional to modern hedonism (Campbell 1987). Manipulation by manufacturers and imaginative hedonism explains the dynamism that pervaded all aspects of consumption in the village, though a prerequisite for the perpetual inflation of wants is the arbitrary nature of the sign.

A recurrent theme in this book were generational differences in the meanings that employment and consumption had. These differences reflected both historical change, for instance in experiences of the labour market and in consumer expectations, and stage of the life course. The latter related to whether reference groups were within or beyond the village, how much one had invested in one's own reputation and how much knowledge one had accumulated about the respectability of other villagers.

For the young (under 30) being without a job was experienced primarily in terms of boredom and poverty: there was little shame at an unfulfilled ethic that valued disciplined work. Conversely, people over about 60 generally had a very strong employment ethic and a great pride in maintaining "an independence", most graphically demonstrated by the willingness of some to continue in their jobs although earning no more than they would receive in benefits. For them the virtue of work remained even though the necessity had gone.

To complete the puzzle of what employment means a third piece should be added to the states of employment and unemployment: that of retirement. This was not within my scope. One of many questions to be answered is whether the difference between the work ethic described here and that found by Williams (1990) amongst the old in Aberdeen can be explained by regional differences or by people's reinterpretation of employment when retired, once the immediate experience of alienation fades away.

Studying the meaning of consumption and employment for the unemployed did more to reveal the fundamental concepts underlying the whole culture of Cauldmoss than it did to show any significant changes in values between those in jobs and those without them. Despite over 30 per cent male unemployment the principal differences in values within the community were not between those in or out of work, but between different age groups. The inability of the unemployed to reproduce social categories through appropriate behaviour and shared activities was clearly not going to lead to the disintegration of the community in the short term.

In the early 1980s the unemployed in Cauldmoss did not identify with each other as a distinct group, nor did they identify much with the unemployed in the rest of Britain. There were several reasons for this. Older men tended to have less social contact with each other when unemployed and more with their immediate relatives. About a third of the unemployed moved in and out of work over the years and even the remaining two thirds were deeply reluctant to accept their situation as long term, which would have meant little differentiated them from "the wasters". A further factor that discouraged identification with others "on the bru" was that alternative sources of income to formal wages, in particular work on the side, could (for the lucky ones) bring the unemployed's spending levels close to those of the employed. This, together with the enormously high marginal tax rates for the low paid, had the important consequence that some unemployed households had incomes similar to those of some households with members in employment. As a result of these factors there was virtually no recognition in Cauldmoss of one of the most important social divisions that had emerged in Britain in the late twentieth century, that between a 'middle mass' and a 'deprived underclass' (Pahl 1984: 320). Yet there were several factors that were likely to exacerbate this incipient class divide: welfare benefit regulations which discouraged the unemployed from doing part time jobs or their spouses getting employment; last in, first out, redundancy policies in many firms; the preference employers had for appointing people currently in work, and, perhaps more important, the vicious circle of the unemployed's diminishing information networks about vacancies.

Since the unemployed in Cauldmoss did not see themselves as a distinct group they were unlikely to generate a new evaluation of resources, creating a counter culture. Even the young unemployed did not adopt punk fashion as a way of coping with restricted income, reversing the normal hierarchy of signs (commodities) as a way of distancing themselves from mainstream society. Rather, the conventional values were maintained and the unemployed felt compelled to consume at what was generally regarded to be a respectable level. Similarly the obligations of reciprocity still had to be met, and rather than fail in this the unemployed withdrew from social involvement.

Nor did the values associated with paid work change much in response to unemployment. For instance, there was a persisting equation of wages with personal worth which inhibited the unemployed from doing voluntary work. Related to this equation was the deeply entrenched notion that time which was not sold had little value. When this was combined with an understanding that commodities were desired for their culturally ascribed value, not some mythical use value abstracted from culture, then it is clear why the unemployed did not resort to self-provisioning in a comprehensive way (as some sociologists had speculated, e.g. Gershuny and Pahl 1980). To save their limited money and use their extra time productively by growing vegetables, making beer, or creating their own entertainment, as an older generation had done in the 1930s, would have meant evaluating their resources very differently: they would have been in a different culture.

Unemployed men with more traditional values felt demeaned in their public consumption because it could no longer express their role as workers. This was most evident in the pub where unemployed drinkers were sometimes resented and it was regarded as "ignorant" to drink only one pint. For such men the one strategy which resolved many of the problems of unemployment was working on the side. Even when working for very low pay, which was frequently the case (such as £1 an hour), this went a long way to fulfilling the employment ethic. Those who had less restricted status aspirations and wider reference groups suffered unemployment more acutely through poverty. For them commodities were crucial in demonstrating their position in a stratified society. Whereas for older unemployed men the only significant way to restore their dignity was to find a job, for some younger men every increase in income enhanced their standing. Thus amongst young unemployed men fiddling and, to a lesser extent, theft were not exceptional means of achieving greater social esteem. Money gained in these ways did not have the same meaning as earned income, but it was got through their own skill, not simply a handout, and therefore boosted their masculine identity and self-respect.

It is worth considering the wider political consequences of these alternative means by which the unemployed augmented their incomes. First, they enabled the unemployed to reproduce the cultural values which were ascribed to consumption, maintaining the importance of the conventional material lifestyle and so contributing to the wider economic system (contrast, for instance, the New Age travellers). Second, they inhibited a radical response to unemployment. Illegal activities exacerbated the isolation of the unemployed, compromised their moral outrage, and provided a financial (and sometimes emotional) shock-absorber which all discouraged militancy. As Seabrook argues (1985), the enterprising poor (who probably have the greatest political initiative) are more ready to take private action to better themselves than to seek a long-term solution for their poverty through collective political action. Third, to businesses mass unemployment and widescale work on the side were doubly advantageous, in that they created an increasingly subservient legal workforce and also access to a cheap unprotected source of labour that could be used or ignored at will. This might lead one to suspect that the government has in practice a benign view towards informal economic activities, whatever its rhetoric.

The implications of these findings for wider social concerns are complex, most disturbing, and yet not without hope. For instance, one interpretation of this analysis of consumption could be that it demonstrates how powerful is the impetus for constantly inflated material desires, there being several separate sources for this dynamic. Those despondent about the public acceptability of redistribution through increased direct taxation, or, at a global level, those concerned about the increasing demands on natural resources, would be dismayed by this conclusion. A less pessimistic interpretation, however, would focus on the social construction of need and see some hope in the diverse sources of consumer demand. The existence of locally generated constraints on consumer aspirations (though currently much diminished), the way in which moral persuasion is implicit in patterns of consumption, and the move from 'traditional' to 'modern' hedonism show that consumption patterns could possibly become, or be modified to be, less ecologically destructive and restrictive of political options.

This study does, however, have some very clear conclusions. It shows how central employment is to men's moral identities and reaffirms the need for a radical redistribution of employment (cf. Leach and Wagstaff 1986). It also demonstrates that to conceive of poverty as relative, far from belittling its consequences, recognises how material and social deprivation pervade all aspects of life. Indeed, recent research suggests that inequalities in health can be partially attributed to *relative* deprivation (Wilkinson 1992). That either of these conclusions needs re-stating is a sad indictment of the political climate in the late twentieth century.

Bibliography

Abel, Thomas and Cockerham, William C. (1993) 'Lifestyle or
    Lebensführung? Critical remarks on the mistranslation of Weber's *Class,
    Status Party*', *Sociological Quarterly* (forthcoming).
Aitken, A. J. and McArthur, T. (1979) *Languages of Scotland*. Edinburgh:
    Chambers.
Allan, Graham, A. (1979) *A Sociology of Friendship and Kinship*. London: Allan
    and Unwin.
Ardener, Shirley (1978) *Defining Females: The Nature of Women in Society*.
    London: Croom Helm.
Ashley, Pauline (1983) *The Money Problems of the Poor: a literature review*. SSRC,
    DHSS Studies in Deprivation and Disadvantage 11. London: Heinemann
    Educational Books.
Atkinson, A. B. and Micklewright, John (1985) *Unemployment Benefits and
    Unemployment Duration*. London School of Economics and Political
    Science: Suntory - Toyota International Centre for Economics and Related
    Disciplines.
Bailey, P. (1978) *Leisure and Class in Victorian England*. London: Routledge
    and Kegan Paul.
Bakke, E. Wight (1933) *The Unemployed Man: A Social Study*. London: Nisbet
    and Co. Ltd.
Barbalet, J. M. (1986) 'Limitations of Class Theory and the Disappearance of
    Status: the problem of the New Middle Class.' *Sociology* Vol. 20 No. 4,
    Nov. 1986.
Barker, Diana (1972) 'Young people and their homes: spoiling and "keeping
    close" in a South Wales town' *Sociological Review* 20 (4) pp. 569-90.
Barker, D. Leonard and Allen, S. (1976) (eds) *Sexual Divisions and Society*.
    London: Tavistock.
Barrett, Michele (1980) *Women's Oppression Today*. London: Verso.
Baudrillard, Jean (1975) *The Mirror of Production*. St Louis, Mo., USA: Telos
    Press.
Baudrillard, Jean (1981) *For a Critique of the Political Economy of the Sign*. St
    Louis, Mo., USA: Telos Press.
Baudrillard, Jean (1983) *Simulations*. New York: Semiotext(e).

Bayley, Stephen (1986) *Sex, Drink and Fast Cars: the creation and consumption of images*. London: Faber.

Beechey, Veronica (1977) 'Some Notes on Female Wage Labour in the Capitalist Mode of Production.' *Capital and Class*. No. 3, 1977.

Berger, P. (1975) 'The Human Shape of Work.' In G. Esland *et al.* (ed.) *People and Work*. Holmes McDougall.

Beynon, Huw (1973) *Working for Ford*. Suffolk: Allen Lane and Penguin Education.

Blaxter, M., Mullen, K. and Dyer, S. (1982) 'Problems of Alcohol Abuse in the Western Isles: a community study.' *Scottish Health Services Studies* No. 44, Scottish Home and Health Department, Edinburgh.

Bostyn, Anne Marie (1990) '"Ah Know Whit Like An 'Oor Is": The meaning of time in a Scottish Lowland Community.' Unpublished PhD thesis, Department of Social Anthropology, Edinburgh University.

Bott, Elizabeth (1957) *Family and Social Network*. London: Tavistock.

Bourdieu, Pierre (1977) *Outline of a Theory of Practice*. Cambridge: Cambridge University Press.

Bourdieu, Pierre (1984) *Distinction*. London: Routledge and Kegan Paul.

Brennan, T., Cooney, E.W. and Pollins, H. (1954) *Social Change in South West Wales*. London: Watts and Co.

Brown, Muriel and Madge, Nicola (1982) *Despite the Welfare State*. SSRC/DHSS London: Heinemann.

Brown, Richard K. (1985) 'Attitudes to Work, Occupational Identity and Industrial Change' in Roberts, Finnegan, and Duncan (eds) 1985.

Bruce, Steve (1985) *No Pope of Rome: Anti-Catholicism in Modern Scotland*. Edinburgh: Mainstream.

Buchan, Norman and Hall, Peter (1973) (eds) *The Scottish Folksinger*. London: Collins.

Bulmer, Martin (1975) (ed.) *Working Class Images of Society*. London: Routledge and Kegan Paul.

Burghes, Louie (1980) *Living From Hand to Mouth: a study of 65 families living on supplementary benefit*. FSU/Child Poverty Action Group.

Burgoyne, Jacqueline (1987) 'Material Happiness'. *New Society* 10 April 1987 Vol. 80 No. 1267, pp. 12-14.

Byron, Reg (1981) Unpublished letter to Jeremy Biossevain, 23 February 1981.

Callender, Claire (1987) 'Women Seeking Work' in Fineman (ed.) 1987.

Campbell, Beatrix (1984) *Wigan Pier Revisited: Poverty and Politics in the Eighties*. London: Virago.

Campbell, Colin (1987) *The Romantic Ethic and the Spirit of Modern Consumerism*. Oxford: Basil Blackwell.

CCCS (1976) 'A Critique of 'Community Studies' and Its Role in Social Thought, Stencilled Occasional Paper, General Series: SP No. 44, Centre for Contemporary Cultural Studies, Birmingham University.

Chapman, Malcolm (1978) *The Gaelic Vision in Scottish Culture*. London: Croom Helm.

Charles, Nickie and Kerr, Marion (1988) *Women Food and Families*. Manchester: Manchester University Press.

Chodorow, Nancy (1978) *The Reproduction of Mothering*. Berkeley: University of California Press.

Clarke, John, Critcher, Chas and Johnson, Richard (eds) (1979) *Working-Class Culture: Studies in history and theory*. London: Hutchinson in association with the Centre for Contemporary Cultural Studies, University of Birmingham.

Clarke, M. (1978) 'The Unemployed in Supplementary Benefit: Living Standards and Making Ends Meet on a Low Income.' *Journal of Social Policy* 7 (4), 385-410.

Clarke, R. (1982) Work in Crisis: Dilemma of a Nation. Edinburgh: St Andrew's Press.

Clemitson, I. and Rodgers, G. (1981) *A Life to Live: Beyond Full Employment*. London: Junction Books.

Coffield, Frank, Borrill, Carol and Marshall, Sarah (1986) *Growing Up At The Margins: Young Adults in the North East*. Milton Keynes: Open University Press.

Cohen, Anthony P. (1978) 'Ethnographic Method in the Real Community.' *Sociologia Ruralis* XVIII (1): 1-22.

Cohen, Anthony P. (1979) 'The Whalsay Croft.' in Wallman (ed.) 1979.

Cohen, Anthony P. (1985) *The Symbolic Construction of Community*. Chichester: Ellis Horwood and London: Tavistock.

Cohen, Phil (1972) 'Sub-cultural Conflict and Working Class Community.' Working Papers in Cultural Studies 2, University of Birmingham.

Condry, Edward (1983) *Scottish Ethnography*. Association for Scottish Ethnography Monograph No. 1 Department of Social Anthropology, University of Edinburgh.

Coulter, Jim, Miller, Susan and Walker, Martin (1984) *A State of Siege: Politics and Policing of the Coalfields: Miners' Strike 1984*. London: Canary Press.

Cowie, Celia and Lees, Sue (1987) 'Slags and Drags' in *Sexuality: A Reader* (ed.) Feminist Review. London: Virago.

Crawford, Alex (1986) 'Attitudes About Alcohol; A Review' paper presented to the Alcohol Epidemiology Section, ICAA, Dubrovnik, 9-13 June 1986.

Critcher, Chas (1979) 'Sociology, cultural studies and the post-war working class.' In Clarke, Critcher and Johnson (eds) 1979.

Culler, Jonathan (1976) *Saussure*. Glasgow: Fontana/Collins.

Daniel, W. W. (1981) 'Unemployment.' *Unemployment Unit Bulletin* No. 1, August 1981.

Darlington, T.E.G. and Byrne, J.M. 'How Young People Form Their Drinking Habits and Choose Brands.' Report by Research Associates: Stone, Staffordshire, England.

Dauncey, Guy (1983) *Nice Work If You Can Get It*. Cambridge: National Extension College.

Daunton, M.J. (1983) 'Public Place and Private Space: The Victorian City and The Working-Class Household.' in Fraser, D. and Sutcliffe, A. (eds) *The Pursuit of Urban History*. London: Edward Arnold.

Davis, A. (1948) *Social Class Influences Upon Learning*. Cambridge, Mass.: Harvard University Press.

Davis, K. (1942) 'Conceptual analysis of stratification' *American Sociological Review* 7, pp. 309-21.

De Beauvoir, Simone (1972) *The Second Sex*. Harmondsworth: Penguin.

Dennis, Norman, Henriques, Fernando, M. and Slaughter, Clifford (1956) *Coal Is Our Life*. London: Eyre and Spottiswoode.

Dixie, Rachael with Talbot, Margaret (1982) *Women, Leisure and Bingo*. Leeds: Trinity and All Saints College.

Douglas, Mary (1970) *Natural Symbols*. London: Barrie and Rockliffe.

Douglas, Mary (ed.) (1987) *Constructive Drinking: Perspectives on drink from anthropology*. Cambridge: Cambridge University Press.

Douglas, Mary and Isherwood, Baron (1979) *The World of Goods: Towards and anthropology of consumption*. Suffolk: Allen Lane.

Dubin, Robert (1976) (ed.) *Handbook of Work, Organisation and Society*.
    Chicago: Rand McNally.
Durkheim, Emile (1952/1897) *Suicide*. London: Routledge and Kegan Paul.
Durkheim, Emile (1964/1893) *The Division of Labour in Society*. London: Free
    Press/Macmillan.
Edwards, M. (1981) 'Financial Arrangements within Families.' *Social Security*.
    December 1981 (Australia).
Eisenstein, Hester (1984) *Contemporary Feminist Thought*. London: Unwin
    Paperbacks.
Ekeh, Peter P. (1974) *Social Exchange Theory: the two traditions*. London:
    Heinemann.
Eldridge, J. E. T. (1974) *Sociology in Scotland - What Needs to be Done?*
    Unpublished manuscript.
Emmet, I. (1982) 'Place community and bilingualism in Blaenau Ffestiniog' in
    Cohen, Anthony (ed.) *Belonging*, Manchester University Press, pp. 202-222.
Engels, Frederick (1942) *The Origin of the Family, Private Property and the State*.
    London: International Publishers.
Evans-Pritchard, E. E. (1940) *The Nuer*. Oxford University Press.
Evans-Pritchard, E. E. (1973) 'Some Reminiscences and Reflections on
    Fieldwork.' *Journal of the Anthropology Society of Oxford*. Vol. IV No. 11-12.
Fabian, J. (1983) *Time and the Other. How Anthropology Makes its Object*. New
    York: Columbia University Press.
Featherstone, Mike (1987) 'Lifestyle and Consumer Culture' in *Theory,
    Culture and Society*. Vol. 4 No. 1 February 1987, 55-70.
Featherstone, Mike (1991) *Consumer Culture and Postmodernism* London: Sage.
Fiegehen, G.C., Lansley, P.S. and Smith, A.D. (1977) *Poverty and Progress in
    Britain 1953-73*. Cambridge University Press.
Fineman, Stephen (1987) (ed.) *Unemployment: Personal and Social
    Consequences*. London: Tavistock.
Firth, Raymond (1956) *Two Studies of Kinship in London*. LSE Monographs on
    Social Anthropology No. 15 London: Athlone Press University of London.
Firth, Raymond (1973) *Symbols: Public and Private*. London: Allen and Unwin.
Frankenberg, Ronald (1966) *Communities in Britain*. Harmondsworth:
    Penguin.
Frisby, David (1985) 'Georg Simmel: First Sociologist of Modernity', *Theory,
    Culture and Society* Vol. 2 No.3, pp. 49-67.
Fromm, Erich (1962) *The Sane Society*. New York: Rinehart.
Fryer, David and Payne, Roy (1986) 'Being Unemployed: A Review of the
    Literature on the Psychological Experience of Unemployment.' in Cooper,
    C. L. and Robertson, I. (eds) *International Review of Industrial and
    Organizational Psychology*. Chichester: Wiley.
Fryer, David and Ullah, Philip (1987) (eds) *Unemployed People: Social and
    Psychological Perspectives*. Milton Keynes: Open University Press.
Galbraith, Kenneth (1979) *The Affluent Society*. Harmondsworth: Penguin.
Gans, Herbert J. (1970) 'Poverty and Culture: Some Basic Questions about
    Methods of Studying Life-Styles of the Poor'. In Townsend (ed.) 1970.
George, Margaret (1973) 'From 'Goodwife' to 'Mistress': The transformation
    of the female in bourgeois culture.' *Science and Society*. 37 (2), 1973, 152-177.
Gershuny, Jay I. (1978) *After Industrial Society?* London: Macmillan.
Gershuny, Jay I. and Pahl, Raymond E. (1979) 'Work Outside Employment:
    Some Preliminary Speculations.' *New Universities Quarterly* 34: 120.
Gershuny, Jay I. and Pahl, Raymond E. (1980) 'Britain in the Decade of the
    Three Economies.' *New Society*. 3 January 1980, pp. 7-9.

Giddens, Anthony (1979) *Central Problems in Social Theory: Action, structure and contradiction in social analysis.* London: Macmillan.

Girling, F.K. (1957) 'Joking Relationships in a Scottish Town.' *Man.* 57: 102.

Goffman, Erving (1971) *The Presentation of Self in Everyday Life.* Harmondsworth: Penguin.

Gofton, Leslie (1984) 'Work, Drink and Gender: Ale Drinking in North-East England.' Paper presented at Conference on Food Sharing, Werner Reimers Stiftling, Bad Homburg Germany, 4 December (proceedings in press).

Gofton, Leslie and Douglas, Stewart (1985) 'Drink and the City.' *New Society.* Vol 74 Nos 1199/1200 20/27 December 1985, pp. 502-4.

Goldthorpe, John (1979) 'Intellectuals and the Working Class in Modern Britain.' Fuller Lecture, Department of Sociology, University of Essex.

Goldthorpe, John (1985) 'The end of convergence: corpuralist and dualist tendencies in modern western societies.' In Roberts, Finnegan and Gallie (eds) 1985.

Goldthorpe, John and Lockwood, David (1963) 'Affluence and the British Class Structure.' *Sociological Review.* 11. pp. 133-63.

Goldthorpe, John, Lockwood, David, Bechhofer, F. and Platt, J. (1968) *The Affluent Worker: Industrial Attitudes and Behaviour; (1969) The Affluent Worker: Political Attitudes and Behaviour.; (1970) The Affluent Worker in the Class Structure.* Cambridge: Cambridge University Press.

Gorz, Andre (1982) *Farewell to the Working Class.* London: Pluto Press.

Guardian, The (11 January 1984) '£15m for YTS Switched to Community Jobs Scheme'

Guardian, The (25 January 1984) 'No Job - So What?'

Guardian, The (1 February 1984) 'Jobless Under Morale Microscope'.

Gullestad, M. (1984) *Kitchen - Table Society.* Oslo: Universitets furlaget.

Hamnett, Chris (1989) 'Consumption and class in contemporary Britain' in *The Changing Social Structure* (eds) Hamnett, C., McDowell, L. and Sarre, P. London: Sage.

Hall, Stuart and Jefferson, Tony (1976) (eds) *Resistance Through Ritual* London: Hutchinson.

Hammersley, Martyn and Atkinson, Paul (1983) *Ethnography: Principles in Practice.* London: Tavistock.

Haraszti, M. (1977) *A Worker in a Workers' State.* Harmondsworth: Penguin.

Harding, Philip and Jenkins, Richard (1989) *The Myth of the Hidden Economy: Towards a new understanding of informal economic activity.* Milton Keynes: Open University Press.

Harris, C. C. (1969) *The Family.* London: Allen and Unwin.

Harris, C. C. (1983) *The Family and Industrial Society.* London: Allen and Unwin.

Harrison, Brian (1971) *Drink and the Victorians: The Temperance Question in England 1815-1872.* London: Faber

Harrison, Tom (1943) (ed.) *'Mass Observation' The Pub and the People: A Worktown Study.* London: Gollancz.

Harvie, C. (1981) *No Gods and Precious Few Heroes: Scotland 1914-1980.* London: Edward Arnold.

Hebdidge, Dick (1979) *Subculture: The Meaning of Style.* London: Methuen.

Henry, Stuart (1978) *The Hidden Economy.* London: Martin Robertson.

Heughan, Hazel E. (1953) *Pit Closures at Shotts and the Migration of Miners.* University of Edinburgh Social Sciences Research Centre, Monograph No. 1, Edinburgh.

Hey, Valerie (1986) *Patriarchy and Pub Culture.* London: Tavistock.

Hillery, G.A. (1955) 'Definitions of community: Areas of agreement.' *Rural Sociology.* Vol. 20, No. 2, pp. 111-23

Hirsch, Fred (1977) *Social Limits to Growth.* London: Routledge and Kegan Paul.

Hoggart, Richard (1957) *The Uses of Literacy.* London: Chatto and Windus.

Howe, Leo (1986) 'Unemployment: historical aspects of data collection and the black economy in Belfast.' Unpublished paper, Department of Social Anthropology, Queens University, Belfast. Presented to ASA Conference 1986.

Hudson, J.A. (1948) *The Church in Great Britain.* USA and Britain: The Old Paths Book Club.

Hunt, Geoffrey P. and Satterlee, S. (1983) 'The Pub, The Village and The People.' Interim paper. Polytechnic of North London, Department of Sociology.

Jahoda, Marie (1982) *Employment and Unemployment: A social-psychological analysis.* Cambridge: Cambridge University Press.

Jahoda, Marie (1987) 'Unemployed Men at Work' in Fryer and Ullah (eds) 1987.

Jameson, F, 'Postmodernism and the Consumer Society' in Foster, H. (ed.) *Postmodern Culture.* London: Pluto Press.

Jenkins, C. and Sherman, Barry (1979) *The Collapse of Work.* London: Eyre Methuen.

Jenkins, Richard (1983) *Lads, Citizen and Ordinary Kids: Working-class youth life-styles in Belfast.* London: Routledge and Kegan Paul.

Jenkins, Richard (1992) *Pierre Bourdieu.* London: Routledge and Kegan Paul.

Jennings, Hilda (1962) *Societies in the Making: A Study of Development and Redevelopment Within a County Borough.* London: Routledge and Kegan Paul.

Jephcott, P. (1967) *Time of One's Own: Leisure and Young People.* University of Glasgow Social and Economic Studies Occasional Papers No. 7, Edinburgh: Oliver and Boyd.

Kelvin, P. (1980) *Work, Unemployment and Leisure: Myths, Hopes and Realities.* Edinburgh University Tourism and Recreation Unit, Conference Proceedings No. 4 April, 1982.

Kent, Ray (1980) 'The Rational Credit User: Myth or Reality? The Case of Check Trading.' Unpublished paper, Department of Sociology, Stirling University.

Kerr, Madeline (1958) *The People of Ship Street.* London: Routledge and Kegan Paul.

Kerr, Marion and Charles, Nicola (1986) 'Servers and providers: the distribution of food within the family.' Sociological Review. Vol. 34, No. 1, February 1986, pp. 115-57.

Klein, Josephine (1965) *Samples from English Cultures.* London: Routledge and Kegan Paul.

Knight, Chris (1991) *Blood Relations: Menstruation and the Origins of Culture.* London: Yale University Press.

Kolvin, Israel, Miller, F.J. W., Scott, D. Mcl., Gatzanis, S. R. M., Fleeting, M., (1990) *Continuities of Deprivation? The Newcastle 1000 Study.* Aldershot: Avebury.

Kornhauser, A. (1965) *Mental Health of the Industrial Worker.* New York: Wiley.

Land, Hilary (1976) 'Women: Supporters or Supported?' in Barker and Allen (eds) 1976.

Leach, Donald and Wagstaff, Howard with Bostyn, Anne Marie, Pritchard, Colin and Wight, Daniel (1986) *Future Employment and Technological Change*. London: Kogan Page.

Leach, Edmund (1982) *Social Anthropology*. Glasgow: Fontana.

Lee, David and Newby, Howard (1983) *The Problem of Sociology: An introduction to the discipline*. London: Hutchison.

Lefebvre, Henri (1971) *Everyday Life in the Modern World*. London: Harper and Row Torchbooks.

Leiss, William (1978) *The Limits to Satisfaction: On Needs and Commodities*. London: Marion Boyars.

Leonard, D. (1980) *Sex and Generation: A Study of Courtship and Weddings*. London: Tavistock.

Lewis, I. M. (1976) *Social Anthropology in Perspective*. Harmondsworth: Penguin.

Linhart, R. (1976) *L'Etabli*. Paris: Editions de Minuet.

Littlejohn, James (1964) *Westrigg: The Sociology of a Cheviot Parish*. London: Routledge and Kegan Paul.

Lockwood, David (1958) *The Black Coated Worker: A Study in Class Consciousness*. London: Allen and Unwin.

Lockwood, David (1966) 'Sources of Variation in Working Class Images of Society.' *Sociological Review*. 14(3), 1966, pp. 249-67.

Lockwood, David (1981) 'The Weakest Link in the Chain: Some Comments on the Marxist theory of action.' *Research in the Sociology of Work*. 1, 1981, pp. 435-81.

Louch (1966) *Explanation and Human Action*. Oxford: Basil Blackwell.

Lowerson, J. and Myerscough, J. (1977) *Time to Spare in Victorian England*. Sussex: Harvester Press.

Maan, Bashir (1992) *The New Scots: The Story of Asians in Scotland*. Edinburgh: John Donald.

MacAndrew, C. and Edgerton, R.A. (1969) *Drunken Comportment: A Social Explanation*. Chicago: Aldine.

MacGregor, S. (1981) *The Politics of Poverty*. London: Longman.

McKee, Lorna and Bell, Colin (1985) 'Marital and Family Relations in Times of Male Unemployment.' in Roberts, Finnegan and Gallie (eds) 1985.

McKee, Lorna and Bell, Colin (1986) 'His unemployment, her problem: the domestic and marital consequences of male unemployment.' In Allen, S., Waton, A., Purcell, K. and Woods, S. (eds) *The Experience of Unemployment* pp. 134-48, Basingstoke: Macmillan.

McLaughlin, Eithne (1991) 'Work and Welfare Benefits: Social Security, employment and unemployment in the 1990's, *Journal of Social Policy* Vol. 20 No. 4 pp. 485-508.

McRobbie, Angela and Garber, Jenny (1976) 'Girls and Subcultures.' In Hall and Jefferson (eds) 1976.

Malcomson, R. W. (1973) *Popular Recreations in English Society 1700-1859*. Cambridge University Press.

Malinowski, Bronislaw (1923) 'The Problem of Meaning in Primitive Languages.' Supplement 1 in Ogden, C. K. and Richards, I. A. *The Meaning of Meaning*. London:Routledge and Kegan Paul.

Mandelbaum, D.G. (1965) 'Alcohol and Culture.' *Current Anthropology 6*, pp.281-93.

Manpower Services Commission (1979) *A Study of the Long-Term Unemployed*. London.

Marcuse, Herbert (1964) *One-Dimensional Man*. London: Sphere.

McKendrick, N. (1983) 'Commercialisation and the economy.' In McKendrick, N., Brewer, J. and Plumb, J. (eds) *The Birth of a Consumer Society*. London: Hutchinson.

Mars, Gerald and Altman, Yochanan (1987) 'Alternative mechanism of distribution in a Soviet economy' in Douglas, Mary (ed.) *Constructive Drinking: Perspectives on drink from anthropology*. Cambridge: Cambridge University Press.

Marsden, Dennis (1970) 'Fatherless Families on National Assistance.' in Townsend (ed.) 1970.

Marsden, Dennis (1982) *Workless*. London: Croom Helm.

Marsden, Dennis and Duff, Euan (1975) *Workless: Some Unemployed Men and their Families*. Harmondsworth: Pelican.

Marshall, T. H. (1953) *Clan, Citizenship and Social Development*. New York: Doubleday.

Martin, Bernice (1981) *A Sociology of Contemporary Cultural Change*. Oxford: Basil Blackwell.

Martin, Bernice (1984) 'Mother Wouldn't Like It; Housework as Magic.' Theory Culture and Society. Vol. 2 No. 2 1984 pp. 19-36.

Marx, Karl (1844) 'Economic and Philosophical Manuscripts' in *Marx-Engels Gesamtausgabe*. Section 1 Vol. 3.

Mauss, Marcel (1954) *The Gift*. London: Gohen and West.

Mead, Margaret (1949) *American Museum of Natural History*. New York.

Miller, Daniel (1987) *Material Culture and Mass consumption*. London: Basil Blackwell.

Miller, S. M. and Roby, Pamela (1970) 'Poverty: Changing Social Stratification.' In Townsend (ed.) 1970.

Mills, Jane (1991) *Womanwords: A vocabulary of culture and patriarchal society*. London: Virago.

Mitchison, Rosalind (1970) *A History of Scotland*. London: Methuen.

Mogey, J. M. (1956) *Family and Neighbourhood: two studies in Oxford*. Oxford University Press.

Morgan, David H. J. (1992) *Discovering Men*. London: Routledge.

Morris, Lydia D. (1985) 'Renegotiation of the Domestic Division of Labour in the Context of Redundancy.' In Roberts, Finnegan and Gallie (eds) 1985.

Morris, Lydia (1987a) 'The household and the labour market' and 'Domestic circumstances.' In Harris, C. C. (ed.) *Redundancy and Recession in South Wales*. pp. 127-55 Oxford: Basil Blackwell.

Morris, Lydia (1987b) 'Local social polarization: a case study of Hartlepool, *International Journal of Urban and Regional Research*, Vol. 11, pp. 331-50.

Moylan, Sue (1983) 'Research of the Effects of Unemployment on Living Standards.' Paper for SSRC Employment and Unemployment Workshop 11 November 1983 concerning a DHSS sponsored research project.

Mukerji, Chandra (1983) *From Graven Images: Patterns of Modern Materialism*. New York: Columbia University Press.

Murray, C. (1979) 'The Work of Men, Women and the Ancestors.' in Wallman (ed.) 1979.

Nadel, S. F. (1951) *The Foundations of Social Anthropology*. London: Cohen and West. *New Statistical Account of Scotland, The* (1841). Edinburgh.

Newby, Howard (1983) *The State of Research into Stratification in Britain*. Social Science Research Council, London.

Noble, Mary, Bostyn, Anne Marie and Wight, Daniel (1986) *The Moral Implications of Unemployment and the Hidden Economy in a Scottish Village*. ESRC final report (G00232114).

Notes and Queries on Anthropology (1967) London: Routledge and Kegan Paul.

O'Connor, J. (1978) *The Young Drinkers*. London: Tavistock.

O'Higgins, M. (1980) *Measuring the Hidden Economy: A Review of Evidence and Methodologies*. London: Outer Circle Policy Unit.

Okely, Judith (1975) 'The Self and Scientism.' *Journal of the Anthropology Society of Oxford*. Vol. VI No. 3 pp. 171-88.

Okely, Judith (1992) 'Anthropology and autobiography: participatory experience and embodied knowledge', in Okely, J. and Callaway, H. (eds) *Anthropology and Autobiography, ASA Monograms 29*, London: Routledge.

Okely, Judith and Callaway, Helen (eds) (1992) *Anthropology and Autobiography, ASA Monographs 29*, London: Routledge.

Orwell, George (1962/1937) *The Road to Wigan Pier*. Harmondsworth: Penguin.

Page Arnot, R. (1955) *A History of the Scottish Miners*. London: George Allen and Unwin.

Pahl, Jan (1979) 'Patterns of Money Management within Marriage'. Unpublished paper, University of Kent.

Pahl, Raymond (1984) *Divisions of Labour*. Oxford: Basil Blackwell.

Pahl, Raymond and Wallace, Claire (1985) 'Forms of Work and Privatisation on the Isle of Sheppey.' In Roberts, Finnegan and Gallie (eds) 1985.

Palm, G. (1977) *The Flight from Work*. Cambridge: Cambridge University Press.

Parades, A. and Hood, W. R. (1975) 'Sobriety as a Symptom of Alcohol Intoxication: a clinical commentary on intoxication and drunkeness.' *British Journal of Addiction* 70 pp. 233-43.

Parker, Hermione (1982) *The Moral Hazard of Social Benefits*. Institute of Economic Affairs, Research Monograph 37, London.

Parker, S. R. and Smith, M. A. (1976) 'Work and Leisure.' In Dublin (ed.) 1976.

Parkin, D. (1979) 'The Categorisation of Work.' In Wallman (ed.) 1979.

Parkin, F. (1971) *Class Inequality and Political Order*. London: MacGibbon and Kee.

Parkin, F. (1979) *Marxism and Class Theory: A Bourgeois Critique*. London: Tavistock.

Parsons, Talcott (1943) 'The Kinship System of the Contemporary United States.' In Parsons (ed.) *Essays in Sociological Theory*. New York: Free Press.

Pearson, Geoffrey and Twohig, John (1976) 'Ethnography Through The Looking-Glass: The Case of Howard Becker.' In Hall and Jefferson (eds) 1976.

Piachaud, David (1981) 'Peter Townsend and the Holy Grail.' *New Society*. 10 September 1981 10 pp. 419-21.

Pitt-Rivers, J. A. (1971) *The People of the Sierra*. Chicago University Press.

Plant, Martin A. (1979) *Drinking Careers: Occupations, Drinking Habits, and Drinking Problems*. London: Tavistock.

Plant, Martin A., Peck, D. F. and Samuel, Elaine (1985) *Alcohol, Drugs and School Leavers*. London: Tavistock.

Pocock, David (1975) *Understanding Social Anthropology*. London: Hodder and Stoughton.

Pope, W. (1976) *Durkheim's Suicide - a Classic Analysed*. Chicago: University of Chicago Press.

Preteceille, Edmond and Terrail, Jean-Paul (1986) *Capitalism, Consumption and Needs*. (Translation by Sarah Matthews) Oxford: Basil Blackwell.

Rees, Alwyn D. (1950) *Life in a Welsh Countryside*. Cardiff: University of Wales Press.

Reid, Douglas (2976) 'The Decline of Saint Monday 1766-1876,' *Past and Present*. 71, 1976, pp. 76-101.

Rein, Martin (1970) 'Problems in the Definition and Measurement of Poverty.' In Townsend (ed.) 1970.

Rex, J. and Moore, R. (1967) *Race, Community and Conflict.* Oxford: Oxford University Press.

Roberts, Bryan, Finnegan, Ruth, and Gallie, Duncan (1985) (eds) *New Approaches to Economic Life.* Manchester University Press.

Roberts, K. (1978) *Contemporary Society and the Growth of Leisure.* London: Longman

Robertson, D. (1968) *Religion and Social Class in Scotland.* PhD Thesis, University of Edinburgh.

Ruether, Rosemary R. (1974) (ed.) *Religion and Sexism.* New York.

Runciman, W. G. (1966) *Relative Deprivation and Social Justice.* London: Routledge and Kegan Paul.

Ryan, Tom (1985) 'The Roots of Masculinity' In Metcalf, A. and Humphries, M. (eds) *The Sexuality of Men.* London: Pluto.

Sahlins, Marshall (1974) *Stone Age Economics.* London: Tavistock.

Sahlins, Marshall (1976) *Culture and Practical Reason.* Chicago: University of Chicago Press.

Salaman, G. (1975) 'Occupations, Community and Consciousness.' In Bulmer (ed.) 1975.

Saunders, P. (1978) 'Domestic property and social class'. *International Journal of Urban and Regional Research.* Vol. 2 pp. 233-51.

Saussure, Ferdinand de (1966/1915) *Course in General Linguistics.* New York: McGraw Hill.

Schwartz, Jack (1958) 'Men's clothing and the Negro'. M.A. dissertation, Committee on Communication, University of Chicago.

Schwimmer, E. (1979) 'The Self and the Product.' In Wallman (ed.) 1979.

Seabrook, Jeremy (1982) *Unemployment.* London: Quartet Books.

Seabrook, Jeremy (1985) 'The Society which Offers Hope on the Underworld Lottery.' *The Guardian.* 25 March 1985.

Seabrook, Jeremy (1986) 'Life in the Sun'. *New Society.* Vol. 76 No. 1215 p. 25, 11 April 1984.

Seabrook, Jeremy (1987a) 'Surviving.' In Fineman (ed.) 1987).

Seabrook, Jeremy (1987b) 'What the papers show.' *New Society.* Vol. 80 No. 1275 pp. 16-18, 5 June 1987.

Showler, Brian and Sinfield, Adrian (1981) (eds) *The Workless State: Studies in Unemployment.* Oxford: Martin Robertson.

Sinfield, Adrian (1970) 'Poor and Out of Work in Shields.' In Townsend (ed.) 1970.

Sinfield, Adrian (1981) *What Unemployment Means.* Oxford: Martin Robertson.

Sissons, P. L. (1973) *The Social Significance of Church Membership in the Burgh of Falkirk.* Edinburgh: the Church of Scotland.

Smart, Carol and Smart, Barry (1978) (eds) *Women, Sexuality and Social Control.* London: Routledge and Kegan Paul.

Smith, Adam (1892/1776) *An Inquiry into the Nature and Causes of the Wealth of Nations.* London: Routledge.

Smith, Michael A. (1981) *The Pub and The Publican: A Participant Observer Study of a Public House.* University of Salford, Centre for Leisure Studies.

Smith, S. (1986) *Britain's Shadow Economy.* Oxford: Clarendon Press.

Smout, T. C. (1987) *A Century of the Scottish People 1830-1950* London: Fontana Press.

Swallow, D. A. (1974) 'The Anthropologist as Subject' in 'Women in Anthropology' *Cambridge Anthropology.* Vol. 1 No. 3.

Stein, M. (1964) *The Eclipse of Community*. New York: Harper and Row.

Talbot, Margaret (1979) *Women and Leisure: A state of the art review*. London: SSRC/Sports Council.

Tawney, R. H. (1948) *Religion and the Rise of Capitalism*. Harmondsworth: Penguin.

Thompson, Edward P. (1968) *The Making of the English Working Class*. Harmondsworth: Penguin.

Townsend, Peter (1970) (ed.) *The Concept of Poverty: Working papers in methods of investigation and life-styles of the poor in different countries*. London: Heinemann.

Townsend, Peter (1979) *Poverty in the United Kingdom*. Suffolk: Allen Lane.

Turnbull, Colin (1973) *The Mountain People*. London: Cape.

Turner, Brian S. (1988) *Status*. Milton Keynes: Open University Press.

Turner, Robert (1979a) 'Scottish Fishers and Miners: the Dynamics of a Cultural Frontier.' Seminar paper, University of Edinburgh.

Turner, Robert (1979b) 'Legitimations and Belief in a Scottish Fishing Village.' Seminar paper.

Turner, Robert (1980) 'We're a' Jack Tamson's Bairns: Central Lowland Scotland as a Culture Area.' Slightly abridged version published in *Proceedings of the Association for Scottish Ethnography*. Vol. 1 1984. Department of Social Anthropology, University of Edinburgh.

Turner, Robert, Bostyn, Anne Marie and Wight, Daniel (1984) *Work and Non-Work in a Small Scottish Lowlands Town*. SSRC Final Report HR7700 F00230066.

Turner, Victor (1967) *The Forest of Symbols*. Ithaca, New York State: Cornell University Press.

Veblen, Thorstein (1924/1899) *The Theory of the Leisure Class*. London: Allen and Unwin.

Wadel, Cato (1973) *Now Whose Fault Is That? The struggle for self-esteem in the face of chronic unemployment*. Newfoundland Social and Economic Studies no. 11, Memorial University of Newfoundland.

Wadel, Cato (1979) 'The Hidden Work of Everyday Life.' In Wallman (ed.) 1979.

Wallman, Sandra (1979) (ed.) *A Social Anthropology of Work*. London: Academic Press.

Weber, Max (1922/1972) *Wirtschaft und Gesellschaft*. Tübingen: Mohr.

Weber, Max (1930) *The Protestant Ethic and the Spirit of Capitalism*. London: Unwin University Books.

Weber, Max (1948) *From Max Weber: Essays in Sociology*. Edited with an introduction by Gerth, H. H. and Mills, C. W. London: Routledge and Kegan Paul.

Westergaard, John (1965) 'The Withering Away of Class: A Contemporary Myth' in Eaton, John, *Towards Socialism*. New Left Review.

Westergaard, John and Resler, Henrietta (1975) *Class in a Capitalist Society*. London: Heinemann.

Which Benefit? in *Money Which?* (December 1982) pp. 696-703. The Consumer Association.

Whitehead, Ann (1976) 'Sexual Antagonism in Herefordshire.' in Barker, D. and Allen, S. (eds) *Dependence and Exploitation in Work and Marriage*. London: Longman.

Wight, Daniel (1987) 'Hard Workers and Big Spenders facing the Bru: Understanding men's employment and consumption in a de-industrialised Scottish village.' Unpublished PhD thesis, Department of Social Anthropology, Edinburgh University.

Wilkinson, Richard (1992) 'Income Distribution and life expectancy'. *British Medical Journal*. Vol. 304 No. 6820 pp. 165-8.

Williams, Raymond (1965) *The Long Revolution*. Harmondsworth: Pelican.

Williams, Raymond (1976) *Keywords*. Glasgow: Fontana/Croom Helm.

Williams, Rory (1990) *A Protestant Legacy: Attitudes to death and illness among older Aberdonians*. Oxford: Clarendon Press.

Willis, Paul E. (1977) *Learning to Labour: How working class kids get working class jobs*. Farnborough: Saxon House.

Willis, Paul E. (1984) 'Youth Unemployment.' *New Society* Vol. 67 No. 1114 pp. 475-7, 29 March, Vol. 68 No. 1115 pp. 13-15, 5 April, and Vol. 68 No. 1116 pp. 57-9, 12 April 1984.

Willis, Paul E. (1985) *The Social Condition of Young People in Wolverhampton in 1984*. Civic Centre, Wolverhampton.

Willis, Roy and Turner, Robert (1980) *An Ethnographic Study of a Scottish Lowlands Village*. Final Report to SSRC Project HR 5571/1.

Yates, F., Hebblethwaite, D and Thorley, A. (1984) 'Drinking in Two North East Towns: a survey of the natural setting for prevention.' Final report of a Health Education Council funded project, Centre for Alcohol and Drug Studies, St Nicholas Hospital, Newcastle-Upon-Tyne, England.

Zweig, Ferdynand (1961) *The Worker in an Affluent Society*. London: Heinemann.

Index

housing, 9, 24, 29, 61, 63, 72, 74–6, 82,
   108–9, 211, 233
   attitudes towards home ownership,
   192–3
   see also home–owners
housing officer, council, 30
Howe, L., 220

illegal economic activity, 11, 13, 219–24,
   226–30, 237–8
incomers, 10, 11, 12, 28–30, 35, 38, 45, 48,
   53, 72–3, 75, 80, 82, 132, 154, 185,
   200, 210
Isherwood, B., 122–3, 124

Jahoda, M., 97
Jenkins, R., 219, 223

Kerr, M., 119
kinship, 36, 41–2, 47–53, 65, 80, 93, 126,
   145, 146, 147, 220, 229, 232
   support, 224–5
Knight, C., 139

Leach, E., 145
Lee, D., 3, 30–1
leisure, 10, 14, 39–41, 63, 64, 72, 77, 80, 82,
   83, 88, 93, 97, 98, 120, 136, 147, 165,
   192, 212, 233
   collective, 185–7
Lockwood, D., 2, 69, 86, 187

McLaughlin, E., 214, 218
Malinowski, B., 12
marriage, 29, 41–2, 46, 234
Martin, B., 8, 36, 46, 77, 83, 98, 126, 127,
   128, 131, 136
Marx, K., 95, 111
masculinity, *see* gender
Masonic Lodge, 40, 49, 55, 58–9, 82, 151
Mauss, M., 142
methods of research, 9–22
Miller, D., 124–6
miners' strike (1984–5), 67, 187
mining, 25, 26, 27, 31, 54, 67, 68, 88, 98,
   99, 100, 163, 187
Mitchinson, R., 28, 54
mobility, geographical, 48, 52–3, 72
   social, 61, 154, 172, 174, 181–3, 184,
   194–5, 234

Newby, H., 3, 30–1, 69
'nice folk', *see* status, groups
Noble, M., 15
non-respectable, *see* status, groups,
   'wasters'

occupation, 7, 31, 51, 60, 61, 62, 74–6, 82,
   88, 92, 99, 100, 184–5, 218, 233

Orange Order, 49, 54–6, 58
   Orange march 32, 55–6, 204

Pahl, R., 5, 68, 220
parenthood, 41, 141, 145, 146, 164, 175,
   207–9, 217, 225
   see also child care
Parkin, F., 70
Parsons, T., 50
Payne, R., 4, 224
poaching, 226, 228
politics, 66–8, 83, 224, 237–8
poverty, 18, 28, 133–4, 201–7, 208, 210,
   212, 229, 230, 232, 235, 237, 238
prestige, 69–70, 71, 76, 80, 154, 233
pubs, 10, 24, 31, 72, 77, 82, 93, 149, 150–6,
   164–5, 166–7, 169, 171, 185, 203, 204,
   213

racism, 59, 96
reciprocity, 82, 83, 108–9, 141–7, 166–8,
   172, 205, 233, 236
Rees, A., 35
reflexivity, 16–18
religion, 20, 27, 53–9
   bigotry, 54, 59; *see also* Orange order
   Catholics, 24, 27, 53–4, 57–8, 59, 78, 151
   church attendance, 27–8, 35, 77–8, 82
   Church of Christ, 24, 27, 54, 79, 82
   Church of Scotland, 24, 53, 78
   Protestants, 54–7, 151, 186
reputation
   moral, 9, 74, 79–81, 84, 196, 224
   sexual, 43, 76, 82, 233
respectability, *see* status, groups, 'nice
   folk'
rubbish, 133

Sahlins, M., 8, 122, 123–4, 139, 145, 210
Seabrook, J., 65, 238
self-provisioning, 5, 13, 237
   fuel, 13, 226–8
   vegetables, 237
sexuality, 17, 43, 45, 76–7
   see also gender; reputation
Sinfield, A., 213, 214
smoking, 143, 144, 166, 202, 205, 210, 225
Smout, T., 66
'snobs', *see* status, groups
social security fraud, *see* welfare benefits
solvency, 133–6
   see also credit
status, 7, 19, 49, 61, 62, 66, 68–73, 121,
   154, 168, 169–71, 181, 184, 192, 194,
   214, 233, 234
   see also esteem; prestige
   community, 72–3, 83
   groups, 8, 69–70, 71, 80, 83, 169, 174,
   183